Moncure Daniel Conway

Emerson at Home and Abroad

Moncure Daniel Conway

Emerson at Home and Abroad

ISBN/EAN: 9783337138431

Printed in Europe, USA, Canada, Australia, Japan

Cover: Foto ©ninafisch / pixelio.de

More available books at **www.hansebooks.com**

EMERSON

AT HOME AND ABROAD

BY

MONCURE DANIEL CONWAY

Author of "The Sacred Anthology," "The Wandering Jew,"
"Thomas Carlyle," &c.

BOSTON:
JAMES R. OSGOOD AND COMPANY.
1882.

COPYRIGHT, 1882,
BY JAMES R. OSGOOD AND COMPANY.

All rights reserved.

Electrotyped by
ADDISON C. GETCHELL.

Printed by
W. F. BROWN & C

Dedicated

TO

MRS. RALPH WALDO EMERSON,

AND HER CHILDREN,

ELLEN, EDITH AND EDWARD,

WHO MADE KINDLY AND BEAUTIFUL

MY SECOND BIRTHPLACE.

CONTENTS.

		Page
A VIGIL		1
I.	MAYFLOWERINGS	19
II.	FORERUNNERS	28
III.	THREE FATES	41
IV.	A BOSTON BOY	47
V.	STUDENT AND TEACHER	51
VI.	APPROBATION	58
VII.	DISAPPROBATION	67
VIII.	A SEA-CHANGE	74
IX.	A LEGEND OF GOOD WOMEN	81
X.	THE WAIL OF THE CENTURY	90
XI.	CULTURE	96
XII.	EAGLE AND DOVE	127
XIII.	DAILY BREAD	132
XIV.	THE HOME	139
XV.	NATURE	146
XVI.	EVOLUTION	154
XVII.	SURSUM CORDA	162
XVIII.	THE SHOT HEARD ROUND THE WORLD	167
XIX.	SANGREAL	173
XX.	BUILDING TABERNACLES	184
XXI.	A SIX YEARS' DAY-DREAM	194
XXII.	LESSONS FOR THE DAY	209
XXIII.	CONCORDIA	229
XXIV.	NATHANIEL AND SOPHIA HAWTHORNE	256
XXV.	THOREAU	279
XXVI.	"THE COMING MAN"	290
XXVII.	THE PYTHON	299
XXVIII.	EMERSON IN ENGLAND	316
XXIX.	THE DIADEM OF DAYS	347
XXX.	LETHE	378

A VIGIL.

IT is the vigil of Emerson. To-morrow (May 25, 1882) he will be seventy-nine years of age. I cannot bear to write "he would be." This day, gazing on a picture of Emerson's funeral, picking out from beneath their grey hairs faces of some with whom I have sat at his feet, there comes home to me the secret of that longing out of which were born myths of men that never died, of Yami and Arthur, of Enoch and Saint John. The love of a Madonna is in his own interpretation. "The fable of the Wandering Jew is agreeable to men, because they want more time and land in which to execute their thoughts. But a higher poetic use must be made of the legend. Take us as we are with our experience, and transfer us to a new planet, and let us digest for its inhabitants what we could of the wisdom of this. After we have found our depth there, and assimilated what we could of the wisdom of the new experience, transfer us to a new scene. In each transfer we shall have acquired, by seeing them at a distance, a new mastery of the old thoughts, in which we were too much immersed. In short, all our intellectual action not promises, but bestows a feeling of absolute existence. We are taken out of time and breathe a purer air."

Such duration did Emerson devise; but one source

of the longing for immortality he could not know so fully as we who cannot leave his grave. It needed this night to bring out the star of that hope.

"I send you," a friend writes, "a sprig from the evergreen that bordered Emerson's grave as his coffin was lowered into it this afternoon. I dropped a piece in after the school-children had covered the coffin with their tributes, and kept the rest, of which this is a part."

Is this bit of evergreen, already dust, all the Amen Nature can give to the faith of its greatest heart? Ye pines and oaks of Sleepy Hollow, awake! Wrestle, as Herakles for Alcestis, grapple with Death for your poet and lover! Search with every rootlet for the seed of that brain, and lift it again to upper air!

Alas! Nature has been faithless. He trusted her April smiles and she chilled him with death; and now she seems to contradict his living word, drawing those he taught to live in the present to find their paradise in the past he made so beautiful.

But the ground laurel on his grave and the whispering oaks and pines waving above it have sent abroad their message to those who with him have walked that sacred grove, saying, "What he has been to thee that shalt thou tell. Into the grave of memory shalt thou search and lift by what art thou canst every gracious word he gave thee, every thought he inspired, and all the beautiful life thou didst witness, to its resurrection and life, that he may, through love, be as immortal as a mortal can be."

Once, as I walked with John Stuart Mill alone, he questioned me concerning Emerson and his influence on

American youth. All I could tell him of Emerson was what he had been to me. When my story was told he said, "That is a thing to be written on a man's tomb." Emerson has a tomb in many homes. He has one in mine; and the inscription on it is here recorded for my fellow-pilgrims in life.

From this vigil beside the grave of Emerson, memory passes over the time of a generation, and across long stretches of sea and land, to a secret nook near my Virginian home, to whose crystal fount and flowers my eighteenth spring carried a wintry heart. Near that wooded slope the Rappahannock spread silvery in the sunshine, placid after its falls foam-white in the distance, streaming past its margin of meadows to the peaceful homes and spires of Fredericksburg. Fresh from college, now from every career planned by parent or friend I had recoiled: some indefinable impediment barred each usual path: the last shadow settled around me when the law-book was closed to be opened no more. Utterly miserable, self-accused amid sorrowful faces, with no outlook but to be a fettered master of slaves, I was then wont to shun the world, with gun for apology, and pass the hours in this retreat. So came I on a day, and reclined on the grass, reading in a magazine casually brought. The laugh and chatter of negroes pushing their flat-boats loaded with grain, the song of birds, the sound of church-bells across the river, all smote upon a heart discordant with them, at discord with itself. Nature had no meaning, life no promise and no aim. Listlessly turning to the printed page, one sentence caught my eye and held it; one sentence quoted from Emerson, which changed my world and me.

A sentence only! I do not repeat it: it might not bear to others what it bore to me; its searching subtle revelation defies any analysis I can make of its words. All I know is that it was the touch of flame I needed. That day my gun was laid aside to be resumed no more. But how crude I was! The nearest mould into which my new life could run was a Methodist itinerancy. A human aim had arisen; souls were to be saved; and in that work must begin my small "Wanderjahre." My horse was got ready: my bible, filled with maternal inscriptions holy as its texts, was taken for compass in my wanderings; I only longed to add some book by Emerson. But the Index Expurgatorius of slavery had excluded Northern books so long and so well, that the bookseller in Fredericksburg offered me "Emerson's Arithmetic," and denied the existence of any other Emerson. For a long time I had only my one sentence; but how large it grew!

My cousin and literary friend, John Moncure Daniel, was editor of the "Richmond Examiner," in which paper I was delighted by finding one day a long extract from one of Emerson's Essays. About that time Edgar A. Poe was lecturing at Richmond on Poetry, and my cousin supplemented his selections by printing Emerson's "Humble Bee." Poe had conceived a dislike of Emerson, and the severest criticism upon himself are his paragraphs about the man he most needed. I remember that restless face and demon-driven figure, and have felt that if he could only have appreciated the true teacher of his time, the career of that wanderer might have been less tragical.

Soon after leaving home for the charge assigned me by the Baltimore Methodist Conference, I obtained the first series of Emerson's Essays, and presently his other works. They were read, between my nineteenth and twentieth birthdays, on horseback, while travelling the roads and woods of a "circuit" in Maryland. I preached seven times in the week, and in some cases had to ride more than twenty miles to an appointment. But with Emerson for companion, my horse, walking the distance with reins on neck, arrived but too soon.

Presently the shadow cast by this light began to travel beside me. Strange that I should have been so long — nearly a year — unconscious of the abyss between what I was thinking and what I was doing! My congregations grew ominously still; elders shook their heads, and were on more anxious seats than the sinners; so I grew perplexed. One Sunday a pious lady awaited my descent from the pulpit and said, "Brother, you seemed to be preaching to us from another world." Then I preached no more.

Having resigned my profession, I returned for a brief time to Virginia: there I was lonely, but still happy, though not able to see my way very far. At this time I was thrilled by learning that a youth from the North — no doubt seeking health in our warmer climate — had died in our neighbourhood, and with his last words begged that his love should be conveyed to Emerson, "who," he said, "has done more for me than any other on earth." This message I undertook to forward, and did, but not at once, for I hoped to find out more about this wayfarer who had died so near a comrade without knowing it.

Of course I had written to Emerson. I was nineteen, alone with my new thoughts, and was seized with a longing to realise my master's existence. So I wrote my brief love-letter, and posted it with a feeling that it was addressed to some impersonal spirit, dwelling in a spiritual realm harmoniously called Concord, whom it would never reach. But — joy! — speedily came the response, read in sweet secrecy then, and how often since!

"CONCORD, Mass., 13*th November*, 1851.

"DEAR SIR, — I fear you will not be able, except at some chance auction, to obtain any set of the 'Dial.' In fact, smaller editions were printed of the later and latest numbers, which increases the difficulty.

"I am interested by your kind interest in my writings, but you have not let me sufficiently into your own habit of thought, to enable me to speak to it with much precision. But I believe what interests both you and me most of all things, and whether we know it or not, is the morals of intellect; in other words, that no man is worth his room in the world who is not commanded by a legitimate object of thought. The earth is full of frivolous people, who are bending their whole force and the force of nations on trifles, and these are baptized with every grand and holy name, remaining, of course, totally inadequate to occupy any mind; and so sceptics are made. A true soul will disdain to be moved except by what natively commands it, though it should go sad and solitary in search of its master a

thousand years. The few superior persons in each community are so by their steadiness to reality and their neglect of appearances. This is the euphrasy and rue that purge the intellect and ensure insight. Its full rewards are slow but sure; and yet I think it has its reward on the instant, inasmuch as simplicity and grandeur are always better than dapperness. But I will not spin out these saws farther, but hasten to thank you for your frank and friendly letter, and to wish you the best deliverance in that contest to which every soul must go alone. — Yours, in all good hope,
"R. W. EMERSON."

Here I had my marching orders, and gradually comprehended them. Struggles were necessary to cut myself loose from Southern polities and from orthodoxy, but they became light when I whispered to myself, "Yours, in all good hope." My heart learned this note, and sang it to me in many a night of loneliness and poverty.

At last the day came when I stood at the door of Emerson. I had entered the Divinity College at Cambridge, and carried a letter from one of his friends; but I was nervous, and it was some relief to hear he was not at home. His little daughter and son, however, brought me an invitation from Mrs. Emerson to return soon, and meantime they took me on a beautiful walk, — a walk amid apple trees, where we sat and told tales in a lovely Lost Bower.

I was taken to Emerson by his children and gave him my note of introduction. He remembered, and said, "Surely you are my Virginian correspondent."

With that he extended his hand and welcomed me with a smile — his smile, not to be lightly lost by one it has warmed. For me, who never before had seen a great man, who yet in my minority was cut off from every relative and had alienated every early friend, this welcoming word and smile was the break of a new day. I could not answer. Many years after I read that one in paradise was asked how he got there and replied, "One day as Buddha passed by he smiled upon me."

Twenty-eight years later, on that spot where I first met Emerson I parted from him to see him no more. It was with the old grasp of hand, and with that smile on his face to win which would at any time have meant to me success. It is before me now, and shall not be changed to a frown by any sentence in this little book.

It is the birthday of Emerson. This twenty-fifth of May he is seventy-nine years of age. Or must I concede that he lives no more! Here are letters before me; reports of words spoken at his house, in church, at the grave. Here is a note written on the day before his funeral. "The main street as well as that on which he lived are to be draped with black, and a great crowd of people is expected to-morrow. The Fitchburg railroad will run special trains, contrary to the law against Sunday travelling. We are doing our best to get what may pass for wild flowers, namely, maple and willow blossoms, to mingle with the pine and hemlock around the pulpit." Another writes on the funeral day: "The assembly of neighbours and friends thronged the church, and the village, for the church could hold but part; the ten carloads of people that went up from Boston and elsewhere would alone have filled it." In that home where he had lived forty-six years, his family gathered around him, and with them the venerable Dr. Furness, Emerson's friend in his college days, still dearer friend by his lifelong faithfulness to every human cause. In the church founded by his fathers, freed from their creed by his larger thought, the Sage lay in state, white-robed, while around him fell the first tears he had ever caused to friend or neighbour. Above was a canopy of pine boughs. His youth sang of the embowered home he was to find —

"beneath the pines,
Where the evening star so holy shines."

When the evening star was near to its setting, for a moment his mind wandered, and he asked to be taken home. Then he beheld his grandchildren, blessed them with his smile, and his words — " Good boy ! " " Good little girl ! "

Now again, carried from his own to the village home, he was stretched beneath the pines, and life's evening star rose before those tearful eyes around him to be a morning star. On front of the pulpit was a harp made of golden flowers. On the high wall was an open book, formed of pinks, pansies, and white roses ; on its page, written in flowers, the word " Finis." His aged friend, Bronson Alcott, read touching lines. Valiant, largehearted Freeman Clarke — he who surrendered his pulpit rather than exclude Theodore Parker from it — said, " Our souls have been fed by him, and although he has left his dust behind, his life does not die ; he himself was the best argument for immortality." Then the grey hairs of Judge Hoar were bent over the face of his beloved friend, companion of all his life, and his voice, which had so often commanded a nation's attention, now was broken with grief. "That lofty brow, the home of all wise thoughts and noble aspirations; those lips of eloquent music; that great soul, which trusted in God, and never let go its hope of immortality; that great heart, to which everything was welcome that belonged to man; that hospitable nature, loving and tender and generous, having no repulsion or scorn for anything but meanness and baseness,— oh! friend, brother, father, lover, teacher, inspirer, guide, is there no more we can do now than to give thee our hail and farewell?"

Nothing more! Through the village streets, which his presence had made beautiful as pathways in Beulah for the pilgrims with whom he walked, they now bore his flower-laden body into the grove of primeval trees, and upward to the higher ground where lay the bride so early lost — "Ellen in the South" — and little Waldo, enshrined in his Threnody, and Thoreau, and Hawthorne; thither they bore him. And there he was laid.

The next day was May Day. That blithe day which his Muse had celebrated dawned upon his grave. What ear was left to hear the pine wind-harps of Sleepy Hollow as he heard them? The ear made fine by grief. In many a solitude was heard that day themes caught from his "May Day," from its Æolian harp, by the boughs waving over Emerson's grave: —

"One musician is sure,
His wisdom will not fail;

> He has not tasted wine impure,
> Nor bent to passion frail.
> Age cannot cloud his memory,
> Nor grief untune his voice,
> Ranging down the ruled scale
> From tone of joy to inward wail."

But here a heart-string breaks. I remember well the days when Emerson began writing "May Day." He told me that a single breath of spring fragrance coming into his open window and blending with strains of his Æolian harp had revived in him memories and reanimated thoughts that had perished under turmoil of the times. His voice of that happy day is audible in these lines: —

> "Not long ago, at eventide,
> It seemed so listening, at my side
> A window rose, and, to say sooth,
> I looked forth on the fields of youth:
> I saw fair boys bestriding steeds,
> I knew their forms in fancy weeds,
> Long, long concealed by sundering fates,
> Mates of my youth, — yet not my mates,
> Stronger and bolder far than I.
> With grace, with genius, well attired,
> And then as now from far admired.
> Followed with love
> They knew not of,
> With passion cold and shy.
> O joy, for what recoveries rare!
> Renewed, I breathe Elysian air,
> See youth's glad mates in earliest bloom, —
> Break not my dream, obtrusive tomb!
> Or teach thou, Spring! the grand recoil
> Of life resurgent from the soil
> Wherein was dropped the mortal spoil."

Never were truer emblems than those flowers that formed the harp and the book beside the dead body of Emerson. Once, when he read from Swedenborg that he had observed in heaven that whenever an angel uttered a truth a twig held in his hand blossomed, it occurred to me that I had observed the same thing in Concord.

The grove where Emerson lies will spread far beyond Concord. In the "Cincinnati Commercial," printed the day after his death, I found this paragraph: "It is a coincidence that on the day Ralph Waldo Emerson died at his home in Concord, a large number of the public-school children of Cincinnati, under the leadership of their superintendent, and in observance of a forestry holiday, were planting an Author's Grove, one of the most prominent objects of which is a group named in honour of Emerson. The Emerson trees are six in number, an elm, two oaks, and four rock-maples. The boys of Hughes' High School formed an inner circle to finish their setting, and the girls of the same school an outer circle. Thus arranged, they sang national songs and gave appropriate recitations. As they performed this worthy and poetic task, the world-renowned philosopher whose name the group will bear lay dying, and as evening came on he passed away. Eden Park is likely to contain no more noted trees than those planted for Emerson on the day he died."

No noble thing in nature that grows, and is strong and beautiful, but may be fit emblem of Emerson, and find its poetic interpretation in some page of his.

When those Emerson maples in Eden Park are glowing like embers, his thought will burn brighter : —

> "The scarlet maple-keys betray
> What potent blood hath modest May;
> What fiery force the earth renews,
> The wealth of forms, the flush of hues;
> Joy shed in rosy waves abroad
> Flows from the heart of Love, the Lord."

And under shade of the Emerson oaks, the children who planted them may teach their finest symbolism in the words which he spoke thirty-nine years ago concerning the conserving and the reforming spirit: — "Nature does not give the crown of its approbation, beauty, to any action, or emblem, or actor, but one which combines both these elements; not to the rock which resists the wave from age to age, nor to the wave which lashes incessantly the rock; but the superior beauty is with the oak, which stands with its hundred arms against the storms of a century, and grows every year like a sapling."

Emerson personally planted the spiritual germs of those trees set in Eden Park by the children of Cincinnati. Twenty-three years ago he visited us there, and gave a course of lectures from my pulpit. Evening after evening the church was filled with the families which gave that city, the "Queen of the West," the intellectual character it has preserved. There the best chapters in "The Conduct of Life" were given, and many a child there is this day more fortunate than any wealth can ever make him, because of that visit from the sower of new souls. Soon afterwards I started there a monthly magazine, the "Dial." This effort to light our Western torch at the finest flame of our East, — announced in reproducing the title of the old transcendental Quarterly, — received sympathy from Emerson, who contributed to it his essay on "Domestic Life," "Quatrains," and "The Sacred Dance." All these have since appeared in his works, the last-named in "May Day," as the "Song of Seid Nimetollah of Kuhistan." The Civil War put an end to that little venture of mine, the "Dial," for we all had sterner work to do; but there are many homes in Cincinnati where it carried a regenerating spirit in that matchless essay on "Domestic Life."

What Emerson became to these distant homes in which he was read, and to the hearts that cherished his every thought, could never be comprehended by himself. Here is an incident which might have given Carlyle a paragraph on the unconsciousness of genius. I have a letter from Emerson, which came with the manuscript of "Domestic Life," in which he speaks of another essay he had thought of sending, and says:—"Then I kept it to put into what will not admit anything peaceably, my 'Religion' chapter, which has a very tender stomach, on which nothing will lie. They say the ostrich hatches her egg by standing off and looking at it, and that is my present secret of authorship. I long ago rolled up and addressed to you an ancient MS. lecture called 'Domestic Life,' and long ago, you may be sure, familiar to Lyceums, but never printed, except in newspaper reports. But I feared you would feel bound to print it, though I should have justified you if you had not printed a page." Reading these last words, remembering the joy with which I sent forth the "Dial" (October, 1860) with that scripture of the sun, and the many grateful responses that came, I have reflected on the number of Beauties that must be sleeping among Emerson's manuscripts, hedged by the thorns of his self-criticism.

It was to a home in Cincinnati, which he had helped to make happy, that Emerson wrote the following letter: —

"CONCORD, 6th October, 1861.

"MY DEAR SIR AND MY DEAR LADY, — I have your note, and give you joy of the happy event you announce to me in the birth of your son. Who is rich or happy but the parent of a son? Life is all preface until we have children; then it is deep and solid. You would think me a child again if I should tell you how much joy I have owed, and daily owe, to my children, and you have already known the early chapters of this experience in your own house. My best thanks are due to you both for the great good-will you shew me in thinking of my name for the boy. If there is room for choice still, I hesitate a good deal at allowing a rusty old name, eaten with Heaven knows how much time and fate, to be flung hazardously on this new adventurer in his snow-white robes. I have never encountered such a risk out of my own house, and, for the boy's sake, if there be time, must dissuade. But I shall watch the career of this young American with special interest, born as he is under stars and omens so extraordinary, and opening the gates of a new and fairer age. With all hopes and all thanks, and with affectionate sympathies from my wife.

"Yours ever, R. W. EMERSON."

"My wife declares that name or no name her spoon shall go."

Alas! this note and the silver cup that came with it, are now memorials of a little grave in England. Could we only have found something not only beloved and beautiful, like the child, but imperishable, to name after Emerson!

I will follow the children of the Queen of the West, who gave his name to their group of trees in Eden Park. In my garden grows a sapling of the Glastonbury Thorn. It was sent me by a friend years ago, that its famous habit of flowering at Christmas might be proved beyond all doubts. Sure enough, at the close of the last year this thorn clothed itself with green leaves, and the blossoms peeped through their sheath. Legend associated it with Joseph of Arimathea, who wandered from the East eighteen centuries ago, whose staff blossomed amid the snow on the vigil of Christ, and so marked the site for Glastonbury Abbey. But this descendant of it shall connect the deep sense of its mythology, — the budding rod of Aaron, the staff of silent Christopher, which converted men by its fruits, the thorn that canopied Patrick with blossoms, — with his name. Some day the wayfarers, seeing it flourishing in winter amid other trees denuded and black, shall say, "Its legend is from the West. It was planted there and named by one who, amid his winter of loneliness and doubt, was surprised by a spring whose leaf never withered, whose blossoms mingled with every snow; a great teacher brought him this fortune and happiness, and wherever he wandered in the world he sought to plant some germ of his teacher's wisdom, that hearts might suffer no blight in life's winter, that faith might flourish amid decay of creeds, and love know the secret of perpetual youth. This is the Emerson tree!"

EMERSON AT HOME AND ABROAD.

I.

MAYFLOWERINGS.

THERE is an incident in the life of the Plymouth Pilgrims too trifling to be included in the regular annals of those times. One morning Captain Miles Standish, and John Alden, and Priscilla, whose relations to each other are well known to readers of Longfellow, were walking through a field together. A light snow lay on the ground, but Priscilla's eye perceived a little flower peeping through it. "Stay, Captain Standish," she said, but was too late to prevent his heavy boot from treading on it. John Alden made haste to pick the flower, which the maiden tenderly nursed. Standish cast a vexed glance at Alden and said, "Puritan soldiers have something else to look after besides flowers." "Nay," rejoined Priscilla, "but we need not trample down any beautiful gift of God's earth. Look at it, Captain; it is fragrant as well as pretty; and is it not a sturdy little soldier too, battling with the snow?" The Captain strode on and was presently leading another attack on the Indians; but Priscilla and John wandered about the fields and gathered many of these blossoms, and found in them a still small voice of courage amid the bleakness of that wintry coast. Such courage had led the pilgrims across the sea in the season of snowstorms; so Priscilla named the blossom "Mayflower," after the ship on which they had voyaged, and wore a spray of them at her breast when she was married to John Alden.

Of this marriage came at last the sweet singer Longfellow, who gathered in his song so many blooms which rough captains of the world had trampled on. But before the poet, who in Washington's headquarters wrote the lyrics of peace and hymns of humanity, could come, — the "sweet and beautiful soul," as Emerson described him, standing at his grave, in whose poetry the Puritan and the Indian first found harmony, — many gentle maidens and lovers, from generation to generation, must gather spiritual Mayflowers amid Calvinistic snows. Cromwell once engaged passage for New England, but never sailed; yet, in a sense, his tread was there for many a day, heavy on the Mayflowers; while Milton was there, too, gathering them up tenderly as John Alden.

The modern pilgrim to Plymouth finds a beautiful town beside the sea where floated that first ship, so freighted with human destinies. The undulating hills and the cliffs, girt about with their autumnal coat of many colours, make fit scenery for the historic vision. "But Plymouth Rock, — I must first see that." A friend guides me toward the water to a kind of wharf, and then begins scraping the ground. Thinking he must have dropped something, I ask, "What are you looking for?" "I am trying to show you Plymouth Rock," he remarks. Angels and ministers of grace defend us! — clearing away the mud to show Plymouth Rock! Presently I do see something like a flagstone; but looking up, the breaking waves dashing high, seen by the mind's eye from childhood, have sunk to a placid pond, and the firm and rock-bound shore on which they dashed has shrunk to a molehill. Dr. Channing told Mrs. Hemans of the thousand voices he had heard singing on Forefathers' Day her famous hymn about the breaking waves and rock-bound shore, and she wept; but she might have smiled through her tears could she have seen that gentle beach, no rock visible, where the pilgrims really landed. However, a stone weighing perhaps a ton was removed from the spot to the museum, and a graceful monument now stands in its place.

The granite heart of the colony was the true Plymouth Rock. "These poor men," says Carlyle, "driven out of their own country, and not able to live in Holland, determined on settling in the New World. Black, untamed forests are there, and wild savage creatures, but not so cruel as a Star-Chamber hangman. They clubbed their means together, hired a ship — the little ship 'Mayflower' — and made ready to sail. Hah! these men, I think, had a work. The weak thing, weaker than a child, becomes a strong thing if it be a true thing. Puritanism was only despicable, laughable then; but nobody can manage to laugh at it now. It is one of the strongest things under the sun at present."

Little by little Plymouth Rock crumbled away; the last fragment survived visibly only at the museum. And meanwhile the sweet Mayflowers bloomed on.

The hard dogmas grew to be stems of fragrant virtues. When I stood in the first church of Plymouth, founded by the Pilgrims on that old Puritan rock, these little flowers were sacramental symbols for worshippers who reverenced the teachings of Channing, Parker, and Emerson. Contemporary Priscillas and Aldens had taken me to gather them. Lilies of the valley cannot surpass this little trailing arbutus (*Epigea repens*), with its hyacinthine shape and delicate pink-faint flush. I have seen Theodore Parker, in the course of a discourse, lift up a bunch of these, which some gatherer had affectionately laid on his pulpit-desk, and he gave them fresh beauty and fragrance in using them as symbols of certain sweet traits of New England character that grew amid the frost of Calvinism, unconscious that he himself was an illustration of his thought. Emerson, too, in early life, addressing the people of Concord concerning their forefathers, said, "The little flower which at this season stirs our wood and roadsides with its profuse blossoms might attract even eyes as stern as theirs with its humble beauty."

But a second and more important pilgrimage lay between Plymouth Rock and Theodore Parker at Lexington, nursing the delicate flowers of his heart amid toil and orthodoxy, and ere Emerson could be reached farther on, the flower of New England history.

This year, 1882, on the 12th July, Benjamin Bulkeley fresh from Divinity College, Harvard University, was settled as minister of Concord church. Concord and its church were both founded by his ancestor and Emerson's ancestor, the Rev. Peter Bulkeley, an Oxonian of noble family, Rector of Odell, Bedfordshire, who had been silenced by Archbishop Laud. In 1635 Peter Bulkeley, and some families with him, emigrated and settled themselves at Musketaquid, which they named Concord. John Eliot, the English "apostle to the Indians," had made the red faces friendly. Bulkeley had brought with him the large sum of six thousand pounds, which he devoted to the welfare of those who accompanied him. He gave a good library to Harvard College. In that same year, 1635, also emigrated Thomas Emerson, of an honourable family in Durham, whose son married one of the Bulkeley family at Concord.

The marching of Peter Bulkeley and his friends to the place where their descendants still reside was through and into a wilderness. It is described by one of their number as "a toyle of some dayes." "This poore people, populate this howling desert, marching manfully on, the Lord assisting, through the greatest difficulties, and greater labours than any with such weak means have done." There was "hard work for many an honest gentleman." In 1835 Emerson was invited to deliver an address on the occasion of the 200th anniversary of the settlement of Concord, and in the course of it he gave a touching picture of the little band of founders: —

"They proceeded to build, under the shelter of the hill that extends for a mile along the north side of the Boston road, their first dwellings. The labours of a new plantation were repaid by its excitements. I seem to see them with their pious pastor addressing themselves to the work of clearing the land. Natives of another hemisphere, they beheld with curiosity all the pleasing features of the American forest. The landscape before them was fair, if it was strange and rude. The little flower, which at this season stirs our woods and roadsides with its profuse blossoms, might attract even eyes as stern as theirs with its humble beauty. The useful pine lifted its cone into the frosty air. The maple, which is already making the forest gay with its autumn hues, reddened over those houseless men. The majestic summits of Wachusett and Monadnoc, towering in the horizon, invited the steps of adventure westward.

"As the season grew later they felt its inconveniences. Many were forced to go barefoot and bareleg, and some in time of frost and snow, yet 'were they more healthy than now they are.' The land was low but healthy; and if, in common with all the settlements, they found the air of America very cold, they might say with Higginson, after his description of the other elements, that 'New England may boast of the element of fire more than all the rest; for all Europe is not able to afford to make so great fires as New England. A poor servant, that is to possess but fifty acres, may afford to give more wood for fire, as good as the world yields, than many noblemen in England.' Many were their wants, but more their privileges. The light struggled in through windows of oiled paper, but they read the word of God by it. They were fain to make use of their knees for a table, but their limbs were their own. Hard labour and spare diet they had, and off wooden trenchers, but they had peace and freedom, and the wailing of the tempest in the woods sounded kindlier in their ear than the smooth voice of the prelates at home in England. ' There is no people,' said their pastor to his little flock of exiles, ' but will strive to excel in something. What can we excel in, if not in holiness?' "

When the war of the Revolution broke out, Concord bore an important part. It contained at that time about 1300 inhabitants, and no other place of its size in America furnished so much aid to Washington. In its records is this entry : — " Since General Washington at Cambridge is not able to give but $2.48 the cord for wood for the army, it is voted that this town encourage the inhabitants to supply the army by paying $2 per cord over and above the General's price to such as shall carry wood thither." They furnished hay to the army in the same generous way, and when Boston was suffering, they relieved its people with grain and money. A provincial Congress was held at Concord in 1774. During the year 1775–76, when Washington had his headquarters at Cambridge, he used the Harvard buildings for barracks, and the university was for the time transferred to Concord.

In his address Emerson reviewed with just pride the history of his town. It was fortunate and favoured, he said, in having received so large an infusion of both of the most important periods of the country — the Planting and the Revolutionary. Its true story would exhibit a community almost exclusively agricultural, distinguished by simplicity, contentment, love of justice, and religious character. And yet " more sacred influences have mingled here with the stream of human life," he says; the merit of its famous men " sheds a perfume less sweet than do the sacrifices of private virtue." There are many old stories told in Concord which justify the high character claimed for it by Emerson. For instance, when, after their repulse at Concord Bridge, some of the retreating British soldiers fell wounded at various points along the road leading toward Boston, they were taken into the homes of those whom they had invaded and tenderly nursed. Some of them recovered and remained through life in the town, captives of this practical love of enemies. In Hawthorne's posthumous tale, the conversation between Septimius and Rose as they see the British soldiers approaching, their horror at the thought of enmity with such brave fellows, is conceived in the true spirit of the Concordians of that day.

"Here," said Emerson, " are no ridiculous laws, no eavesdropping legislators, no hanging of witches, no ghosts, no whipping of Quakers, no unnatural crimes. The tone of the records rises with the dignity of the event. These soiled and musty books are luminous and electric within. The old town-clerks did not spell very correctly, but they contrive to make pretty intelligible the will of a free and just community. Frugal our fathers were, very frugal, though for the most part they deal generously by their minister, and provide well for the schools and the poor. If at any time, in common with most of our towns, they have carried this economy to the verge of a vice, it is to be remembered that a town is, in many respects, a financial corporation. They economise that they may sacrifice. They stint and higgle in the price of a pew that they may send two hundred soldiers to General Washington to keep Great Britain at bay. For splendour there must somewhere be rigid economy. That the head of the house may go brave, the members must go plainly clad, and the town must save that the State may spend."

The earnestness with which Emerson dwells upon the details of the story reveals that therein lay the root of his own character. And when, in the end, he expressed the hope that " the little society of men who now for a few years fish in this river, plough the fields it washes, mow the grass, and reap the corn," might be worthy of such ancestors and antecedents, we can recognise, what his hearers of 1835 then could not, that the young Harvard scholar was to repeat in a higher plane the heroism of his ancestor — the Pastor Bulkeley — to lead a band from old theologic settlements, and make the wilderness bloom with nobler thoughts and aims.

II.

FORERUNNERS.

OF the founder of Concord, Peter Bulkeley, a very interesting account is given by Mr. W. Hale White in the "Athenæum" of May 13, 1882: — "He wrote Latin verse with ease, and yet he was as fervent as Bunyan in all matters touching the soul and the soul's welfare. He loved his learning, and never forsook it, but it was subdued into the service of a Divine Master. His neighbours observed of him that whenever they came into his company, no matter what the business might be, he would 'let fall some holy, serious, divine, and useful sentences on them ere they parted;' and it is also recorded of him that, 'by a sort of winning and yet prudent familiarity, he drew persons of all ages to come and sit with him.' There was a quarrel in the church while he was minister over it, but he healed it at last, and afterwards he told his friends that he 'thereby came — 1. to know more of God; 2. to know more of himself; 3. to know more of men.' His contemporaries seem to have been impressed with his kindness to his servants, for it remains on record, although the details of his life are so few. When they had lived with him a number of years, it was his practice to dismiss them, and bestow farms upon them.

'Thus he cast his bread both upon the waters and into the earth, not expecting the return of this his charity to a religious plantation until after many days. With all his culture and gentleness, it is distinctly said of him by Neal, in a chance notice of him in the 'History of New England,' that he was a ' thundering preacher.' In other words, although he had in him something of the ' Essays,' there was also in him something of the temper which more than two centuries and a half afterwards re-appeared in the ' Voluntaries' of one who felt

> 'Only the fiery thread
> Leading over heroic ground
> Walled with mortal terror round.'

"'The Gospel Covenant,' the only book Dr. Bulkeley wrote, is a series of Puritan sermons on faith, justification, and the law. It is now almost unreadable, but I remember a passage in it which is a prophecy of what was to come. It is as follows : —

"'And hence, while the mind is possessed with these things, because so great a businesse as making a covenant of peace with the High God, and about so great an affair as the life and salvation of our soule cannot be transacted in a tumult, therefore, in the fourth place, faith takes the soule aside and carries it into some solitary place, that there it may be alone with God, with whom it hath to doe. This business and multitude of other occasions cannot be done together, and therefore the soule must be alone, that it may the more fully commune with itself, and utter itself fully before the Lord. Thus the poor Church in the time of her affliction, when the Lord seemed to hide himself from her, she sate alone, as she speakes Lament. 3, 28, 29, and Jer. 15, 17, *I sate aione because of thy plague: The way of the Lord is prepared in the desart*, Esay 40. 3. When the Lord will come to the soule and draw it into communion with himselfe, he will have his way hereto prepared in the desart; not in the throng of a city, but in a solitary desart place, he will allure us and draw us into the wildernesse from the company of men, when he will speak to our heart, and when He prepares our heart to speak unto Him."

Two centuries after the old pilgrim sailed to the American wilderness with these thoughts and hopes, his great descendant returned from a pilgrimage to teachers in the Old World with such melodies as these in his heart:—

> "Whoso walketh in solitude,
> And inhabiteth the wood,
> Choosing light, wave, rock, and bird,
> Before the money-loving herd,
> Into that forester shall pass
> From these companions power and grace;
> Clean shall he be, without, within,
> From the old adhering sin."

Professor Tyler (*Hist. American Literature*, i. 218) says of "The Gospel Covenant:" "The whole work carries momentum with it. It gives the impression of an athletic, patient, and orderly intellect. Every advance along the page is made with the tread of logical victory. No unsubdued enemies are left in the rear. It is a monumental book. It stands for the intellectual robustness of New England in the first age. It is an honour to that community of pioneers, drudging in the woods of Concord, that these profound and elaborate discourses could have been produced, and endured among them."

Dr. Bulkeley, it is to be feared, was over-logical when the "prophetess" Anne Hutchinson came to New England with her transcendentalism about the real presence of the Holy Spirit in true believers. He was Moderator of the Boston Synod, which immoderately drove her away to Rhode Island, where the Naragansett Indians permitted her to set up her community, in which no one was accounted a delinquent for doctrine.

Thomas Emerson emigrated from England to America in 1635. It may have been from York, where a Ralph Emerson was knighted by Henry VIII. (1535), or from Durham, where the mathematician of that name lived, whose heraldic arms were the same as those of the knight. The lions from this coat of arms are still traceable upon the tomb of Nathaniel (son of Thomas) Emerson at Ipswich, Massachusetts. Thomas became a farmer and baker at Ipswich. He was thrifty and made money. His will, dated May 31, 1653, distributes a large property among his family. He gives to his "loving wife" Elizabeth the annual rent of his farm and six head of cattle; and if she shall marry again, she is to have six pounds annually (a considerable sum in that time and place), also "the little feather-bed, and one bolster, and two pairs of sheets, and two cows," and half the fruit of the orchard. The loving wife is also appointed sole executrix, while Lieutenant-Governor Symonds and General Dennison are to be overseers of the estate.

His son John, who married the Lieutenant-Governor's daughter, went to Harvard College after his marriage, and there graduated in 1656, having earned the money to pay for his own education. He became minister at Gloucester, Massachusetts, and from him descended the anti-slavery orator, Wendell Phillips; the most eloquent American clergyman, Phillips Brooks; and the Hon. Alphonso Taft, sometime Attorney-General of the United States, and now American Minister at Vienna.

For James, a son in England, the will of Thomas Emerson provides that he shall have forty pounds if he shall come to America, or send a certificate of his being alive within two years after his mother's death. The house of Thomas is still standing at Ipswich, near "Labor-in-vain" Creek. His son Joseph, born in England the year that the "Mayflower" sailed, married Miss Woodmancy, and settled at Wells, Maine, as a teacher. He was a distinguished citizen of that place, and when the Massachusetts Commissioners went to settle the rule of their colony over Maine, they were received in his house. About fourteen years after settling in Wells, Joseph became the preacher there; but under his ministry occurred a schism, the cause of which is unexplained; and in 1667 we find him preaching at Milton, Massachusetts. Meantime, in 1665, he had married Elizabeth Bulkeley of Concord, granddaughter of the founder of that town. In 1669 he became the minister of Mendon, in the same State. This Joseph, the great-great-grandfather of Ralph Waldo Emerson, was the first minister at Mendon, and there is something notable in his contract with the people there. The township had been partitioned by the settlers in estates of forty acres each. The minister is to become an equal citizen by having also his forty acres, on which they are to build him a house. And it is contracted that if for any reason he should be dismissed from or compelled to separate from the church, this property was to continue his possession, or, if he should die, belong to his family. There may have been some reminiscence of experiences in Maine which led to this carefulness, but there is also in it that substantial relation with affairs which Lowell recognized in Joseph's great descendant —

"A Greek head on right Yankee shoulders, whose range
  Has Olympus for one pole, for t'other the Exchange."

The Emersons were always as generous as they were thrifty; and, securing their independence as to means, they returned more to their fellow-citizens than they got. It was the rule in the family to distribute their possessions equally between the members of their families, and so no large Emerson fortune was accumulated. When Mendon was destroyed in King Philip's war, the Rev. Joseph Emerson moved to Concord, where he died in 1680. His son Edward became a merchant at Charlestown, Boston. He was born in 1670, and in 1697 married Rebecca Waldo of Chelmsford, Massachusetts. This lady, a descendant of a family of the Waldenses who had become London merchants, was some years older than her husband, and outlived him, reaching a great age. His son Joseph, minister at Malden, Massachusetts, married Mary Moody, daughter of a minister. They had ten children, of whom two became ministers. Joseph, the second child, became minister of Pepperell; and the ninth of the family, William, was pastor of Concord when the Revolution began.

It is pleasant enough to believe that the vigorous English stock which had given intellectual and moral leaders to seven New England towns, and to several their founders, was meanwhile represented in the mother country by that William Emerson whose marble effigy remains in St. Saviour's Church, Southwark, and Thomas, his grandson, whose charitable bequest (1620) still brings comfort to twelve aged pensioners in London. The epitaph on the tomb is, "Here under lyeth the body of William Emerson, who lived and died an honest man. He departed out of this life the 27th of June anno 1575, in the year of his age 92. Ut sym sic eris." The pensioners sit together every Sunday in St. Saviour's, in seats marked "Emerson's Pensioners," and after the morning service receive from one of the wardens each their weekly three-and-ninepence. With this same old church was connected Mr. Harvard, who was a Governor of its Grammar School, and father of the founder of Harvard University. Lately I walked from St. Saviour's to the old Emerson estate in the Borough, passing along Park Road to Summer Street, and there found Emerson Place and Emerson Terrace, the quietest spot of that crowded region. All Boston names! Yet the helpful chaplain of St. Saviour's cannot find the family arms of this benefactor, and one can only conjecture that the recurrence of the names "William" and "Thomas" and the name of the estate ("God's Providence"), indicate a common origin with the American family.

There is less reason to doubt that the Emersons who gave America the first of that name also gave England the famous Durham mathematician, William Emerson (1701–82), whose arms were the same. When I mentioned this to Emerson he said, "Then he must have appropriated all my mathematics, for I can't multiply 7 by 12 with security." To which I returned a sentence spoken by him many years before — "The vine which intoxicates the world is the most mathematical of plants." Some characteristics of the Durham mathematician were certainly Emersonian; notably his fondness for the solitude of his paternal estate, his severe independence, and his exceeding care about the proof of his books. Having walked all the way from Durham to London, when he had a work in press, he revised every sheet as it appeared, and could not endure an error. He was suspected of familiarity with the black art. Carlyle told me the story of a poor woman whose husband had not returned from sea at the usual time, and who went to consult William Emerson. He happened to meet her at the door, and when with a curtesy she asked where her man might be, "*In hell*," was the old man's answer, emphasised by his door's sharp slam.

Ralph Waldo was more courteous when he was supposed to be dealing in uncanny knowledge.

William Emerson, the grandfather of Ralph Waldo, was the first with whom liberal religious ideas may be clearly connected. It was at the end of a controversy in Concord over the theology of Jonathan Edwards that the Arminians found themselves strong enough to elect an opponent of extreme Calvinism, and as the result William Emerson was chosen minister of the church. There are, however, indications that the Emersons had historically represented the vanguard of the pilgrimage from Puritanism. William Emerson was born in 1743, graduated at Harvard in 1761, settled over the Concord congregation in 1764, and, having married in 1766, built the famous Old Manse for his residence, in 1767. He was chaplain of the Continental Congress in the Revolution, and in that war he did great service, arousing the people by his eloquence and fine enthusiasm. He died of a fever caught while accompanying the army in 1776.

The next minister at Concord was Dr. Ezra Ripley. He married the widow — and, so to say, the church — of William Emerson, and occupied the Old Manse. He lived long enough to be a bridge between the Arminian and the Unitarian doctrine, with which last the church became identified during his ministry. He was especially remarkable for his personal and patriarchal relations with every man, woman, and child in Concord, and not one of them could be afflicted without being prayed for by name. An anecdote related by Dr. George Ellis shows that the old man must have been a sort of "survival." "Dr. Channing told me expressly always, in the public prayer of the church, to recognise the afflicted. 'Afflicted and sorrowing persons are always around us. Make reference to them as tenderly as you wish, but never specify any case,' was his advice. Very shortly after I was settled — it must have been forty years ago — I went up to exchange with Barzillai Frost, who was the colleague of the good and venerable Dr. Ripley, who, of course, followed the old ways. He was very marked for the quality of specific personal references in his prayers. Some of you may remember that Mr. Emerson, in paying his tribute to Dr. Ripley after his death, spoke of that quality of individualising in prayer. A man had died in his parish who did not bear a very good name, but was a very strong man; and on two occasions he had been of service at fires, and saved life or furniture. At the funeral Dr. Ripley prayed, 'We thank thee, O Lord, that thy departed servant was good at fires.' I had an experience with this Dr. Ripley. I went, as I say, to exchange with Mr. Frost. It was a great breach of courtesy on my part that I did not go to the home of the aged pastor to attend him to meeting; but I accompanied Mrs. Frost, and got into the pulpit first. After a while I heard the steps of the venerable man slipping along; and, as he got toward the stairs of the pulpit, he asked aloud, 'Has the minister gone up yet?' I stood up and opened the door to welcome him in. He handed me two notes. They had no names attached, but referred to families in the congregation. I, of course, knew nothing about them. I followed my rule in the prayer of general reference. Dr. Ripley was hard of hearing, and leaned up against me, with his hand behind his ear, while I prayed, making me very uncomfortable. The 'Amen' was scarcely out of my mouth before he said aloud, 'You said nothing about our afflicted friends.' I had to raise my voice to make him hear, as I replied, 'I make it a rule not to make any special references in prayer.' 'It's a very poor rule, and the sooner you change it the better!' he shouted in answer. I told Mr. Frost that, so long as Dr. Ripley lived, I must decline going into that pulpit again."

"He seemed," said Emerson of Dr. Ripley, who died in 1841, "in his constitutional leaning to their religion, one of the rearguard of the great camp and army of the Puritans; and now, when all the platforms and customs of the church are losing their hold in the affections of men, it was fit that he should depart; fit that, in the fall of laws, a loyal man should die."

William Emerson, the father of Ralph Waldo, was born in the Old Manse in 1769. He was six years old when the shuddering family gazed upon the Concord fight beneath their windows. He was an only son, and at eleven years of age, by his mother's marriage with Dr. Ripley, came under the care of that kindly old minister. The Old Manse was the seat of a fine hospitality, and William was able to listen to the best conversation. His career, which would probably have added a shining name to American letters had he not died prematurely, singularly coincides with that of his son Ralph. He graduated at Harvard at seventeen with a similar reputation for excellence in composition, rhetoric, and classical studies. He taught school, studied theology irregularly, and as a preacher made a strong impression. He was the most liberal preacher who had yet appeared in Boston, when he was installed there over the First Church (1799), and devoted himself to what was universal and ethical in Christianity.

He is described as a blond, handsome man, graceful and benignant, with a melodious voice, and in every respect simple and scholarly. In a sketch of William Tudor, in Duyckinck's "Cyclopædia of American Literature," we have a remarkable anticipation of the time of the Transcendental Club and the "Dial." This journal, which bore the name of "The Monthly Anthology," was originally commenced in November, 1803, by Mr. Phineas Adams, a graduate of Harvard, and at the time teacher of a school in Boston. At the end of six months it fell into the hands of the Rev. William Emerson, who, joining a few friends with him, laid the foundation of the "Anthology Club." The magazine was then announced as edited "by a society of gentlemen." By the theory of the club every member was to write for the "Anthology," but the rule was modified, as usual, by the social necessities of the company, and the journal was greatly indebted to outsiders for its articles. The members, however, had the privilege of paying its expenses, which in those days could hardly have been expected to be met by the public. In giving an account of this work subsequently, Mr. Tudor remarks: "Whatever may have been the merit of the 'Anthology,' its authors would have been sadly disappointed if they had looked for any other advantages to be derived from it than an occasional smile from the public, the amusement of their task, and the pleasure of their social meetings. The publication never gave enough to pay the moderate expense of their suppers, and through their whole career they wrote and paid for the pleasure of writing." Whereon we may reflect in the saying of one born in the same year as his father's "Anthology"—"Sport is the sign of health." The magazine enlisted the best pens, John Quincy Adams, Channing, George Ticknor, Richard H. Dana, Andrews Norton, and Buckminster. It died in 1811, when its editor died, his son, Ralph Waldo Emerson, being then eight years old.

III.

THREE FATES.

A FINE copy of the famous picture long ascribed to Michael Angelo, the "Parcæ," hung over the fireplace in Emerson's study, a work of art mystically associated with him by his friends. Sometimes he wove the thread spun and clipped by the old women into his conversation. It meant many things to him, and it used to warn some of his friends not by any idle visit to clip the golden thread of thought which ran through the morning that always shone in that study. But gradually, as I learned the story of Emerson's early life, the three formidable faces softened to those of the young and fair women who had presided over his destinies, and who remained young and fair even in old age.

The mother of Emerson, who had been Ruth Haskins of Boston, was a lady of refined culture, of gracious and religious nature, with the blended sweetness and dignity of manner so characteristic of the son. She builded her household in beauty and wisdom when it was left to her on her husband's death. Five sons were thrown upon her care, of whom Ralph was the second. He was born in that happy and cultured home in Boston, and was eight years old when his father died. Mary Emerson was second of the fostering Fates, having devoted herself to the assistance of her brother's widow in bringing up her children. Besides being of an earnest and conscientious nature, she must be described as a woman of some genius. With a rather formidable eye for all social shams and pretences, a lively interest in all large subjects, and an individuality that verged on eccentricity, her influence was a stimulant to self-reliance. She was almost passionately fond of philosophical studies and well acquainted with the chief European works of that character. There was a considerable survival of the ascetic temper in her, and of theological bias, though she did not accept traditional views in the traditional way. In the discussion of metaphysical problems she had few equals, and her criticisms were often quoted in the controversies which attended the development of heresy in New England. She used to claim that she was "in arms at the battle of Concord," being two years old at the time, and held up by her mother to see it; but in the theological struggles of a later period her share was less equivocal.

The third of Emerson's Parcæ was Sarah Bradford. She was as fine a Greek scholar as America has produced, an accomplished mathematician, and possessed scientific attainments of which professors were glad to ask aid. Of this wonderful woman — not less admirable for her simplicity and womanly charm than for her scholarship — more will be said hereafter; it may be mentioned here, that when Emerson, just after his father's death, entered the grammar school, and afterward when he was studying in the Latin School at

Boston, she corresponded with him about every book and lesson, and revised his translations. From this period she accompanied his entire progress in culture, and to the last was the intimate friend of his thought.

These three women, all refined and cultivated — representing the religious sensibility, the self-reliance, and the philosophical thought and scientific scholarship of the New England renaissance, so to say — had charge of the Emerson boys. Never were maternal Parcæ more triumphant. The annals of Harvard may be searched in vain to find more brilliant careers than those of several of these youths. It was even for a time doubtful which of them was to be "the coming man." Affectionate with each other, sympathetic in their studies and opinions, devoted to their mother and her two friends (of whom indeed any youths might have been proud), they were born free of the besetting vices of young men, while full of humour and enterprise.

The family, without being straitened in circumstances, had to observe strict economy for the supreme object of education, and when the elder had graduated they taught school to pay the way of the younger through college. William was to have entered the ministry, and went to Germany to pursue his studies for that end. He there formed the acquaintance of Goethe, and studied German criticisms until his opinions became sceptical concerning Christianity, and he was compelled to disappoint his mother in his selection of a profession. He died a few years ago, after a successful career in New York as a barrister. It required a good deal of moral courage in the elder son to disappoint his mother and the eminent clergymen around her, who were looking forward to another William Emerson, to make good the promise of the brilliant father.

The third son, Edward Bliss, also studied law, and in the office of Daniel Webster; but lost his health in early life, and went to Porto Rico, where he died. "The Last Farewell," written by him in 1832, while sailing out of Boston harbour on the voyage from which he never returned, was printed in the first number of the "Dial," and is included in "May Day, and other Poems," followed by Emerson's "In Memoriam." Robert Bulkeley was enfeebled by scarlet fever, and died in middle life.

Charles Chauncy died in 1836. This was a particularly heavy bereavement, not only to the family, but to a large circle of friends. He was betrothed to Elizabeth Hoar of Concord, then as afterwards an intimate and cherished friend of Emerson.

In the "Dial" some literary fragments left by Charles Emerson were published as "Notes from the Journal of a Scholar," preceded by lines from Persius —

"Nunc non e manibus illis
Nunc non e tumulo, fortunataque favilla
Nascuntur violæ?"

Those who read these casual but most suggestive paragraphs concerning Homer, Shakespeare, Burke, will not wonder at the enthusiasm of his friends, which anticipated for him a brilliant career. Dr. Oliver Wendell

Holmes, who was his class-mate, wrote concerning Charles Emerson these beautiful lines: —

"Thou calm, chaste scholar! I can see thee now,
The first young laurels on thy pallid brow;
O'er thy slight figure floating lightly down
In graceful folds the academic gown;
On thy curled lip the classic lines, that taught
How nice the mind that sculptured them with thought,
And triumph glistening in the clear blue eye,
Too bright to live, — but oh, too fair to die!"

I quote a passage from Charles Emerson's journal, from which one may gather that he did not die, but was caught up into the spirit of the brother who mourned his loss so profoundly.

"This afternoon we read Shakespeare. The verse so sank into me, that as I toiled my way home under the cloud of night, with the gusty music of the storm around and overhead, I doubted that it was all a remembered scene; that humanity was indeed one, a spirit continually reproduced, accomplishing a vast orbit, whilst individual men are but the points through which it passes.

"We each of us furnish to the angel who stands in the sun a single observation. The reason why Homer is to me like dewy morning is because I too lived while Troy was, and sailed in the hollow ships of the Grecians to sack the devoted town. The rosy-fingered dawn as it crimsoned the top of Ida, the broad sea-shore dotted with tents, the Trojan hosts in their painted armour, and the rushing chariots of Diomed and Idomeneus — all these too I saw; my ghost animated the frame of some nameless Argive. And Shakespeare in 'King John' does but recall me to myself in the dress of another age, the sport of new accidents. I, who am Charles, was sometime Romeo. In Hamlet, I pondered and doubted. We forget what we have been, drugged with the sleepy bowl of the present; but when a lively chord in the soul is struck, when the windows for a moment are unbarred, the long and varied past is recovered. We recognise it all. We are no more brief, ignoble creatures; we seize our immortality, and bind together the related parts of our secular being."

It will be seen that the elemental Fates did but partially second the faithful and wise human Providences which had watched over these young men. It may partly have been the pain suffered in the loss of his brothers which taught Emerson his peculiar horror of ill-health, which he spoke of as a ghoul, and dreaded as the hermits did any sign of a demon invading their solitude. It may also have been in part the love, wisdom, and character represented in his three Fates — Ruth, Sarah, Mary — which made him among the earliest to demand that the equality of woman with man should be represented in politics and the laws.

IV.

A BOSTON BOY.

THE later life of Emerson furnishes various foregrounds from which his early life may be seen in right perspective. That which I select is the great New Year's Day of 1863, which brought President Lincoln's proclamation of freedom to the American slaves, when Emerson read to a large assembly his noble Boston Hymn.

The proclamation found the people assembled in Boston and Emerson reading to them his Hymn: —

> "The word of the Lord by night
> To the watching Pilgrims came
> As they sat by the seaside,
> And filled their hearts with flame.
>
> " God said, I am tired of kings,
> I suffer them no more;
> Up to my ear the morning brings
> The outrage of the poor."

So it opened, and through the twenty-two verses, so full of majesty, the vast audience listened with hearts aflame.

What a vista was visible behind that scholar who

came from his Concord solitude to rejoice with his fellow-citizens and set their bounding pulses to music! Near that fine Music Hall he was born. Along meadows now covered with mansions he had driven his mother's cow to pasture, pausing on the way to read a little in his Greek or Latin book. As one of his friends lately wrote — Frank Sanborn, a college comrade of my own — of that boyhood in Boston: — "He breathed in its atmosphere and its traditions as a boy while he drove his mother's cow to pasture along what are now the finest streets. He learned his first lessons of life in its schools and churches; listened to Webster and Story in its courts, to Josiah Quincy and Harrison Gray Otis in its town-meetings at Faneuil Hall; heard sermons in the Old South Meeting-house." Some years ago, in a speech made at a little gathering of grey-haired gentlemen who had been his companions at the Latin School, Emerson referred to the time when the city was in alarm at the rumoured approach of the British in the war of 1812. The master invited the boys to go out to a neighbouring island and help in throwing up earthern defences against the enemy. He remembered a pleasant holiday on Noddle Island, but not any work done by the boys. Whether Great Britain altered her plans on discovering this movement in the Latin School he could not say. Amid such events the Boston Hymn was in process of composition, line by line. The scion of English noblemen was learning his lesson in nobility.

The Rev. Mr. Cooke, in his book on Emerson, tells a pretty story of these early years. He once brought home the first volume of a novel from the circulating library, having paid six cents for it. His aunt Mary reproved him for spending his money in that way, when it was so hard for his mother to obtain it. He was so affected by this appeal that he returned the volume and did not take out the other; nor was the end of the romance ever read.

The two leaders of Boston, in those early years, were Webster and Channing. The traditions of the great struggle for American independence were still fresh in many memories, and Daniel Webster gathered up these in his powerful intelligence, and was their organ on every national occasion. His oratory was of the New England type, not passionate after the style of Southerners, but grave and impressive, and sometimes rising to a poetic strain. There was a grandeur in his personal appearance, such as is ascribed to Goethe, and the tones of his voice were as majestic. When I heard him in the United States Senate, it was after he had begun to surrender the high principles of New England, and there was an undertone of insincerity which excited distrust; but in the Supreme Court, where I have also heard him speak, he was still the true orator. Emerson has often told me of the effect of Webster upon his mind in boyhood, when he filled up his ideal of the Olympian Jove.

Channing had not as yet become the leader of the theological revolution afterwards associated with him, but he was the most eloquent preacher in Boston. He was ordained minister of a congregation there in 1803, the year of Emerson's birth, at the age of twenty-three, and during Emerson's boyhood was chiefly remarkable for his eloquent discourses against war, intemperance, and other evils. The Emerson family attended Channing's church, and Ralph might have heard, in 1814, that brilliant thanksgiving for the overthrow of Napoleon. Channing was intimate in the Emerson home, and the youths always thought of him as a dear relative. The younger brothers of Channing also — Edward, a fine scholar and writer, and Walter, an eminent physician, both professors at Harvard — were of the circle of friends and instructors surrounding Emerson's early life. It was indeed a time favourable for the touching of fine spirits. The controversial era had not fully arrived. The enthusiasm of Channing was for Wordsworth, whose "Excursion" was to him a revelation. The talk was of poetry, heroism, humanity, the love of nature; and one of the earliest ideals that rose before the mind of Emerson was Wordsworth, with his plain living and high thinking, his recognition of all grandeurs, whether of nature or human character, in the scenery and the lowly people around his own home. He always spoke of Wordsworth as "the great modern poet," and once told me that he still found himself unable to compare any early intellectual experience with the effect produced on his mind by the poet's description of the influence of nature upon the mind of a boy.

V.

STUDENT AND TEACHER.

EMERSON was by no means the pedagogue's model boy. He valued studies from books held beneath the bench in the Latin School as much as those exacted. His schoolmates retained affectionate memories of him as a genial and spirited companion. The widow Emerson went to reside at Cambridge when her elder sons were prepared to enter Harvard University. Emerson became the President's freshman there at the age of fourteen. The office, long since abolished, was of some importance: the holder of it was in the President's confidence, and conveyed his will or admonitions to other students. The position was not favourable to an intimate relation with other students. His brother William was a senior at the time, and possibly Ralph Waldo preferred the company of the older youths. The proximity of his room to that of the President prevented its being much affected by other students, and he had more time for quiet reading. He had at this time come under the fascination of Montaigne and Shakespeare, and was never able to devote himself to the college curriculum. But he gained much from the eminent men who taught in the university at that time. Dr. Kirkland had become (1810) President of the university, which entered upon a new era — less religious and more scholarly — under his administration. He greatly enlarged its course of studies, increased the number of professorships, and improved the library. Some have dated the New England "Renaissance" from his presidency. He was a philosophical thinker, a man of fine personality, who preferred moulding minds to writing books. As a writer he possessed a remarkable power of generalisation. Among the professors was George Ticknor, historian of Spanish Literature. The most important men to Emerson were Edward Everett, professor of Greek; Levi Frisbie, professor of moral philosophy, the great representative of the intuitive system of ethics; and Edward Channing, professor of rhetoric and oratory. Edward Everett was the most graceful speaker in America at that time, and taught by example what Professor Channing taught by precept. In both of these studies, Greek and oratory, Emerson gained prizes. Among the students to whom he was attached were Josiah Quincy, afterwards an eminent personage in Boston; Charles W. Upham, the historian of Salem Witchcraft; George Ripley, the founder of Brook Farm Community; and W. H. Furness, the eminent philanthropist and author who conducted Emerson's funeral. Mr. Bancroft Hill has recorded the following : —

"While he was pursuing his college course, his mother moved to Cambridge, and some of the students boarded at her table. So he was boarding at home in his sophomore year when his class had a fight with the freshman at supper in Commons Hall — a fight described in the mock-heroic poem 'The Rebelliad.'

Some of the sophomores were expelled for their share in the disturbance, and thereupon the whole class indignantly withdrew from college. Emerson remained at home until his class came to terms with the authorities. This trouble had the result of binding the class closely together, and creating a warm sympathy which after years could not chill. On their return from banishment, Alden, the wag of the class, established the Conventicle Club — a convivial club of which Kingsbury was archbishop, Alden bishop, and John B. Hill parson. . . . Emerson was one of the number. Although his quiet nature kept him out of most of the convivial societies, he was always genial, fond of hearing or telling a good story, and ready to do his share towards an evening's entertainment." Emerson was also the leading spirit of a book-club among the students which purchased the English Reviews, and other current literature not found in the college library. He graduated in 1821, and was the "Class Poet" at Commemoration. The memorable class of that year held its annual reunion at Cambridge for fifty years.

Emerson graduated with a fine reputation in the university for general literary ability, classical culture, and eloquence. About this latter, however, opinions appear to have been divided. The Boylston professorship of rhetoric and oratory at Harvard included all English compositions, and attended to refinements of style with very great care. Emerson twice won Bowdoin prizes for dissertations, and in his senior year the second Boylston prize for elocution. His rival was Josiah Quincy, in whose journal is found the entry: "July 16, 1821. Attended a dissertation of Emerson's in the morning, on the subject of ethical philosophy. I found it long and dry." No doubt it was so as compared with the conventional oratory of the period. Josiah Quincy had the kind of oratory which could make a man mayor of Boston, and so made him. But Emerson had a new idea of eloquence and of its aim; and it is creditable to Professor Channing that even the second prize could have been awarded it sixty years ago. For it is now well known that his style of speaking was already of the quiet, self-restrained, and simple kind, whose striking effects were the result of artistic touches rather than elaborate statement or highly coloured illustrations. Writing of his college years, Mr. Bancroft Hill says: "His mind was unusually mature and independent. His letters and conversation already displayed something of originality; and if his two Bowdoin essays were published, I feel sure we should find in them many characteristic turns of thought and expression." He had an enthusiastic admiration for Edward Everett, then just returned from a European tour, in which he had made the acquaintance of Scott, Byron, Jeffrey, Davy, Romilly, Mackintosh, and had prepared himself for his new professorship by studying in Italy and Greece. His first lectures on Greek literature and art at Harvard were heard by Emerson with great admiration. Yet Emerson's style of lecturing was totally different from Everett's from the first. The measured gesture, the deliberate following of classical models, the never-concealed art of Everett soon palled upon the taste. In his famous lecture upon George Washington, I remember his taking up a glass of water, holding it for a moment, and dexterously spilling some of it as he spoke of Washington's purity and cleanliness of soul. There were no tricks of any kind in Emerson's discourse; he had no gesture or manner, but depended upon clearness of thought and simplicity of statement. He once told me that when he graduated, his ambition was to be a professor of rhetoric and elocution; and when I smiled at this, thinking only of what he had actually become, maintained that it was a great art. He recalled Saadi's gratitude for the one gift Allah had given him — "sweetness of speech" — and thought that many discords and controversies might be avoided if preachers and public speakers had adequately cultivated the art of putting things felicitously. He expressed the belief that an educated Boston congregation — and none could be more conservative just then — would call to their pulpit and listen to a really eloquent man whatever his opinions. "An atheist?" "Yes." But he must not be a pedant; he must have a genuine conviction, and speak from his own heart and mind. "The North suffers in debate with those eloquent Southern Congressmen at Washington because it has not a senator or representative who can speak as well for Northern as they for Southern principles." I named several Northern men I had heard at Washington, considered eloquent, but he said, "Yes, but they speak too much after the Southern style. The adequate answer must be characteristic of the people it comes from. I don't want a man there of the same type, though that is fit for its place and purpose." Daniel Webster was dead when Emerson said this; Edward Everett had long been over-compliant to the South, and his oratory had declined. Senator Sumner was much esteemed by Emerson, but was too much of an egoist to satisfy him. The men he would have been glad to send to Washington were Garrison and Wendell Phillips. Of Phillips he said, "It is one of the picturesque incidents of the anti-slavery effort that such a man as Wendell Phillips should be devoting himself to popular gatherings in Massachusetts, and facing mobs with an eloquence that would be admired in any country. He is an ornamental person, with a culture and wealth that presuppose European society and art galleries." Of Dr. Channing he spoke with warm admiration. "The charm of his preaching is not to be discovered by reading his sermons; whenever he spoke it seemed to an occasion; the heart of his audience rose to meet him; here was something sufficient; the multitude found it good to be there, and went away fed, satisfied."

Not his own inclination at the time, but his family affections, determined the first step of Emerson after graduation. William Emerson had set up a school for girls in Boston, with the view of assisting his brothers through college. Ralph now went to join him. He did not like the work much, being no doubt eager to enter upon further studies, but his sympathy with young people and instinct for individualisation made him an excellent teacher. The severest discipline administered is said to have been sending a pupil now and then to his mother's room to pursue her studies. The school was near the Federal Street Church (Channing's), and Emerson witnessed the most striking example of the power possible to the American pulpit. It was in the year of Emerson's graduation (1821) that the new impulse

given to the liberal tendencies of America began to be
generally felt. In that year Channing gave his Dud-
leian lecture at Cambridge on the " Evidences of
Christianity." Every word spoken in that Boston
church was now heard throughout the country. He
saw Channing to be a " necessary " person, as he said
long afterwards, one affirming the verdict of the human
faculties, and passing solemn sentence upon guilty
dogmas by simply stating their offence against the
moral sentiment.

VI.

APPROBATION.

THE determination of his brother William not to enter the ministry, which caused his mother sorrow, may have inclined Emerson to that profession, but probably Dr. Channing was the determining influence. He began the study of theology when he was twenty years of age — not entering Divinity College, but keeping abreast of its classes — and after three years was "approbated to preach" by the Middlesex Association of Preachers. Unitarianism had no written creed, but it had certain forms, concerning which Emerson already had doubts. It looks as if he had not quite kept Lord Bacon's prescription for health, "Never to do anything contrary to your genius," for Emerson went South for his health, and probably his first public sermon was given in Charleston, which then had the only Unitarian pulpit south of the Potomac. In college his room-mate had been a South Carolinian (John Gourdin), and Emerson always had a pleasant feeling towards the South ("except those bonds"), and in after life would have gladly passed some winters in Florida, where the author of "Uncle Tom's Cabin" now finds a congenial home. Part of that winter (1826-27) was indeed passed in beautiful Florida, whose fragrance is in his early song, "To Ellen at the South."

On his return from the South, in the spring of 1827, his first sermons were given at New Bedford. The impression made by Emerson at this time on best persons was remarkable. His earliest sermons are almost forgotten in the charm of his personality and in the warm glow of his sympathies, in his *das Dämonische*, which, in Emerson, was known in a peculiar joy felt in his presence. In the privately printed Life of the late Mrs. Lyman of Northampton, written by her daughter, Mrs. Lesley, there are some pages that show the young preacher's footprints already traceable in flowers. They who know anything of the late Mrs. Lyman need not be told that one fourteen years her junior must have possessed extraordinary character and powers to make such an impression upon her as appears in this volume, which my friend who wrote it kindly permits me to use. In the autumn of 1827, Mr. Hall, the minister at Northampton, being in ill health, his pulpit was supplied by young ministers from Boston. "During this autumn my mother heard that Mrs. Hall was expecting one of the preachers to stay at her house for a fortnight. She did not even know the name of the expected guest, but she knew Mrs. Hall was not well, so she sent her word that, when the preacher came, she would like to have him transferred to her house. It was Mr. Ralph Waldo Emerson, then a young man, who took up his abode for a fortnight under her friendly roof. I have no power to convey in words the impression she used to give me of this visit, or its effect upon her appreciative mind. To her sister she mirthfully quoted an expression sometimes used by her orthodox neighbours about certain students at Amherst, and wrote, " O Sally ! I thought to entertain 'a pious indigent,' but lo ! an angel unawares ! " Not long after this visit, my brother Joseph became intimate with Charles Emerson at Cambridge, a friendship which my mother hailed as one of the highest and holiest influences in the life of her beloved son. She rarely saw Mr. Emerson in later life ; a few letters passed between them. Once (in 1849) he spent a few days at her house while lecturing in Northampton, and after her removal to Cambridge he called to see her. The personal feeling towards him thus engendered burned henceforth with a flame that threw light upon every passage of his writings, gilded the gloom of many a weary day, and made her fine face shine with responsive sympathy for the author as she read aloud. She was wont to feel a certain property in him and his works ; and I have seen her ready to shed tears when she could not see any appreciation of his thought in her listener. To one I have heard her say, " Well, you call that *transcendental*, and *that's* all you have to say about it. *I* call it the profoundest common sense." To another, " You think it very arrogant of me to pretend to understand Mr. Emerson. Well, I tell you I have the key to him ; and I am not going to pretend I have *not*, whatever any one thinks." And so as the years went by, and volume after volume appeared of the Essays, she hailed them with delight and read them till they became part of herself.

It is the best benefit of searching into genealogies that

it brings us on so many fair fulfilments reversing ill omens. That beautiful and happy wife of Judge Lyman was a descendant of Anne Hutchinson, whose genius re-appeared in her. Emerson's ancestor, Rev. Peter Bulkeley, presided over the Synod which banished Anne Hutchinson to Rhode Island and to death. Now these two meet in near friendship, and in the sorrows that were presently the portion of Anne Lyman the word of consolation and sympathy from Emerson never failed.

The first sentences of Emerson which I have read are in a letter written from Divinity Hall, Cambridge, February 11, 1828, to Mrs. Lyman on the death of her brother-in-law, Judge Howe, resulting from devotion to the duties of his office. "In such a death of such a man, if there must be to his family and friends the deepest grief, there must also be to them a feeling of deep and holy joy. There is something in his character which seems to make excessive sorrow unseasonable and unjust to his memory, and all who have heard of his death have derived from it new force to virtue and new confidence to faith."

In a letter dated "Boston, August 25, 1829," to the same friend, he introduces Mr. George Bradford: "But who is Mr. Bradford? He is Mrs. Ripley's brother, and a fine classical and Biblical scholar, and a botanist, and a lover of truth, and 'an Israelite in whom is no guile,' and a kind of Cowper, and a great admirer of all admirable things; and so I want him to go to your house, where his eyes and ears shall be enriched with what he loves."

It is a little droll to find him in this note speaking of

getting Mr. Upham to point him out the lions on a public occasion at Cambridge. Speaking of some pecuniary losses sustained by their friends, Emerson says: — "God seems to make some of his children for prosperity, they bear it so gracefully, and with such good-will of society; and it is always painful when such suffer. But I suppose it is always dangerous, and especially to the very young. In college, I used to echo a frequent ejaculation of my wise aunt's, 'Oh, blessed, blessed poverty!' when I saw young men of fine capabilities, whose only and fatal disadvantage was wealth. It is sad to see it taken from those who know how to use it, but children whose prospects are changed may hereafter rejoice at the event."

The question of immortality, so anxiously discussed with Carlyle at Craigenputtock, is touched in a letter to Mrs. Lyman, January 6, 1830, on the death of her father, in which he speaks of the "*hopes* which our Saviour has imparted to us." "Take away these hopes, and death is more ghastly to the soul than the corpse to the eye. Receive them, and the riddle of the universe is explained; an account given of events perfectly consistent with what we feel in ourselves when we are best." Six years later, in his first book, Emerson wrote, "Even the corpse has its own beauty."

In a letter to this lady on the occasion of a heavy bereavement, — the death of a lovely daughter, — he writes (1837): — "How gladly have I remembered the glimpses I had of her sunny childhood, her winning manners, her persuading speech, that then made her father, I believe, call her his 'lawyer.' In the pleasant weeks I spent at your house, I rejoiced in the promise of her beauty, and have pleased myself with the hope that she was surmounting her early trials, and was destined to be one of those rare women who exalt society, and who make credible to us a better society than is seen in the earth. I still keep by me one of her drawings which she gave me. I have scarcely seen her face since. But we feel a property in all the accomplishments and graces that we know, which neither distance nor absence destroys. For my part, I grudge the decays of the young and beautiful whom I may never see again. Even in their death, is the reflection that we are for ever enriched by having beheld them, — that we can never be quite poor and low, for they have furnished our heart and mind with new elements of beauty and wisdom.

"And now she is gone out of sight, I can only offer to you and to Judge Lyman my respectful and affectionate condolence. I am sure I need not suggest the deep consolations of the spiritual life, for love is the first believer, and all the remembrances of her life will plead with you in behalf of the hope of all souls. How do we go, all of us, to the world of spirits, marshalled and beckoned unto by noble and lovely friends! That event cannot be fearful which made a part of the constitution and career of beings so finely framed and touched, and whose influence on us has been so benign. These sad departures open to us, as other events do not, that ineradicable faith which the secret history of every year strips of its obscurities, — that we can and must exist for evermore."

In her extreme age, the lady to whom these letters

were written was visited by Emerson and one of his daughters. It was a great joy to her, and she wrote: — "Perhaps I shall never see Mr. Emerson any more. Well, 'I saw his day and was glad.'" To lead on this glad day which her so distant daughter beheld, — the triumph of her noble thought and spirit, — Anne Hutchinson had lived and died.

But we must return now to the beginning of Emerson's ministerial career. After preaching at various places, — among others for some Sundays at Concord, — and meanwhile writing poetry, he was ordained minister of the Second Church in Boston, March 11, 1829. It was at first as colleague of the Rev. Henry Ware, jun., but shortly after he became sole pastor of the church. Eminent Unitarian ministers participated in the ordination services, and Emerson received a hearty welcome. In September of the same year he was married to Ellen Louisa Tucker. He was at once accorded in Boston the highest position, and was listened to with admiration in the church of Channing. A venerable minister gave me an account of a sermon he heard from Emerson in those days, impressed on his memory by the vitality it infused in an old theme, and the simplicity with which it was delivered. The text was, "What is a man profited if he shall gain the whole world and lose his own soul?" The emphasis was on the word "own," and the general theme was that to every man the great end of existence was the preservation and culture of his individual mind and character. Each man must be saved by his own inward redeemer; and the whole world is for each but a plastic material through which the individual spirit is to realise itself. Aspiration and thought become clear and real only by action and life. If knowledge leads not to action, it passes away, being preserved only on the condition of being used. "The last thing," added my informant, "that any of us who heard him would have predicted of the youth, whose quiet simplicity and piety captivated all, was that he would become the religious revolutionist of America."

I once asked Emerson about his sermons, and he told me he had utilised them in his Essays, these being, however, less ethical in form. In a pulpit address delivered in 1830 at Concord, occur characteristic words of Emerson. It was at the ordination of a new minister there. Having recalled the phrase, "Be of one mind," he said: "Thousands of hearts have heard the commandment, and anon with joy receive it. All men on whose souls the light of God's revelation truly shineth, with whatever apparent differences, are substantially of one mind, work together, whether consciously or not, for one and the same good. Faces that never beheld each other are lighted up by it with the same expression. Hands that were never clasped toil unceasingly at the same work. This it is which makes the omnipotence of truth in the keeping of feeble men, this fellowship in all its servants, this swift consenting acknowledgment with which they hail it when it appears God's truth; it is that electric spark which flies instantaneously through the countless bands that compose the chain. Truth, not like each form of error, depending for its repute on the powers and influence of here and there a solitary mind that espouses it, combines hosts for its support, and makes them co-operate across mountains, yea, and ages of time."

Emerson took an active interest in the public affairs of Boston. He was on its School Board, and was chosen chaplain of the State Senate. He invited the anti-slavery lecturers into his church, and helped philanthropists of other denominations in their work. Father Taylor, to whom Dickens gave an English fame, found in him his most important supporter when establishing the Seaman's Mission in Boston. This was told me by Father Taylor himself in his old age. I happened to be in his company once when he spoke rather sternly about my leaving the Methodist Church, but when I spoke of the part Emerson had in it, he softened at once, and spoke with emotion of his great friend. I have no doubt that if the good Father of Boston Seamen was proud of any personal thing, it was of the excellent answer he is said to have given to some Methodists who objected to his friendship for Emerson. Being a Unitarian, they insisted that he must go to hell. "It does look so," said Father Taylor; "but I am sure of one thing, if Emerson goes to hell he will change the climate there, and emigration will se that way."

VII.

DISAPPROBATION.

IN June, 1832, Emerson invited the most active members of his church to his house, "to receive a communication from him in relation to the views at which he had arrived respecting the ordinance of the Lord's Supper." He there made his statement of objections to the existing form, and proposed to "so far change the manner of administering the rite as to disuse the elements and relinquish the claim of authority." He suggested a modification. After hearing this communication a committee was appointed (Deacons Mackintosh and Patterson, Dr. John Ware, George B. Emerson, George A. Sampson, Gedney King, and Samuel Beal) to consider the subject. They reported and submitted: "(1.) That in the opinion of this church, after a careful consideration of this subject, it is expedient to maintain the celebration of the Lord's Supper in the present form. (2.) That the brethren of this church retain an undiminished regard for their pastor, and entertain the hope that he will find it consistent with his sense of duty to continue the customary administration of the Supper." The minister, however, having given an explanatory sermon on the subject, offered a kindly but firm resignation of his charge.

It is significant that the only sermon by Emerson ever published was this of September 9, 1832, in which he announced his resignation of his pulpit and assigned his reasons for it. It is given in full in O. B. Frothingham's "Transcendentalism in New England." Reading it, one cannot but wonder that the Unitarians should have let go such a preacher. The text was Romans xiv. 17, "The kingdom of God is not meat and drink, but righteousness, and peace, and joy in the Holy Ghost." The history of controversies on the subject is condensed in a page, yet in a way which shows that every phase of it had been carefully studied, up to the time when "the Society of Quakers denied the authority of the rite altogether, and gave good reasons for disusing it." Next are given his reasons for believing that Jesus did not intend to establish an institution for perpetual observance when he ate the Passover with his disciples. The only reporter of the incident whose words, "This do in remembrance of me," would bear a different construction, was Luke, who was not present. But what did this expression really signify? "It is a prophetic and an affectionate expression. Jesus is a Jew, sitting with his countrymen, celebrating their national feast. He thinks of his own impending death, and wishes the minds of his disciples to be prepared for it. 'When hereafter,' he says to them, 'you shall keep the Passover, it will have an altered aspect to your eyes. It is now a historical covenant of God with the Jewish nation. Hereafter it will remind you of a new covenant sealed with my blood. In years to come, as long as your people shall come up to Jerusalem to keep this feast, the connection which has subsisted between us will give a new meaning in your eyes to the national festival, as the anniversary of my death.' I see natural feeling and beauty in the use of such language from Jesus, a friend to his friends. I can readily imagine that he was willing and desirous, when his disciples met, his memory should hallow their intercourse; but I cannot bring myself to believe that in the use of such an expression he looked beyond the living generation, beyond the abolition of the festival he was celebrating and the scattering of the nation, and meant to impose a memorial feast upon the whole world." Then follows a statement of the Eastern way of teaching, the readiness of Jesus to spiritualise every occurrence — as in washing his disciples' feet, more emphatically enjoined as an example than any sacrament. The communism of the first disciples, which rendered such a festival natural; the expectation of the second coming of Jesus, which influenced the mind of Paul to preserve the local rite, were considered with great force, and led up to the general view. As to the question of expediency, he thinks the ordinance produces confusion in our views of the relation of the soul to God. "For the service does not stand upon the basis of a voluntary act, but is imposed by authority." "The use of the elements, however suitable to the people and modes of thought in the East, where it originated, is foreign and unsuited to affect us." This alone is a sufficient objection to the ordinance. "It is my own objection. This mode of commemorating Christ is not suitable to me. That is reason enough why I should abandon it. If I believed that it was enjoined by Jesus on his disciples, and that he even contemplated making permanent this mode of commemoration, every way agreeable to an Eastern mind, and yet, on trial, it was disagreeable to my own feelings, I should not adopt it. I should choose other ways which, as more effectual upon me, he would approve more. For I choose that my remembrances of him should be pleasing, affecting, religious. I will love him as a glorious friend, after the free way of friendship, and not pay him a stiff sign of respect, as men do to those whom they fear. A passage read from his discourses, a moving provocation to works like his, any act or meeting which tends to awaken a pure thought, a flow of love, an original design of virtue, I call a true, a worthy commemoration." Freedom, he declares, is the essence of this faith. "It has for its object simply to make men good and wise. Its institutions, then, should be as flexible as the wants of men. That form out of which the life and suitableness have departed should be as worthless in its eyes as the dead leaves that are falling around us." "Although I have gone back to weigh the expressions of Paul, I feel that here is the true point of view. In the midst of considerations as to what Paul thought, and why he so thought, I cannot help feeling that it is time misspent to argue to or from his convictions, or those of Luke and John, respecting any form. I seem to lose the substance in seeking the shadow. That for which Paul lived and died so gloriously; that for which Jesus gave himself to be crucified; the end that animated the thousand martyrs and heroes who have followed his steps, was to redeem us from a formal religion, and teach us to seek our wellbeing in the formation of the soul. The whole world was full of idols and ordinances. The Jewish was a religion of forms. The Pagan was a religion of forms; it was all body — it had no life; and the Almighty God was pleased to qualify and send forth a man to teach men that they must serve him with the heart; that only that life was religious which was thoroughly good; that sacrifice was smoke, and forms were shadows. This man lived and died true to this purpose; and now with his blessed word and life before us, Christians must contend that it is a matter of vital importance, really a duty, to commemorate him by a certain form, whether that form be agreeable to their understandings or not. Is not this to make vain the gift of God? Is not this to turn back the hand on the dial?"

In conclusion Emerson said: "My brethren have considered my views with patience and candour, and have recommended unanimously an adherence to the present form. I have, therefore, been compelled to consider whether it becomes me to administer it. I am clearly of opinion I ought not. This discourse has already been so far extended, that I can only say that the reason of my determination is shortly this: It is my desire, in the office of a Christian minister, to do nothing which I cannot do with my whole heart. Having said this, I have said all. I have no hostility to this institution; I am only stating my want of sympathy with it. Neither should I ever have obtruded my opinion upon other people had I not been called by my office to administer it. That is the end of my opposition, that I am not interested in it. I am content that it stand to the end of the world, if it please men and please Heaven, and I shall rejoice in all the good it produces.

"As it is the prevailing opinion and feeling in our religious community that it is an indispensable part of the pastoral office to administer this ordinance, I am about to resign into your hands that office which you have confided to me. It has many duties for which I am feebly qualified. It has some which it will always be my delight to discharge, according to my ability, wherever I exist. And whilst the recollection of its claims oppresses me with a sense of my unworthiness, I am consoled by the hope that no time and no change can deprive me of the satisfaction of pursuing and exercising its highest functions."

Bishop Huntington, once a Unitarian preacher in Boston, recently said that "to a degree Mr. Emerson's aberrations in religious thought were due to his inaptitude for thinking consecutively and logically on any abstract subject." Dr. Huntington has too readily taken at the foot of the letter Emerson's casual talk of the same kind about himself. The sermon from which I have quoted is an admirable piece of methodical work throughout, and of consecutive logical reasoning. When Emerson had a practical purpose in view, as in this sermon and in several of his essays during the war, he proved himself amply able to follow the logical method. That he did not ordinarily do so was because he was more interested in points not to be so carried.

Although Emerson's congregation were loth to part with a man who had reflected such honour upon them, and showed in various ways their continued love for him, the Unitarian community outside acted far less creditably. Among his warmest friends was the Methodist, Father Taylor, who bravely said, "Mr.

Emerson may think this or that, but he is more like Jesus Christ than any one I have ever known. I have seen him when his religion was tested, and it bore the test." The report was circulated among the Unitarians and believed that Emerson was insane! The extent to which Unitarian churches in Boston have discontinued the Eucharist, and the recent encomiums on Emerson delivered in them, warrant the hope that, some day, the Unitarians will adopt the rule of making an annual pilgrimage to the grave at Concord, in remembrance that when the intellectual flower of the New World rose before them, some cried, "Infidel!" and others "Madman!"

But the impression made by Emerson's brief ministry in Boston was lasting. From that day to this there have been men and women, well known for their leading part in all high works and movements, whose lives and characters were mainly influenced by his sermons.

VIII.

A SEA-CHANGE.

EMERSON'S nerves were a good deal strained by the trouble with his church. He had already formed friendships, in his high way, with individual hearts and minds in his congregation; and though his spiritual sword, with the fine edge of Saladin's, was able to cut even the silken thread of affection if it withheld him from his aim, it was not without the laceration of his sensibility in all such relations. His mother had received another blow to her hopes concerning her sons. William had abandoned the ministry because of sceptical opinions; Edward had been compelled to give up the law and go south on the voyage from which he never returned; and now Ralph Waldo was severed from the traditional profession of the family. All this Emerson felt deeply. There had also come upon him a heavy bereavement. In the February of 1832, a few months before the difficulty with his church, his young wife had died of consumption. Under these troubles, and the sharp words of his disappointed fellow-ministers, his health suffered, and he resolved on an excursion to Europe. He had an ardent desire to converse with the English authors who had become important to him, especially Carlyle,

Coleridge, Landor, and Wordsworth. Above all, he wished Carlyle to know that his voice had been heard in New England, and to bear him a prophecy of the response that awaited him. Early in the spring of 1833 he sailed for Europe, and though he was at home again by the close of August, he had visited Sicily, Italy, France, and England. He visited Landor in Florence. With reference to Emerson's visits to Carlyle and Wordsworth at that time, he wrote at once to Alexander Ireland, whose acquaintance he had made in Edinburgh, and whose friendship was of much value to him. A very interesting account of this visit to Edinburgh, and of the impression made on him by Emerson's sermon in that city, is given in Mr. Ireland's memorial of his friend. I was indebted to Mr. Ireland for Emerson's letter to him, which appears in my book on Carlyle, and from which extracts may be made here.

"The comfort of meeting a man of genius is that he speaks sincerely; that he feels himself to be so rich, that he is above the meanness of pretending to knowledge which he has not, and Carlyle does not pretend to have solved the great problems, but rather to be an observer of their solution as it goes forward in the world. . . . My own feeling was that I had met with men of far less power who had yet greater insight into religious truth. He is, as you might guess from his papers, the most catholic of philosophers; he forgives and loves everybody, and wishes each to struggle on in his own place and arrive at his own ends. But his respect for eminent men, or rather his scale of eminence, is about the reverse of the popular scale.

Scott, Mackintosh, Jeffrey, Gibbon, even Bacon, are no heroes of his; stranger yet, he hardly admires Socrates, the glory of the Greek world; but Burns, and Samuel Johnson, and Mirabeau, he said interested him, and I suppose whoever else has given himself with all his heart to a leading instinct, and has not *calculated* too much. But I cannot think of sketching even his opinions, or repeating his conversations here. I will cheerfully do it when you visit me in America. He talks finely, seems to love the broad Scotch, and I loved him very much at once. . . . I could not help congratulating him upon his treasure in his wife, and I hope he will not leave the moors; 'tis so much better for a man of letters to nurse himself in seclusion than to be filed down to the common level by the compliances and imitations of city society."

Emerson called on Wordsworth at Rydal Mount, and was cordially received, the poet remembering up all his American acquaintance. "He had very much to say about the evils of superficial education, both in this country and in mine. He thinks that the intellectual tuition of society is going on out of all proportion faster than its moral training, which last is essential to all education. He does not wish to hear of schools of tuition; it is the education of circumstances which he values, and much more to this point. . . . He led me out into a walk in his grounds, where he said many thousands of his lines were composed, and repeated to me three beautiful sonnets, which he had just finished, upon the occasion of his recent visit to Fingal's Cave at Staffa. I hope he will print them speedily. The third is a gem. He was so

benevolently anxious to impress upon me my social
duties as an American citizen, that he accompanied
me near a mile from his house, talking vehemently,
and ever and anon stopping short to imprint his words.
I noted down some of these when I got to my inn, and
you may see them in Boston, Massachusetts, when you
will. I enjoyed my visits greatly, and shall always
esteem your Britain very highly in love for its wise
and good men's sake. I remember with much pleasure
my visit to Edinburgh, and your good parents. . . .
It will give me very great pleasure to hear from you,
to know your thoughts. Every man that ever was
born has some that are peculiar."

Carlyle's tones were tenderer even than his words
when, in the evening after his inauguration as Lord
Rector at Edinburgh, he told me of this visit. " He
came from Dumfries in an old rusty gig; came one
day and vanished the next. I had never heard of him:
he gave us his brief biography. We took a walk while
dinner was prepared. We gave him welcome; we
were glad to see him. I did not then adequately
recognise Emerson's genius; but she and I thought
him a beautiful transparent soul, and he was always a
very pleasant object to us in the distance. Now and
then a letter still comes from him, and amid the smoke
and mist of the world it is always as a window flung
open to the azure."

Emerson's hopes in this pilgrimage were too high to
be realised. Though eight years younger than Carlyle,
he was really older. The hermit of Craigenputtock
was still at heart involved in beliefs that Emerson's
fathers had outgrown for him before he was born, and

he was mourning over ruins which did not exist in the landscape of the New World. Then, and for many years after, Emerson urged Carlyle to settle in the New England his genius implied.

> "A thousand years a poor man sat
> Before the gate of Paradise;
> Then, while he snatched one little nap,
> It oped and shut. Ah! was he wise?"

It is a fable that on the evening of their meeting Carlyle gave Emerson a pipe and took one himself, and that the two sat together in perfect silence until bedtime, when they shook hands and congratulated each other on the charming evening they had enjoyed. The conversation was fluent enough that evening and the next day, but in the silence that followed their parting, one of them had discovered that the light he had sought so far had not been imparted.

The little story, which Carlyle allowed me to set afloat years ago, of how, when the first pages of "Sartor" appeared, the general clamour of "Fraser's" readers against it was broken by but two voices — "an Irish Catholic priest and a Mr. Emerson of Concord" — suggests the vaguely contrary elements, combined from the first in that pillar of cloud and fire which rose amid the Scottish moors. Emerson was the first to recognise the sign of a new exodus, but he presently perceived that Carlyle had his eyes fixed on Germany — on the Old and not the New World. They must part. But the American had found Carlyle a grand figure, and loved him. From the time (1836) when he introduced "Sartor" into America, where, I believe, its sale rose over a thousand before its publication as a volume in England, Emerson's chief work was to attend to Carlyle's business. He was perpetually among the booksellers when he had no book of his own to sell, and was visible among foreign exchangers often enough for his head to appear to Lowell, the fabulist of the time, with "Olympus for one pole, and for t'other the Exchange." For every work of Carlyle's, certainly during a period of twenty years, Emerson did far more work than for his own. Carlyle had reason to say, as he once did, that there was something maternal in the way New England took him up, but the paternal part was Emerson's. His friends were also Carlyle's friends; and, among these, Le Baron Russell was chiefly instrumental in publishing, and securing subscriptions for, "Sartor," of which he appears as co-editor. He was assisted by the Rev. William Silsbee.

The personal love between Carlyle and Emerson was deep; it survived all its trials, and the wide differences of opinion on nearly every subject. When I was starting for America in 1880, Carlyle said, "Give my love to Emerson. I still think of his visit to us at Craigenputtock as the most beautiful thing in our experience there." When I met Emerson in that year, his memory was nearly gone but the one name that required no suggestion was that of Carlyle. Out of the far past this arose clearly enough, and when he received the message I brought, his face beamed with the old intelligence.

During the dismal discussion which has gone on over the grave of Carlyle, I heard from a friend a word spoken by Emerson which sends a sunbeam through it all. Just after he had visited Craigenputtock, a friend asked him how he liked Carlyle. His whole reply was, "A marvellous child!"

IX.

A LEGEND OF GOOD WOMEN.

EVERYBODY has been wrong in his guess, except good women, who never despair of an ideal right." These are words from a letter written by Emerson to Carlyle about the American civil war. They are pregnant with a great deal of experience. No man had more reason for his faith in "the moral genius of women" — how well I remember the solemnity of his voice in that phrase! — than Emerson. Something of that, indeed, has been told in a previous chapter, but more remains, and this fine influence will be found shedding its light upon the path of Emerson even to the grave.

The first teachers of Transcendentalism in New England were Anne Hutchinson and Mary Dyer (more than eight generations ago!). The one was its prophetess, the other its protomartyr. They were beautiful and refined, true ladies, of good education. Anne Hutchinson was a woman of genius, however apologists of Puritanism may call it fanaticism. Governor Harry Vane was not far wrong in regarding her as a prophetess; for with her "profitable and sober carriage," which her opponents admitted, she united a far-reaching spiritual instinct, a clear logical intellect, and the eloquence of simple and sweet speech. She had but one religious principle, the indwelling Spirit, setting free the individual from all rites and formulas, and superior to all scriptures. She spoke of the inner immediate revelation, but was careful to guard this against any fanatical notion of its being miraculous. This she pronounced a delusion. It was really a more cultured form of Quakerism, and the best Quakers became identified with it. Among these was Mary Dyer. In 1638, when Anne Hutchinson was banished from the Massachusetts colony, Mary Dyer shared her exile in Rhode Island, but there could not rest. She returned to preach in Boston, was twice sentenced to death and reprieved,— the second time when her three male Quaker comrades had been executed beside her, and the rope was around her neck, — but on her third return suffered death.

Peter Bulkeley, as we have seen, presided at the Synod which banished Anne Hutchinson. It is now visible as Bulkeley banishing Emerson. It is satisfactory, however, to know that the founder of Concord died the year before the execution of Mary Dyer.

Time brought on its picturesque revenge. Anne Hutchinson, with her band of exiles, settled near what is now the beautiful town of Newport. She shares with Roger Williams the glory of having founded the first State on the planet organised on the principles of entire religious liberty. "It was further ordered that none be accounted a delinquent for doctrine." So runs (anno 1638) the constitution of Anne Hutchinson's "democracie" of Aquetnet Island, which she and her friends bought from the Indians, the signet of the State being a sheaf of arrows with the motto, *Amor vincet omnia.* This fair future for love seemed presently overcast when the Puritans pursued her in her retreat. "Her powerful mind still continued its activity," writes Bancroft; "young men from the colonies became converts to her opinions; and she excited such admiration, that to the leaders in Massachusetts it gave cause of suspicion and witchcraft." Among the red men of Naragansett she had found peace and safety; but the Puritans could not endure even the proximity of a colony so liberal, and Anne, with her friends, had to move away into Connecticut, where the Indians confused them with their Dutch oppressors, and slew them.

When the Quakers came back into Massachusetts, it was with these great witnesses from the past around them. Among their settlements there was a flourishing one at New Bedford. At that place Emerson first began to preach in the North. He found the Quakers there in commotion. English Quakers, moved by well-grounded apprehensions that the Amerian societies were departing from orthodoxy, had visited the United States. Wherever they preached, there rose up before them Elias Hicks — one of the great men whose story remains to be truly told — to confront their dogmas. In 1827 the Societies of Friends throughout the country were divided into "Orthodox" and "Hicksite;" and when Emerson, in the same year, preached at New Bedford, the controversy was at its height. He there made the acquaintance of Quakers, and his attention may here have been drawn to the sacramental forms they rejected, and to the simplicity of their doctrine, the inner light. Their view he adopted; it was on this that he separated from his church, and in the end abandoned the ministry. The Quaker poet, Whittier, recently wrote of the reverence with which he regarded the beautiful Boston Common, " knowing that hidden somewhere under its green turf are the graves of the Quaker martyrs." But he might even more reverentially remove his hat as he passes the Second Church in Boston, where the broken body and shed blood of Anne Hutchinson and Mary Dyer revived to be the sacrament of a New World covenant. Nearly thirty years ago, I went on a Sunday afternoon to a Quaker meeting in Milton Street, Boston. There were hardly a dozen persons present, and no word was spoken. They were so few that they met but once a year. That they should sit there, not knowing that their lost life had been found, their broken seed risen to fruitage, was incomprehensible to me until I found, by the journals of Caroline Fox, that the one great man she could not recognise — and does not mention while he was lecturing in England — was that American in whom her spiritual race had flowered!

When Emerson returned from Europe, he straightway went to New Bedford again, and preached there for several months. The struggle between the Orthodox and the Hicksites had ended in the latter connecting themselves with the Unitarian Church, which was prepared to give up the sacraments to which they objected. It was their hope that Emerson would settle with them, but the price of the Sibylline book had been raised; he could consent only if he were permitted to

pray or refrain from prayer as the spirit might move.
This was not conceded. But he remained for the true
Friends their good shepherd. A New Bedford boy,
afterwards distinguished as a journalist in New York,
Charles Congdon, has included in his published "Reminiscences" the following : —

"One day there came into our pulpit the most
gracious of mortals, with a face all benignity, who
gave out the first hymn and made the first prayer as
an angel might have read and prayed. Our choir was
a pretty good one, but its best was coarse and discordant after Emerson's voice. I remember of the sermon
only that it had an indefinite charm of simplicity and
wisdom, with occasional illustrations from Nature,
which were about the most delicate and dainty things
of the kind which I had ever heard. I could understand them, if not the fresh philosophical novelty of
the discourse. Mr. Emerson preached for us for a good
many Sundays, lodging in the house of a Quaker lady
just below ours. Seated at my own door, I saw
him often go by, and once, in the exuberance of my
childish admiration, I ventured to nod to him and to
say 'Good morning.' To my astonishment he also
nodded, and smilingly said, 'Good morning;' and
that is all the conversation I ever had with the sage of
Concord. He gave us afterwards two lectures based
upon his travels abroad, and was at a great deal
of trouble to hang up prints by way of illustration.
There was a picture of the Tribune in the Uffizi
Gallery in Florence, painted by one of our townsmen;
and I recall Mr. Emerson's great anxiety that it should
have a good light, and his lamentation when a good

light was found to be impossible. The lectures themselves were so fine — enchanting, we found them — that I have hungered to see them in print, and have thought of the evenings on which they were delivered as true Arabian Nights."

Mr. Hale White, in his letter to the "Athenæum" already quoted, falls into the familiar mistake of attributing to the Quakers of New England the indecency which was really that of the Puritans, who scourged those women naked through the streets; but he tells a charming story of Emerson's relation to the Friends. "When Mr. Emerson was last in this country, I asked him who were his chief friends in America. He replied, 'I find many among the Quakers. I know one simple old lady in particular whom I especially honour. She said to me: I cannot think what you find in me which is worth notice. Ah!' continued Mr. Emerson to me, 'if she had said yea, and the whole world had thundered in her ear nay, she would still have said yea.' That was why he honoured her."

While connected with the Unitarian denomination, I filled an engagement to preach and lecture in New Bedford, and there met some of these friends of Emerson. In Maryland also I had found the Hicksite Quakers warm sympathisers with the advancing religion of Massachusetts, in which they recognised the travail of George Fox's soul. There was the triumphal tableau of a historic drama in these Friends surrounding the pure flower of New England culture. In New Bedford it was through the insight and faith of good women that the new vision was reaching fulfilment. Anne Hutchinson and Mary Dyer were still living and in great peace, finding their saint in a descendant of the Moderator whose Synod banished them two centuries before. The leading Quaker of New Bedford fifty years ago was Miss Mary Rotch, whose friendship was precious to Emerson, and she must be included among the women whose influence largely moulded his life. She was Margaret Fuller's friend also. It is even doubtful whether it was not the vision of Mary Rotch leaving church when the Last Supper was to be commemorated which first cast a blight upon that rite in Emerson's eyes. She was a woman of culture, quiet humour, and sympathetic voice. Emerson loved to quote the words of Mary Rotch whenever conversation threatened to become theological. On one occasion, I remember an interval of silence, after which he said, " Mary Rotch told me that her little girl one day asked if she might do something. She replied, ' What does the voice in thee say?' The child went off, and after a time returned to say, ' Mother, the little voice says, no.' That," said Emerson, " calls the tears to one's eyes."

Among those who were friends of Emerson's thought in that early period may here be mentioned Elizabeth Peabody. Since Emerson's death a number of ladies in Boston celebrated the seventieth birthday of this lady, and in recalling the time when she came to Boston to teach school, she mentioned her first acquaintance with him. " I had a great desire to study Greek, and Waldo, just through Harvard, was teaching it. Through his brother William he became my teacher; but he was so shy, and I was so shy, we would sit at a table, and he did not dare to look at me, nor I to speak to him.

So we had a hard time of it till one day William Emerson came with Waldo, and said everything necessary to be said. After William had spoken for him, Waldo took courage, things went on easier, and I went on with my Greek." Miss Peabody and her sisters — afterwards Mrs. Hawthorne and Mrs. Horace Mann — Margaret Fuller, Elizabeth Hoar (who had been betrothed to his brother), and Sarah Clarke, were not only true friends, but of high — some of the highest — value to him. And meanwhile amid them still sat the three fair Fates, who had helped to attune that heart and intellect of his to a harmony which drew to him the trust of woman. This he found his panoply against animadversions and misunderstandings, whose severity was, and is, underrated because so cheerily borne by Emerson.

Sarah Bradford, the friend of his childhood, had married Emerson's relative, the Rev. Samuel Ripley, and was settled at Waltham, in the neighbourhood of Boston. A letter of hers to Emerson's aunt, Mary Moody Emerson, shows by its date, Sept. 4, 1883, that Emerson must have sped to that Waltham home immediately after his arrival from Europe. But it shows something more. "We have had a delightful visit of two days from Waldo. We feel about him as you no doubt do. While we regard him still more than ever as the apostle of the eternal reason, we do not like to hear the crows, as Pindar says, caw at the bird of Jove; nevertheless, he has some stern advocates. A lady was mourning the other day to Mr. Francis about Mr. Emerson's insanity. 'Madam, I wish I were half as sane,' he answered, and with warm indignation." This was the Rev. Dr. Conners Francis, for a long time professor in the Divinity College at Cambridge, whose wife was a sister of Mrs. Ripley, and whose sister was Lydia Maria Child, author of various works, among others of the earliest contribution to the science of religions, "The Progress of Religious Ideas."

Thus was Emerson able to spare the applause of bigots, being surrounded by good women, who never fail in their sympathy for "an ideal right." Nor did they fail of their reward. "You question me," writes Margaret Fuller to a friend, "as to the nature of the benefits conferred upon me by Mr. Emerson's preaching. I answer that his influence has been more beneficial to me than that of any American, and that from him I first learned what is meant by the inward life. Many other springs have since fed the stream of living waters, but he first opened the fountain. That the 'mind is its own place,' was a dead phrase to me till he cast light upon my mind. Several of his sermons stand apart in my memory, like landmarks in my spiritual history. It would take a volume to tell what this one influence did for me, but perhaps I shall some time see that it was best to be forced to help myself." In this Margaret Fuller has expressed the grateful experience of the women I have named, while each was a sacred person in the experience of Emerson. To her words may be added these of Goethe:

"Das Ewig-Weibliche
Zieht uns hinan."

X.

THE WAIL OF THE CENTURY.

ONCE when we were conversing about Robert Browning's poetry, Emerson said, "Paracelsus is the wail of the nineteenth century." I was a new student in Divinity College, and was rejoicing so much in having reached a shore so free as Unitarianism, that I did not quite understand Emerson's remark. Afterwards, while rambling along the Plymouth shore, the gently beating waves seemed to repeat

> "The sad rhyme of the men who proudly clung
> To their first fault, and withered in their pride."

Like those voyagers in Paracelsus's fable, who bore their household gods to the wrong shore, the old Plymouth Pilgrims fixed their ideals in rock-caves of dogma.

> "A hundred shapes of lucid stone!
>   All day we built its shrine for each,
> A shrine of rock for every one,
> Nor paused we till in the westering sun
>   We sat together on the beach
> To sing because our task was done.
> When lo! what shouts and merry songs!
> What laughter all the distance stirs!
> A loaded raft with happy throngs
> Of gentle islanders!

'Our isles are just at hand,' they cried,
  'Like cloudlets faint at even sleeping;
Our temple-gates are opened wide,
  Our olive-groves thick shade are keeping
For these majestic forms,' they cried.
Oh, then we awoke with sudden start
From our deep dream, and knew, too late,
How bare the rock, how desolate,
Which had received our precious freight:
  Yet we called out — 'Depart!
Our gifts, once given, must here abide.
  Our work is done; we have no heart
To mar our work,' we cried."

Anne Hutchinson and Mary Dyer and Roger Williams, and their bands of liberal pilgrims, seemed now the gentle islanders. From Rhode Island — where the islets in the harbour and the streets of their settlements bore the names of graces and virtues — they came to tell the Pilgrims how hard and desolate was the dogma that had received their ideals of truth, liberty, and justice, whose exile they had shared. Sternly they were bidden depart, but ever and again they returned.

In the end the Pilgrims had to yield and start on a new pilgrimage, seeking new shrines for their gods. There, on the self-same island where Anne Hutchinson founded her community of free and equal men and women, one hundred and fifty years later was born Channing; and there stands the beautiful memorial church that bears his name, though less beautiful in its architecture than in the fact that Channing objected to the introduction of even a theistic expression of belief into the constitution of the earlier church he dedicated at Newport (1835). He demurred to the words " believing in one God, the Father," lest they should ultimately become a fetter upon some honest seeker of truth. Thus is the church a memorial also of Anne Hutchinson, in the constitution of whose State it was expressly provided "that none be accounted delinquent for doctrine."

In the phraseology of the old Pilgrims, Anne Hutchinson and her gentle islanders had been banished because they were "unfit for the society" which had been constituted at Boston, and because it was feared that they "might, upon some revelation, make a sudden insurrection." But when from Rhode Island her voice came back in the eloquence of Channing, none could be more fit for the society of the citizens, though there was a revelation, and thereon an insurrection. The young scholars followed Channing as far as he could lead, and once more fixed their ideals in the shrines to which he led them.

Unitarianism seemed, indeed, an abode fair enough when seen from the bareness of Plymouth Rock. Its rise and progress are traceable in a fine enthusiasm. It did away with all the horrors of Calvinistic theology — its mercantile atonement, its doctrine of human depravity, its hell and devils. When the lucid ideals had superseded such grim gargoyles of the old churches, the children of the Pilgrims sang because their task seemed done.

But, alas! once again the voice of the gentle islanders was heard, and the new coast was found bare and desolate. It was found that Unitarianism had unsettled everything, settled nothing. It was trying to hold on to the Christian fairy-tales after destroying the faith on which they rested. It clung to the rosy visions of a theologic heaven, whose evidences it invalidated by repudiating its equal revelation of visions not rosy. It was able to give no reason for its surviving faith in God or immortality; and when Abner Kneeland denied these, and was shut up in prison, Unitarianism mingled with its petition for mercy to its abhorred child a cry of helplessness.

It was then shown, also, that temples sprinkled with Unitarian holy water were not only prepared to imprison the human mind, but might be made buttresses of the national inhumanity based upon the Bible. What, then, was Unitarianism? Christianity made easy. New England theology with none of its crosses, but all of its comforts, adapted by scholars to suit spiritual epicures. Between the Universalists, who believed God too good to damn them, and the Unitarians, who believed they were too good to be damned, respectability was able to make itself quite comfortable. But how was it with the real heart and intellect of the country?

The "wail of the nineteenth century," already audible in the Old World, was first heard in the new by Emerson. Even in the peaceful homes of his Quakers, or in that happy retreat at Waltham, it followed him, and to it he must respond. A young man himself, — in years only thirty when he returned from Europe, — he saw the young men of America as if stricken by a mental malady and melancholy, which "strips them of all manly aims and bereaves them of animal spirits."

"The noblest youths," he wrote in a letter printed

in the "Dial," "are in a few years converted into pale caryatides to uphold the temple of conventions. They are in the state of the young Persians when 'that mighty Yezdan prophet' addressed them and said, 'Behold the signs of evil days are come; there is now no longer any right course of action nor any self-devotion left among the Iranis.' As soon as they have arrived at this turn, there are no employments to satisfy them; they are educated above the work of their time and country and disdain it. Many of the more acute minds pass into a lofty criticism of these things, which only embitters their sensibility to the evil and widens the feeling of hostility between them and the citizens at large. From this cause companies of the best-educated young men in the Atlantic States every week take their departure for Europe; for no business that they have in that country, but simply because they shall so be hid from the reproachful eyes of their countrymen, and agreeably entertained by one or two years, with some lurking hope, no doubt, that something may turn up to give them a decided direction. It is easy to see that this is only a postponement of their proper work, with the additional disadvantage of a two years' vacation. Add that this class is rapidly increasing by the infatuation of the active class, who, while they regard these young Americans with suspicion and dislike, educate their own children in the same courses and use all possible endeavours to secure to them the same result."

This, then, was "the wail of the nineteenth century." Undoubtedly there was a cause for the acute form assumed by this malady. Authentic voices from Europe were announcing the departure of old beliefs and the crumbling of old institutions. Kant and Schelling, Jacobi and Schleiermacher, Herder and De Wette, Goethe and Schiller, Cousin and Quinet, Coleridge and Carlyle, were read by students in colleges supposed to be intent upon languages of the dead. Above all, Carlyle had spoken to young Americans, as Emerson said, with an emphasis which deprived them of sleep. Yet, though roused, they were drawn to travel with shamed faces and averted eyes on the traditional paths, albeit these paths had been fringed with fresh flowers by Channing and the early Unitarians. The greatest voices of their time brought them only pain as they "clung to their first fault," heritage from their fathers, who had prisoned the ideals of America in stoniest shrines.

In Plymouth Emerson's first lecture was given, in 1834, and probably in the church founded by the Pilgrim Fathers. The long and brave history that made its foreground, sent impressiveness to the vision to which he pointed the children of the Pilgrims. The Hon. Thomas Russell, then a schoolboy, remembers across the half-century the weight of these words: "Why cannot some little community of men leave others to seem and content themselves to be?"

XI.

CULTURE.

EMERSON'S reference, quoted in the previous chapter, to "that mighty Yezdan prophet" who came to the Iranis in their evil days, may be followed by the legend of how their darkness and doubt were dispelled by Ardá Viráf.

"They say that once upon a time the pious Zoroaster made the religion which he had received current in the world, and till the completion of three hundred years the religion was in purity, and men were without doubts. This religion, namely, all the Avesta and Zend, written upon prepared cowskins and with gold ink, was deposited in the archives of Stákhar Pápakán. But Alexander the Great, who was dwelling in Egypt, burnt them up, and after that there was confusion and contention among the people of the country of Iran. They were doubtful in regard to God, and religions of many kinds and various codes of laws were promulgated.

"And it is related that the wise men and teachers of religion assembled, and agreed that they would give to some one among them a sacred narcotic, that he might pass into the invisible world and bring them intelligence. The lot for this task fell on Ardá Viráf.

"Then those teachers of religion filled three golden

cups with wine and the narcotic Vishtasp; and they gave one cup to Viráf with the word 'Well thought,' and the second cup with the word 'Well said,' and the third cup with the word 'Well done.'

"While Viráf slept, seven women kept the ever-burning fire and the teachers chanted the Avesta. On the seventh day the soul of Viráf returned, and he rose up as from a pleasant sleep, inspired with good thoughts and full of joy. An accomplished writer sat before him, and whatsoever Viráf said he wrote down clearly and correctly, as followeth:—

"'Taking the first footstep with the good thought, the second with the good word, and the third with the good deed, I entered paradise.

"'I put forth the first footstep to the star-track on Húmat, where good thoughts are received with hospitality; and I saw those souls of the pious whose radiance, which ever increased, was glittering as the stars. And I asked Ataro, the angel, "Which place is this, and which people are these?" And he answered, "This is the star-track and these are they who in the world offered no prayers and chanted no liturgies; they also exercised no sovereignty. Through other works they have attained this happiness."

"'I came to a place and saw the souls of the liberal adorned above all others in splendour, and it seemed to me sublime.

"'I saw the souls of the great and truthful speakers, who walked in lofty splendour, and it seemed to me sublime.

"'I saw the souls of agriculturists in a shining place, as they stood and offered praise before the spirits of water and earth, trees and cattle. Great is their throne. The souls of artisans I also saw on embellished thrones. And it seemed to me sublime.

"'I saw the souls of the faithful, the teachers and inquirers, in the greatest gladness, on a splendid throne; and it seemed to me sublime.

"'I also saw the friendly souls of interceders and peace-makers, who thereby ever increased their brilliance, and they ever walked in an atmosphere of light.

"'I also saw the pre-eminent world of the religious, which is the light, full of glory and of joy, with which no one is satiated.'"

Five centuries after this was written down, after much earlier traditions, its vision was fulfilled in Concord. There, in the town of his fathers, Emerson went to reside in 1834. He dwelt in the Old Manse, built by his grandfather, with the venerable Dr. Ripley (for whom his mother was keeping house), until the following year. Then he was married to Lidian Jackson, and purchased the house and farm where he thenceforth lived. His mother came to reside at his house, and there lived until her death, November 16, 1853. His aunt Mary was a frequent inmate until her death in May, 1863. Near by, at Waltham, and subsequently in the Old Manse at Concord, was Sarah Ripley, who died in 1867. And soon came the most brilliant and cultivated woman America ever produced,—Margaret Fuller.

While the teachers chanted their scriptures, and noble women kept the sacred fire ever burning, Ralph Waldo Emerson drank the Vishtasp, and with good thought, good word, good deed, mounted to the star-track, and conversed with the great souls of all ages, as transfigured in the light and liberty of his own genius. When he re-appeared to the world, it was with the vision of one who had seen the invisible, and was able to shed the needed light upon the life and labour of the farmer and the artisan, no less than upon tasks of the teacher and scholar. The age of scepticism was ended, and the plague of pessimism was escaped.

And this Vishtasp, what was it? The life-blood of all noblest hearts and brains, distilled by finest art, and mingled with the wine of his own genius.

When Emerson was last in London, his friend William Allingham guided him to various places in Old London, Chaucer's "Tabard," Guildhall, and also at his special desire to Milton's grave in the Church of St. Giles, Cripplegate. It is in the chancel, the stone partly covered by a pew. Allingham asked, "Do many people come to look at this grave?" "Americans, sir," was the pew-opener's reply. In the cab, Emerson said, "Perhaps nobody has so poor an opinion of my books as I have myself." "That seems to me very likely," answered Allingham with a smile.

Some day an artist will paint the picture of Emerson in St. Giles Church, and inscribe it, "At the grave of his father."

So soon as the pew, which partly covers Milton himself as well as his grave, is removed, it will appear that he has had no successor but in America. One may find in England a fragment of him kneeling here, another fragment singing there; but the whole of him has for some time been discoverable only in the literary fraternity of America, mingling morning lark-songs with the chants of prophecy, and illumining the scroll of human equality with the golden letters of poetry.

Above all was Emerson the flower of the heart of Milton. An unspeakable awe-stricken reverence for virtue and wisdom; a spirit ever kneeling before the universe as the transcendent temple of goodness and truth; a horror at the thought of raising private interests before eternal principles and laws; a faith not to be argued with, absolute, in personal righteousness as the primary condition of all worth, involving a sense of corruption in all qualities however brilliant which have not that foundation. These, however invested, were the essential elements of that Puritanism which in Milton saw the earth and sky aflame with cherubim, and coined winds and seas into anthems of adoration. In the course of two centuries Puritanism had, in the hands of the common people, been moulded and hardened into a grim unlovely dungeon. Abandon it, said Channing; Destroy it utterly, said Parker; but Emerson said, Be not afraid, this also is penetrable to the spirit: and he led the way beyond the dark mouth of the old cavern to tinted halls and fairy grottos, repeating mystically the foliations and clusters of the bright world without

An enterprising house in America has promised a reprint of the "Dial." It may be that those four volumes, long precious to their few fortunate owners, will presently be generally accessible. I will therefore select from them only such passages as may indicate the early impressions made upon Emerson's mind by the masters of literature. Comparison of these early criticisms with later writings will show pretty clearly that some of them are transcripts from his diary kept in youth. Horace Mann reports him as having in a lecture (1837) condensed the commandments, as regards young men, into two: "sit alone" and "keep a journal." "Have a room by yourself, and if you cannot do without, sell your coat and sit in a blanket." Emerson's advice came from his experience.

Let us read what in early years he wrote of Milton:—

"It is the prerogative of this great man to stand at this hour foremost of all men in literary history, and so (shall we not say?) of all men, in the power to *inspire*. Virtue goes out of him into others. Leaving out of view the pretensions of our contemporaries (always an incalculable influence), we think no man can be named whose mind still acts on the cultivated intellect of England and America with an energy comparable to that of Milton. As a poet, Shakespeare undoubtedly transcends and far surpasses him in his popularity with foreign nations; but Shakespeare is a voice merely; who and what he was that sang, that sings, we know not. Milton stands erect, commanding, still visible as a man among men, and reads the laws of the moral sentiment to the new-born race. There is something pleasing in the affection with which we can regard a man who died a hundred and sixty years ago in the other hemisphere, who, in respect to personal relations, is to us as the wind, yet by an influence purely personal makes us jealous for his fame as for that of a near friend. He is identified in the mind with all select and holy images, with the supreme interests of the human race."

A hundred and sixty years after Milton's death came Emerson's first year at Concord (1834); and in these words just quoted is the spirit which still held fast those who supposed that they had broken with the new heretic. He did not so much consider the letter of current beliefs as the sentiments and ideas trying to express themselves through them; these he re-stated with such fulness and beauty that their traditional or dogmatic sheath softly folded away beneath. There was even more of the Puritan than of the Unitarian in him. As Swedenborg made a dictionary of correspondences for the names and words of the Bible, Emerson found a significance in old beliefs. I remember how old religious phraseology sometimes tinged his casual talk, as "the saving grace of common-sense." He looked upon human creeds with the same calmness as upon crystals, flowers, and weeds; they were to him all genuine products of nature; and as a religious naturalist, his instinct led him to develop, recombine, transmute. He was never really alienated from the best spirit of his fathers; and when his mind expanded to its flower, albeit so different from any that the same stem had borne before, there was a corresponding movement of the roots deeper into the Puritan soil from which he had sprung. For every hard dogma he unfolded a fragrant tinted petal of thought. He lost nothing, but raised up all to the last day. This was, I believe, one reason why the religious sentiment of New England was never alienated from Emerson; he seemed to be giving a consummate statement of fundamental beliefs, a prophet of true lineage announcing the fulfilment of every jot and tittle of the faith delivered to the saints.

When the "Mayflower" sailed, it took along no copy of Shakespeare. A good argument may, indeed, be made from Milton for performing Shakespeare's plays even on Sunday (could that covering pew only be removed!), but, in the Puritan measure, he who would write an epic must live an epic; and Shakespeare was not in the list of martyrs. In his early estimate of Milton, Emerson's sentence concerning Shakespeare discloses a survival of this feeling. And with all his enthusiasm for Shakespeare, which began when he was at college, there are recurrences of chagrin at the absence of any personality corresponding to the greatness of the works. It was, perhaps, in some mood of this kind that he omitted from "Representative Men," as mentioned by Mr. Cooke, a passage delivered in the lecture on Shakespeare : —

"There is nothing in literature comparable to Shakespeare's expression for strength and for delivery. Men have existed who affirmed that they heard the language of celestial angels, talked with them; but that, when they returned into the natural world, though they preserved the memory of these conversations, they found it impossible to transmute the things that had been said into human thoughts and words. But Shakespeare is like one who had been rapt into some purer state of sensation and existence, had learned the secret of a finer diction, and, when he returned to the world, retained the fine organ which had been opened above."

Possibly this was felt to assign too high a source for Shakespeare's inspiration. Whatever may have been the cause of the omission of a passage so beautiful and just — which recalls Tieck's pretty fable of the fairies whispering in turn to the sleeping boy the secrets he must afterwards tell, — as encomium it falls beneath others in his estimates of Shakespeare. Yet in all that he has written about Shakespeare we may hear the echo of Milton's sentence: "I was confirmed in this opinion, that he who would not be frustrate of his hope to write well hereafter in laudable things, ought himself to be a true poem." Schiller — as Mr. James Sime has pointed out in his beautiful biography — long found it intolerable that in Shakespeare's writings "the poet would never let himself be caught, would never talk with his reader." "For several years," adds Schiller, "I studied Shakespeare, and gave him my entire reverence, before his individuality became dear to me." But this period was even more slowly passed by Emerson. "It must even go into the world's history," he says so late as 1850, "that the best poet led an obscure and profane life, using his genius for the public amusement." I feel pretty certain that it was some feeling of this kind which led Emerson to lend an ear to the theory, first propounded by Miss Bacon, that the plays were not written by Shakespeare but by Lord Bacon. Emerson did not, I think, imagine that they could have been written by Bacon, though he might not have agreed with Carlyle that Bacon "could as easily have created this planet as written 'Hamlet.'" But he had some scepticism about the authorship of the plays. He introduced Miss Bacon to Carlyle, who wrote back that she was mad, and so she became. Emerson told me that he thought Hawthorne's chapter concerning her, "Recollections of a Gifted Woman," one of the best things he had written, but was not further interested in her theory. Carlyle, as I remember, could never quite forgive Shakespeare for not having written a History of England, and he did not admire him so much as Emerson. In later life, in an extemporaneous speech at Howard University, Washington, Emerson said of Shakespeare, " No nation has produced anything like his equal. There is no quality in the human mind, there is no class of topics, there is no region of thought in which he has not soared or descended, and none in which he has not said the commanding word. All men are impressed, in proportion to their own advancement in thought, by the genius of Shakespeare; and the greatest mind values him the most."

Emerson went thoroughly into old English books, from Chaucer to Sir Thomas Browne and Burton, but valued more highly the earliest of these, and does not hesitate to speak of his reading of such as an " idle habit." He came among these venerable ones like the man with the touchstone in Allingham's poem —

> "Of heirloom jewels, prized so much,
>   Were many changed to chips and clods,
>   And even statues of the gods
> Crumbled beneath its touch."

The nature of his touchstone he has told : " There is no better illustration of the laws by which the world is governed than literature. There is no luck in it. It proceeds by fate. Every scripture is given by the inspiration of God. Every composition proceeds out of a greater or less depth of thought, and this is the measure of its effect."

The chief thing he learned from the philosophers of the past was the characteristic of the best thought of his own time, namely, its realism and tendency to scientific statement. The old wives' prescriptions of spiders' legs and amulets recommended for divers maladies by Lord Bacon and Sir Thomas Browne, the aërial devils with which Burton declares the air swarming, of these and other cobwebs he sees the age of science sweeping the world clear. The schoolboys of to-day cannot conceive how their fathers were content with their pinhole views of the universe.

Christendom has now become a vast reading-room. Every hope, fear, folly, whim, has its organ.

" It prints a vast carcass of tradition every year with as much solemnity as a new revelation. Along with these it vents books that breathe of new mornings, that seem to heave with the life of millions, books for which men and women peak and pine; books which take the rose out of the cheek of him that wrote them, and give him to the midnight a sad, solitary, diseased man; which leave no man where they found him, but make him better or worse; and which work dubiously on society, and seem to inoculate it with a venom before any healthy result appears. The favourable side of this research and love of facts is the bold and systematic criticism which has appeared in every department of literature. From Wolf"s attack upon the authenticity of the Homeric poems dates a new epoch of learning. Ancient history has been found to be not yet settled. It is to be subjected to common sense. It is to be cross-examined. It is to be seen whether its traditions will consist, not with universal belief, but with universal experience. Niebuhr has sifted Roman history by the like methods. Heeren has made good essays toward ascertaining the necessary facts in the Grecian, Persian, Assyrian, Egyptian, Ethiopic, Carthaginian nations. English history has been analysed by Turner, Hallam, Brodie, Palgrave. Goethe has gone the circuit of human knowledge, as Lord Bacon did before him, writing true or false on every article. Bentham has attempted the same scrutiny in reference to civil law. Pestalozzi, out of a deep love, undertook the reform of education. The ambition of Coleridge in England embraced the whole problem of philosophy, to find, that is, a foundation in thought for everything that existed in fact. The German philosophers, Schelling, Kant, Fichte, have applied their analysis to nature and thought with unique boldness. There can be no honest inquiry which is not better than acquiescence. Inquiries which once looked grave and vital no doubt change their appearance very fast, and come to look frivolous beside the later queries to which they give occasion. This sceptical activity, at first directed on circumstances and historical views deemed of great importance, soon penetrated deeper than Rome or Egypt, than history or institutions, or the vocabulary of metaphysics, namely, into the thinker himself, and into every function he exercises. The poetry and the speculation of the age are marked by a certain philosophic turn which discriminates them from the works of earlier times. The poet is not content to see how 'fair hangs the apple from the rock,' 'what music a sunbeam awoke in the woods,' nor of Hardiknute, how 'stately steppes he east the way, and stately steppes he west,' but he now revolves, What is the apple to me? and what the birds to me? and what is Hardiknute to me? and what am I?"

Through all this it is felt that the writer is not one of the sceptical phalanx in whose work he rejoices. There is the undertone in it of a man who holds some affirmation for which the way must be cleared. He does not love the transitional, but finds in the motion promise of a fairer repose. And it seems to me undeniable that the impression which Emerson has made upon his age is mainly due to his great convictions. His idealism rises like a rock, almost alone amid the waves of misgiving and doubt, which in these days have covered nearly all others.

I find from these early papers, as compared with his collected writings, that Emerson's theology changed to a spiritual positivism, and then to a poetical philosophy. His mental keynote is in the first sentence of his first Essay — "There is one mind common to all individual men." From this point of view he finds history to be a vast expression of the powers and passions of every heart and brain; self-reliance to be self-surrender to the Over-soul, that unity within which every man's particular being is contained and made one with all other. The essay on the Over-soul is the fullest expression which this central idea of his philosophy has reached. In a paper in the "Dial" this Over-soul is at first generalised by him as "the feeling of the infinite," a semi-theological phrase which passes into semi-philosophic statement. "Another element of the modern poetry, akin to this subjective tendency, or rather the direction of that same on the question of resources, is the Feeling of the Infinite. Of the perception now becoming a conscious fact, — that there is One Mind, and that all the powers and privileges which lie in any, lie in all; that I as a man may claim and appropriate whatever of true or fair or good or strong has anywhere been exhibited; that Moses and Confucius, Montaigne and Leibnitz, are not so much individuals as they are parts of man and parts of me, and my intelligence proves them my own, — literature is far the best expression."

This "feeling of the infinite" is essentially one with that "depth of thought," from which, as it more or less comes, every scripture is more or less immortal, already described as the touchstone with which Emerson went among the great names of literature. He finds in it, indeed, the dawn of a coming literature, and estimates the writers of the past according to some gleam caught by them here and there of this ascending glory.

The poet, by Emerson's estimate, was he who stood at the shining point where all things converge to One. Fancy may deal with fragments of the universe, and invest them with fine conceits; but the imagination is conversant with the whole, and sees truth in universal relations. The poet attained by insight the goal to which all other knowledge is finding its way, step by step, and has anticipated Buffon's declaration, " there is but one animal," and Faraday's faith that in the end there will be found but one element with two polarities. The globule of blood and the rolling planet are one; a little heat more or less makes of a bit of jelly a fish or a human brain. The poet was therefore necessarily a pantheist, and it looks like a theological "survival" that Emerson did not recognise the " authentic fire " in Shelley. In Wordsworth, with whom pantheism was unconscious, overpowering his intellectual beliefs — a feeling rather than a philosophy — he recognised " the great modern poet." It is not wonderful that the poet of Rydal Mount should have been a companion of those dreamy walks through the vales around Concord, at a time when the young seer's mind was burgeoning toward its spring. "The 'Excursion' awakened in every lover of nature the right feeling. We saw stars shine, we felt the awe of mountains, we heard the rustle of the wind in the grass, and knew again the ineffable secret of solitude. It was a great joy."

The exhaustive unity which dominated this phase of Emerson's culture found a happy expression in his philosophisings concerning Art. Here also he begins with a statement of the law of identity — a theme of which no other writer has furnished so many and such exquisite variations. Trade, politics, letters, science, religion, art, are the rays of one sun; they translate each other's laws into new languages. The law as it appears in art is this: the Universal Soul is the alone creator of the useful and the beautiful; therefore, to make anything useful or beautiful, the individual must be submitted to the universal mind. He speaks first of the omnipotence of nature in the useful arts. "All powerful action is performed by bringing the forces of Nature to bear upon our objects. We do not grind corn or lift the loom by our own strength, but we build a mill in such a position as to set the north wind to play upon our instrument, or the elastic force of steam, or the ebb and flow of the sea. So in our handiwork, we do few things by muscular force, but we place ourselves in such attitudes as to bring the force of gravity, that is, the weight of the planet, to bear upon the spade or the axe we wield." The same law prevails over the fine arts. "A masterpiece of art has in the mind a fixed place in the chain of being, as much as a plant or a crystal." "The delight which a work of art affords, seems to arise from our recognising in it the mind that formed Nature again an active operation. . . . Arising out of eternal reason, one and perfect, whatever is beautiful rests on the foundation of the necessary. . . . In the mind of the artist, could we enter there, we should see the sufficient reason for the last flourish and tendril of his work, just as every tint and spine in the seashell pre-exists in the secreting organs of the fish."

After illustrating the subject by the discovered origin of the Doric, Gothic, and other architectures in the characteristics of Nature as surrounding the peoples among whom they arose, the essay concludes with these pregnant thoughts: —

"In this country, at this time, other interests than religion and patriotism are predominant, and the arts, the daughters of enthusiasm, do not flourish. The genuine offspring of our ruling passions we behold. Popular institutions, the school, the reading-room, the post-office, the exchange, the insurance company, and an immense harvest of economical inventions, are the fruit of the equality and the boundless liberty of lucrative callings. These are superficial wants; and their fruits are these superficial institutions. But as far as they accelerate the end of political freedom and national education, they are preparing the soil of man for fairer flowers and fruits in another age. For beauty, truth, and goodness are not obsolete; they spring eternal in the breast of man; they are as indigenous in Massachusetts as in Tuscany or the Isles of Greece. And that Eternal Spirit whose triple face they are, moulds from them for ever, for his mortal child, images to remind him of the Infinite and Fair."

For some years after he had left the pulpit and entered upon the study of philosophy and poetry, Emerson did not conceal his sense of a certain frivolity attaching to the "profession of letters." This trait, perhaps, was partly hereditary. For seven or eight horizons back of him there had been no literature but what one part of the population preached to the other, or, as he himself said, "ministers and ministers." Even in Emerson's time the Puritan suspicion of intellect remained, and to be simply literary was yet slightly revolutionary. Few of his admirers probably would be satisfied to have him described as a "man of letters," though all would feel that his style is more that of the purely literary than of the metaphysical class. My belief is that from the time Emerson met with the writings of Walter Savage Landor his tone became less fervid and prophetic, and more secular. Whatever eccentricity threatened him was dismissed in the presence of the clear and classic style of Landor. There is something almost naïve in an apology for literature with which he introduces a paper on Landor.

"This sweet asylum of an intellectual life must

appear to have the sanction of nature, so long as so many men are born with so decided an aptitude for reading and writing. . . . Let us not be so illiberal with our schemes for the renovation of society and nature as to disesteem or deny the literary spirit. Certainly there are heights in nature which command this; there are many more which this commands. It is vain to call it luxury, and, as saints and reformers are apt to do, decry it as a species of day-dreaming. What else are sanctities, and reforms, and all other things? Whatever can make for itself an element, means, organs, servants and the most profound and permanent existence in the hearts and heads of millions of men, must have a reason for its being. Its excellency is reason and vindication enough. If rhyme rejoices us, there should be rhyme, as much as if fire cheers us we should bring wood and coals. Each kind of excellence takes place for its hour and excludes everything else. Do not brag of your actions as if they were better than Homer's verses or Raphael's pictures. Raphael and Homer feel that action is pitiful beside their enchantments. They could act too if the stake were worthy of them; but now all that is good in the universe urges them to their tasks. Whoever writes for the love of truth and beauty, and not with ulterior ends, belongs to this sacred class."

Of this class he regarded Landor as chief among his contemporaries, and with him he went, as it were, upon a summer excursion into the land of letters, somewhat as he might in summer pass a few weeks with Agassiz, Holmes, and others in the Adirondack mountains.

"As it is not from the highest Alps or Andes, but from less elevated summits, that the most attractive landscape is commanded, so is Mr. Landor the most useful and agreeable of critics.

"In the character of Pericles he has found full play for beauty and greatness of behaviour, where the circumstances are in harmony with the man. These portraits, though mere sketches, must be valued as attempts in the very highest kind of narrative, which not only has very few examples to exhibit of any success, but very few competitors in the attempt. The word Character is in all mouths; it is a force which we all feel; yet who has analysed it? What is the nature of that subtle and majestic principle which attaches us to a few persons, not so much by persons as by the most spiritual ties? What is the quality of the persons who, without being public men, or literary men, or rich men, or active men, or (in the popular sense) religious men, have a certain salutary omnipresence in all one life's history, almost giving their own quality to the atmosphere and the landscape? A moral force, yet wholly unmindful of creed and catechism, intellectual, but scornful of books, it works directly and without means, and though it may be resisted at any time, yet resistance to it is a suicide. For the person who stands in this lofty relation to his fellow-men is always the impersonation to them of their conscience. It is a sufficient proof of the extreme delicacy of this element, evanescing before any but the most sympathetic vision, that it has so seldom been employed in the drama and in novels. Mr. Landor, almost alone among English living writers, has indicated his perception of it."

Two early essays, "The Comic" and "The Tragic," in some of their sparkling passages might represent that Concord table-talk which so many remember. The first of these opens with a paragraph which would have made Lavater rub his eyes.

"It is a nail of pain and pleasure, said Plato, which fastens the body to the mind. The way of life is a line between the regions of tragedy and comedy. I find few books so entertaining as the wistful human history written out in the faces of any collection of men at church or court-house. The silent assembly thus talks very loud. The sailor carries in his face the tan of tropic suns and the record of rough weather; the old farmer testifies of stone walls, rough wood-lots, the meadows, and the new barn. The doctor's head is a fragrant gallipot of virtues. The carpenter still measures feet and inches with his eye, and the licensed landlord mixes liquors in motionless pantomime. What good bargains glimmer on the merchant's aspect! And if beauty, softness, and faith in female forms have their influence, vices even, in slight degree, are thought to improve the expression. Malice and scorn add to beauty. You shall see eyes set too near, and limited faces, faces of one make and invariable character. How the busy fancy inquires into their biography and relations! They pique, but must tire. Compared with universal faces, countenances of a general human type, which pique less, they look less safe. In such groups the observer does not think of heroes and sages. In the silentest meeting the eye reads the plain prose of life, timidity, caution, appetite, ignorance, old houses, musty savours, stationary, retrograde faculties puttering around (to use the country phrase) in paltry routines from January to December."

Having laid down the precincts of comedy, he maintains that whilst a taste for fun is nearly universal with the human species, the lower orders neither do nor perceive anything ridiculous. Concord has no zoological garden. Is it not certain that an old fox or opossum, an ostrich, an ape, and, measurably, a donkey, are among nature's jokes?

The brief paper on "The Tragic" is somewhat in the same vein with his essay on "Fate." He regards the tragical elements of life and nature as superficial and transient. The bitterest of them are derived from a belief in a brute fate — that the order of nature is controlled by a law not adapted to man, nor man to that, but which holds on its way to the end, serving him if his wishes chance to lie in the same course, crushing him if his wishes lie contrary to it, and heedless whether it serves or crushes him. "This is the terrible idea that lies at the foundation of the old Greek tragedy, and makes Œdipus and Antigone and Orestes objects of such hopeless commiseration. They must perish, and there is no over-god to stop or to mollify this hideous enginery that grinds or thunders, and takes them up into its terrific system." In all this, penalties are not grounded on the nature of things, but on arbitrary will; or, indeed, this destiny is not will at all, but an immense whim. It is discriminated from the doctrine of philosophical necessity in that the last is an optimism, wherein the sufferer finds his good consulted in the good of all of which he is a part. The old idea of fate disappears with civilisation, and so the antique tragedy can never be reproduced.

"Time, the consoler, time, the rich carrier of all changes, dries the freshest tears by obtruding new figures, new costumes, new roads, on our eye, new voices on our ear. . . . Nature will not sit still; the faculties will do somewhat; new hopes spring, new affections twine, and the broken is whole again. . . . The intellect is a consoler, which delights in detaching or putting an interval between a man and his fortune, and so converts the sufferer into a spectator, and his pain into poetry. It yields the joys of conversation, of letters, and of science. Hence also the torments of life become tuneful tragedy, solemn and soft with music, and garnished with rich dark pictures. But higher still than the activities of art, the intellect in its purity, and the moral sense in its purity, are not distinguished from each other, and both ravish us into a region whereinto these passionate clouds of sorrow cannot rise."

Goethe harmonised with Emerson's innate optimism, with the disposition implied in it of looking upon conventional society with the eye of a naturalist rather than that of a moralist. The devil became a fossil monster for Emerson when Goethe appeared with his sparkling wickedness. Emerson's optimism was a zenith to the Puritan nadir, which held that "the earth is the Lord's and the fulness thereof" in a sense that would change space to a meeting-house and eternity to a Sabbath-daymare. It is interesting to compare his first and later criticisms upon Goethe. A letter to Carlyle (1834) shows him scandalised by Goethe's velvet life. But Goethe "held him with his glittering eye," and his first great effort in German was reading Goethe's fifty-five volumes. Emerson came to care more for the quantity than the quality of what he could gain from any teacher.

"To look at him (Goethe) one would say there never was an observer before. What sagacity, what industry of observation! To read his record is a frugality of time, for you shall find no word that does not stand for a thing; and he is of that comprehension which can see the value of truth. His love of Nature has seemed to give a new meaning to that word. There was never man more domesticated in this world than he. . . . If we try Goethe by the ordinary canons of criticism, we should say that his thinking is of great altitude and all level; not a succession of summits, but a high Atlantic tableland. Dramatic power, the rarest talent in literature, he has very little. He has an eye constant to the fact of life, and that never pauses in its advance. But the great felicities, the miracles of poetry, he has never. It is all design with him, just thought and instructed expression, analogies, allusion, illustration, which knowledge and correct thinking supply; but of Shakespeare and the transcendent Muse no syllable. . . . Poetry is with Goethe thus external, the gilding of the chain, the mitigation of his fate; but the Muse never assays those thunder-tones which cause to vibrate the sun and moon, which dissipate by dreadful melody all this iron network of circumstance, and abolish the old heavens and the old earth before the free-will and godhead of man."

There are many references to Goethe in Emerson's

writings, and ever and again, when his moral mood has revolted, he returns almost like a penitent. "After taxing Goethe as a courtier, artificial, unbelieving, worldly, I took up this book of 'Helena,' and found him an Indian of the wilderness, a piece of pure nature, like an apple or an oak, large as morning or night, and virtuous as a brier-rose." Finally, in "Representative Men," he stereotypes his judgment. "Goethe can never be dear to men." "He has not worshipped the highest unity; he is incapable of a self-surrender to the moral sentiment." But! "The old Eternal Genius who built the world has confided himself more to this man than to any other."

The burden of his prophecy was on Emerson's shoulders. Goethe had to create his New World out of his brain by magic art, and mount it on a stage tricked out in unyielding walls of a fortress. Emerson is resolved that the poetry of the Old shall be the reality of the New World. He means that the pictures of Raphael and Goethe shall sink to studies of what is to breathe and live in America.

The influence of Swedenborg upon the mind of Emerson is phenomenal. The lecture upon the Mystic in "Representative Men" suggests that he had placed too much faith in the exaggerated claims for Swedenborg's scientific work put forth by enthusiastic writers. Having accepted their interpretations, *e.g.*, that Swedenborg's allusion to seven planets was a prediction of Uranus instead of a bit of astrology, Emerson was prepared to welcome a man who justified the office of the Seer by making more happy discoveries with his scientific eyes shut ($\mu\nu\epsilon\sigma\iota\varsigma$) than when they were open.

Taking a general view of Swedenborg's life, nothing could more completely foreshadow the ideal man of Emerson: a powerful brain, whose first outgrowth is a trunk of practical science, and whose last fruit has converted all that trunk and its roots to visions. Here, at any rate, was the hint and dim outline of a man. He was much charmed by the ingenious writers — Dr. Garth Wilkinson in London, and Sampson Reed in America — who had adapted Swedenborg to modern culture. He wrote to Carlyle in the early years of their friendship about Swedenborg, at the same time deprecating his Hebraism and mechanical theism. Carlyle mentioned this to me, and added, " I speedily discovered that Swedenborg was mad and gave him up." In the end, the Swedenborgians would have been glad if Emerson had done the same. Nothing troubled them more than his lecture, fourteen years later, on " Swedenborg, the Mystic." It was a splendid epitaph on that sect. Nevertheless, it remains true that Emerson was the first to discover the place of Swedenborg in nature, — the ages of tradition that revealed their force and direction in his evolution. " He is the last Father in the Church, and is not likely to have a successor." He had carried the deity of Christ, miracle, angelolatry, demonology, revelation, to that extreme point that they became dying confessions of the Christian system. " Nature reveals her secrets in monsters," said Goethe: Emerson, as a spiritual naturalist, found similar revelations in the monstrosities of Swedenborg — keys to the discredited spiritual mythology.

On Emerson's new horizon, Carlyle, the secrets of

his "art and mystery" gained, appeared an English Prometheus, resolved to bear to men the fire which the Teutonic deities were reserving to themselves. His brave effort to animate the cold still forms of trade and politics was an irresistible appeal to Emerson; and in a paper he wrote on the appearance of "Past and Present" there is the prophecy of Carlyle's career and the omen of revolutions now historical. This paper of seven pages is not so much a criticism as a happy celebration, the principal theme of which is admiration at the generosity of the thinker who had addressed himself to a great human task, with, however, a sharp touch here and there on that thinker's faults.

"Here is Carlyle's new poem, his Iliad of English woes, to follow his poem on France, entitled the 'History of the French Revolution.' In its first aspect it is a political tract, and since Burke, since Milton, we have had nothing to compare with it. It grapples honestly with the facts lying before all men, and with a heart full of manly tenderness offers his best counsel to his brothers. . . . It is not by sitting still at a grand distance and calling the human race *larvæ* that men are to be helped, nor by helping the depraved after their own foolish fashion, but by doing unweariedly the work we were born to do."

"It requires great courage in a man of letters to handle the contemporary practical questions, not because he then has all men for his rivals, but because of the infinite entanglements of the problem, and the waste of strength in gathering unripe fruits. The task is superhuman, and the poet knows well that a little time will do more than the most puissant genius."

He expresses frankly his sense of a fault in Carlyle's "Past and Present." The picture is over-coloured, lacks universality, the tone exaggerated; it is not serene sunshine, but everything is seen in lurid storm-lights. "One can hardly credit, whilst under the spell of this magician, that the world had always the same bankrupt look to foregoing ages as to us — as of a failed world just recollecting its old withered forces to begin again and try to do a little business. . . . Each age has its own follies, as its majority is made up of foolish young people; its superstitions appear no superstitions to itself; and if you should ask the contemporary, he would tell you with pride or with regret (according as he was practical or poetic) that it had none. But after a short time, down go its follies and weakness, and the memory of them; its virtues alone remain, and its limitation assumes the form of a beautiful superstition, as the dimness of our sight clothes the objects in the horizon with mist and colour. The Revelation of Reason is this of the unchangeableness of the fact of humanity under all its subjective aspects, that to the cowering it always cowers, to the daring it opens great avenues. The ancients are only venerable to us because distance has destroyed what was trivial, as the sun and stars affect us only grandly because we cannot reach to their smoke and their surfaces and say, Is that all?"

In private, Emerson remonstrated with Carlyle about his style of writing, and I gathered from his conversation that he never quite recovered from the shock of "Sartor," nor valued that book so highly as his friends did. It took all his optimism to adapt himself to his friend's "clothes," but it was achieved. "We have never had anything in literature so like earthquakes as the laughter of Carlyle. He 'shakes with his mountain mirth.' It is like the laughter of the genii in the horizon. These jokes shake down Parliament-house, and Windsor Castle, temple, and tower, and the future shall echo the dangerous peals. The other particular of his magnificence is in his rhymes. Carlyle is a poet who is altogether too burly in his frame and habit to submit to the limits of metre. Yet he is full of rhythm, not only in the perpetual melody of his periods, but in the burdens, refrains, and grand returns of his sense and music. Whatever thought or motto has once appeared to him fraught with meaning, becomes an omen to him henceforward, and is sure to return with deeper tones and weightier import, now as promise, now as threat, now as confirmation, in gigantic reverberation, as if the hills, the horizon, and the next ages returned the sound."

Probably the most lasting influence of Carlyle upon Emerson was derived from his political writings, which quickened in him the feeling of the practical relation of his genius to his age and country. The creed of the Puritans, that the worker must think, the thinker must work, revived in his perception that literature is a blossom that must pass away unless fulfilled in fruit.

In the first discoverable scrap of Emerson's writing there is found nearly the same literary style as in his last. The only authors whose influence seems traceable in it are Shakespeare and Montaigne; and one may remember that Montaigne's Essays is the only book known to have been in the library of Shakespeare. If one should first meet in an essay by Emerson such sentences as, "Spirits are not finely touched but to fine issues," or "Nature is helped by no mean, but nature makes that mean"— it would hardly make one pause. In his lecture on Montaigne, Emerson says, "A single odd volume of Cotton's translation of the Essays remained to me from my father's library when a boy. It lay long neglected, until, after many years, when I was newly escaped from college, I read the book and procured the remaining volumes. I remember the delight and wonder in which I lived with it. It seemed to me as if I had myself written the book in some former life, so sincerely it spoke to my thought and experience."

There is, however, a felicity about Emerson's expression such as is hinted in a note he wrote on verses sent to the "Dial" by Wentworth Higginson in his youth: "They have truth and earnestness, and a happier hour may add that external perfection which can neither be commanded nor described." The nearest parallel is in the authentic utterances found in the bibles of the world. Emerson was among the earliest students of Oriental scriptures, from which some of the finest passages were inserted in the "Dial." In the paper which we have been mainly reading, "Thoughts on Literature," he writes: "The Bible is the most original book in the world. This old collection of the ejaculations of love and dread, of the supreme desires and contritions of men, proceeding out of the region of the grand and eternal, by whatsoever different mouths spoken, and through a wide extent of times and countries, seems, especially if you add to our canon the kindred sacred writings of the Hindoos, Persians, and Greeks, the alphabet of the nations."

In reading these critical judgments, one may recognise that Emerson had at a very early age liberated himself from all authorities. In his first lecture at Harvard University (1837) he said: "Meek young men grow up in libraries, believing it their duty to accept the views which Cicero, which Locke, which Bacon have given, forgetful that Cicero, Locke, and Bacon were only young men in libraries when they wrote these books." In this spirit he gathered up the literature of the past into himself, but it was transmuted into his own life by his own experience. Herman Grimm ("National Zeitung," June 11, 1882) finds a resemblance in Emerson to Shakespeare in "the precision with which, especially in illustration, he draws from his own experience, without caring to go beyond it." And in reading or hearing his sentences on men and books, I have felt that they were not literary criticism but spiritual biography. The finest writing was worse than wasted on Emerson unless it advanced some actuality a point farther. He would forgive endless weeds where he found one sesame that could open any closed door, but cared not for the most felicitous amplifications. It is not in an ordinary sense that Emerson can be described as a literary man at all. In books he valued so much as was not book but man, and could be so proved by assimilation in another man. That writer who had helped him was the writer he could report about. Not that his spirit was, "Save most of men Count Gismond, who saved me!" But he knew the danger of a counterfeit; he would never pronounce a thing true gold which had not rung on his counter, nor any currency sound which he had not actually converted into the substance of life. "Cut these words and they would bleed," he says of Montaigne. Emerson's literary estimates are sometimes surprising; but his task lay in a realm where "the perfection of man is the love of use;" and where words are known only as they are made flesh, and estimated by experience of their creative power.

XII.

EAGLE AND DOVE.

ON a beautiful day I was walking with Emerson in a wood near Concord. It was in one of my early months at Divinity College, — a period of painful recollections of my once comfortable little Egypt, left for poverty, loneliness, and a spiritual wilderness. He had questioned me about our studies up at Cambridge, and our experiences, and brought upon himself an outpouring of crude questionings and blank misgivings about the universe. He listened with a patience I now see to be divine. After a silence, and a few sympathetic words, he paused and exclaimed, "Ah! there is one of the gods of the wood!" I looked and saw nothing; then turned to him and followed his glance, but still beheld nothing unusual. He was looking with a beaming eye along the path that lay before us through a thicket. "Where?" I asked. "Did you see it?" he said, now moving on. "No, I saw nothing — what was it?" "No matter," said he gently. I repeated my question, but he still said smilingly, "Never mind if you did not see it." I was a little piqued, but said no more, and very soon was listening to discourse which obliterated anxieties about the absolute. The incident was never alluded to again, and it was long before I knew what god of the woods Emerson then surprised, which I saw not.

Many have learned, with George Meredith —

> "What a dusty answer gets the soul
> When hot for certainties in this our life."

But it is the characteristic of our time that the certainties are hotter after mortals than these are for the certainties. Some of us who have known the bitterness of seeing the old stars of faith go down, as we were wandering through the dark wolds of early life, have been guided from it by the tones of Concordia (to remember Schiller's "Bell"); but we may not have considered or remembered through what fires and hard blows Concordia had to pass ere it gained that pure voice in which the stars that had set rose again in our heart and sang together for joy. It is difficult to associate anything but happiness with Emerson; but Heine's fact stands, Wherever genius is, there is Golgotha. When Emerson had gone to dwell in Concord, and when, on the two-hundredth anniversary of the settlement of the town by his ancestors, he built their bones into the poetic monument already described, the faith in which they had so nobly wrought was to him the place of a skull. Scepticism was not in his temperament; he was a born believer; his eye was made for ineffable visions; yet the fatal shaft of criticism had reached the vulnerable point, — his intellectual veracity, — and there remained not a rack of the ancient deities or heavens.

Residing with his prayerful mother, in the home of the venerable minister in whom the pious traditions of his race are all embodied, what sees that walking eyeball with no past at his back?

"As men's prayers are a disease of the will, so are their creeds a disease of the intellect."

"The faith that stands on authority is not faith."

"The word Miracle, as pronounced by Christian churches, gives a false impression: it is Monster."

"The prayers and even the dogmas of our Church are like the zodiac of Denderah, and the astronomical monuments of the Hindoos, — wholly insulated from anything now extant in the life and business of the people."

"The Puritans in England and America found in the Christ of the Catholic Church, and in the dogmas inherited from Rome, scope for their austere piety and their longings for civil freedom. But their creed is passing away, and none arises in its room."

"Christianity became a mythus, as the poetic teaching of Greece and of Egypt before."

"The secret of heaven is kept from age to age. No imprudent, no sociable angel ever dropt an early syllable to answer the longings of saints, the fears of mortals."

"The popular notion of a revelation is that it is a telling of fortunes."

"These questions which we lust to ask about the future are a confession of sin."

In the Wiertz Museum at Brussels is pictured a maiden gazing on her own skeleton; these denials show the skeleton supplanting a form painted with the colours of faith over its shrivelled skin. But what does all this mean for a young, believing, loving, and truthful genius like that of Emerson? for a genius with the world in its winged heart? It means Milton suddenly brought down from his celestial paradise to a small prosaic solitude.

Goethe's fable tells the near result. As the eagle soared, the huntsman's dart pierced its right wing and brought it to the ground. The wound was healed, but alas! the power to soar was gone. Now from the earth, pining, he can only look up to the far heaven, his haughty eye filled with a tear. A dove beholds his sorrow, and, turning for a moment from its mate, flutters to the next bush. "Cheer up, my friend," it says sweetly to the wounded king; "see how near thee are the sources of tranquil bliss. On the brook's mossy brink thy heart can meet the sunset splendours. Amid the dewy flowers thou shalt find delicate food. At the crystal fountain thy thirst may be quenched. O friend! the sweet spirit of content gives all we know of happiness, and finds everywhere its food." The eagle, its lofty eye turned now to the myrtle grove where it had fallen, then into itself, said, "O wisdom, ever thou speakest as a dove!"

Smitten down from his pulpit by the arrow that flieth by day, exiled from the apocalyptic city of God — however radiant in the visions of Dante and Milton — Emerson, with broken wing, still gazed on the ancient heavens. Nay, as we have seen, he flutters away to Highgate, Rydal Mount, Craigenputtock, seeking some helpful strength by which he may rise. "Believe in the Trinity!" cried Coleridge. "Beware of your intellect!" warned Wordsworth. "No step thitherward can be taken!" said Carlyle. Back, then, to

Concord! Back, with however heavy a heart, to listen to what the dove may say at the door of the Old Manse!

As over the chaos of crumbled beliefs this sweet spirit brooded, there arose an Eden which turned the visions, from Patmos to Rydal Mount, into mere fables of its eternal beauty. Those negations quoted above are merest thorns, which Emerson pruned away from his roses, that needed no guard but his love to garner the dawns in that garden. Every essential doctrine of every system deemed religious receives its sentence. Read in their context, the negations are shades setting forth glorious forms of affirmation; they are discords that die in raising the heart to harmonies; they are serpents summoned only to deliver up the fruits of wisdom to him whose heel their head sustains. He has found the immortality that is not postponed; he prays the prayer that is always answered; he meets a god in every bush. His joy now looks back upon the former heaven as a prison. He has learned why nature denied man wings, and takes care that when devised they shall melt or be broken — even that he may soar.

XIII.

DAILY BREAD.

SIR RALPH EMERSON in Yorkshire, if a true ancestor, would never have been prouder of the lions on his shield, had he foreseen "Thomas Emerson, Baker," on the front of that house in New England where the American family was founded. This gentleman, reared under chivalrous traditions, finds himself in a wild settlement of his fellows, and recognises beside "Labour-in-vain Creek" the dragon he is to slay. Barrenness he is to conquer, swamp he is to clear. He is the best-educated man there, and well-to-do; he sees a thing needed — wholesome wheaten bread; and into bread he converts a large quantity of dust and mud. When his monument is built, let his coat of arms be carved quartered with a loaf, over the words, "He made bread for men in the wilderness." And the words of his great descendant might be added, "Real service will not lose its nobleness."

Two centuries later the same English knighthood, its plume changed to a pen, its badge to an invisible charm, is found in Concord, giving to the settlers of an ideal world their daily bread. Nor was he in this less cheerful and earnest because it was a world small and lowly, so far as then visible. From the first Emerson had shown himself remarkably free from ambition for public position, his eagerness being apparent where individual minds were concerned. Of spiritual companionship in Concord, when he first went to reside there, he found very little; and, much as he loved solitude, he longed ardently for intellectual communion. He pleaded with Carlyle very earnestly to come to New England, as we have seen, but in vain. The great lesson of self-reliance which he was to teach, he now learned in all its depths. One of its most important instructions was that others were essentially like himself — or were himself. They would transmute the same ideas and truths, if given them, as they did the same bread and fruit into protoplasm. If he should show these humble country-folk what was in his heart, would they receive it? could they? The question was no sooner asked than answered.

Emerson was under the necessity of earning his own daily bread, but felt no anxiety on that score. His lectures paid only an average of four pounds each, but that, forty-seven years ago, was enough to secure him what he most needed just then, a year or two of freedom for poise before descending on his object. He used to speak of it as leisure, but in the years 1834 and 1835 he gave twenty-two lectures in Boston, the subjects being "Water," "The Relations of Man to the Globe," "Italy (2)," "The Means of Inspiring a Taste for English Literature," "Biography," "Burke," "Michael Angelo," "Luther," "George Fox," "English Literature (10)." He generally wrote these lectures out in the week they were delivered. He also wrote some of his best poems about this time. He was perfectly conscious that there was a field golden with its harvest before him, and that his sickle was able to reap it. He deliberately prepared himself for the work. He studied the works and lives of the men and women who had made revolutions — Socrates and Plato, Plotinus, St. Augustine, Dante, Luther, George Fox, Behmen, Swedenborg, Tauler, Bacon, Newton, Goethe. And meanwhile he kept up his habit of teaching the people, and of sedulously attending to every individual whom his thought drew to him.

Emerson found near Concord (namely, at East Lexington) a congregation which dearly loved to listen to him, and would have dispensed with any forms whatever to have him settle with them. But this he would not do. He used to drive out there from Concord to preach to them on Sundays. This was while he was giving his earliest lectures in Boston, which so many declared incomprehensible. Emerson never lowered his statement for any audience; he prepared for the Lexingtonians as if they were an assembly of Oxonians. Lexington understood him well enough. Elizabeth Peabody told me that an humble woman there, asked whether they meant to settle a preacher, replied, "We are very simple people here, and don't understand anybody but Mr. Emerson."

A youth whose unfolding mind had attracted him was invited from Boston to pass some days at the Old Manse, and has told me of his great happiness in driving with Emerson over to East Lexington, where he heard him preach on a Sunday morning. On the way Emerson repeated George Herbert's hymn, "Sweet day, so cool, so calm, so bright." It would seem a sufficient end of life to pass such a morning in the morning time of life; and, for his young friend, that sweet day has never set.

The discourses which Emerson gave these simple people were the same he had given in Boston, and, as he told me, many of them re-appear in substance in his volumes. But he found the country congregation more open to any innovations he saw fit to make in the services. As we have seen, he could no longer conform to the usage of formal prayer. A friend told me that about this time he heard him give a discourse on the text, "Pray without ceasing." The burden of it was that, when prayer was real, whatever men prayed for they received. If the prayer were unreal, a petition for what was against the nature of things, there could be no heart in it, and no faith; but if it were the genuine aspiration of the whole nature, it would be the unceasing aim, and desire, and effort of the life, and that prayer would move on to its answer and fulfilment. "Our prayers are prophets."

In the same way Emerson gave the people bread made of grain that had grown in them. He differed from the majority of "innovators" in this. He did not undervalue the religious sentiments already in the common people, or their associations. The New England congregations, with their slowly built-up independence; the weekly day of rest, which gave opportunity for moral culture; the simplicity of the services, allowing so much room for quiet modification; all these were recognised by Emerson as forms, in the main, higher than the use commonly made of them. And likewise the popular beliefs — in God, in the eternal consequence of actions, in retribution, in miracle, in the divinity of a man who had lived and died for his fellows — how susceptible all these were of such statement as would make them living bread to mankind! The only need was that men and women should be made to realise that these things were of the essence of their daily lives, when truly lived. What Confucius had taught in ancient China, Emerson applied to his neighbours. "The ode says, As we cut hatchet handles. We use one handle to cut another. The wise man uses what is in man to reform men." So Emerson taught the lowly folk around him that Concord and East Lexington possess the elements of Palestine, that true prayers are always answered, that the world is what we believe it to be, that the future is what we make it, and that the perfect man is God.

He studied the sciences carefully, always keeping abreast of their vanguard, and brought every ray of light from Germany, France, England, to illumine the things around him, and around those he taught. The discoveries of philology lit up the every-day speech of the rustic, surprised at finding his words were poems: the gods and goddesses of mythology were seen in the procession of dawns, days, clouds, seasons; the trees were heard singing and sighing as if an Ariel were in each; nature was touched and tinted all over with new light, its secrets told, until everything seemed supernatural. To make life, for each whom he could reach, rich, beautiful, divine, was to Emerson an object so assiduously pursued, that to simple minds he was irresistible.

New England Puritanism had intertwined its theology

with every-day life. The children bore scriptural names; a text was cited for everything, whether shooting an Indian, executing a witch, or planting peas and beans. The perpetual round of biblical duties gave the week seven sabbaths. It has been said that if a fool would only be consistent in his folly he would cease to be a fool. When the Judaic delusion of Puritanism had gone to a suicidal extreme, when the strain on human nature began to give way, and a generation came that could venture to smile, the jokes became textual. The author of "The Biglow Papers," replying to a charge of irreverence, says: "Will any one familiar with the New England countryman venture to tell me that he does *not* speak of sacred things familiarly?" Corresponding to this was that outcome of the Puritan measure which now, by the voice of Emerson, insisted on an actual and every-day application of the principles which had taken the place of the dogmas. They should not be shelved for Sunday use. Whatever was affirmed must be religiously applied. The typical old lady of Boston, who, when asked her opinion of the doctrine, observed that "Total depravity is a good thing if only lived up to," found an unexpected supporter in the new thinker. Every doctrine which had faintly "survived" in the Unitarian movement, every theory it affirmed, was now tested as to its applicability to the existing time and place, and its harmony with the highest aims that men and women could set before themselves. The churches saw danger in this doctrine when enunciated by one who had found even the creedless church of Channing too narrow, and whose pale of communion had widened to include science and art, and the secular work of the world. But the common people heard him gladly. Pisgah and Tabor rose up against the horizon around Concord and Lexington. In his twenty-second year Emerson, at the anniversary of the Concord fight, proposed the toast, "The little bush that marks the spot where Captain Davis fell : 'tis the burning bush where God spake for his people." Now he kindles every bush for the people. He persuades the farmer, so anxious not to be cheated, that when he is equally anxious not to cheat, his market-cart will shine like a chariot of the sun. The correspondences which Swedenborg saw between biblical and natural forms are fossils beside those which Emerson shewed between nature and the heart, mind, life, of every man ; over every flower hovered its soul, and the farm was a sermon that never wearied. Thus the descendant of Thomas Emerson, baker, did not seek to feed the hunger of his villagers with tidings of heavenly bread harvested in ancient times and far lands. Beside his " Labour-in-vain Creek," as the retrospective fathers found it, he lived and laboured as in the living garden of a living God, and gave of its fruits to all whom he met; and such made it manifest that his prophecy was true — that which was ecstasy shall become daily bread.

XIV.

THE HOME.

A WISE old friend of mine used to say that in marriage one should seek a soul that came into the world about the same time as himself." So Emerson once said to me. Lidian Jackson, whom he married in September, 1835, exceeded him a little in age, and the spiritual breath of the same era was upon her. Born beside Plymouth Rock, she had become of such marked devoutness in the Church there founded by the Pilgrims,— dedicated by her ancestors to the God of Calvin, and ascended to the God of Channing,— and so unwearied in her charities that she was known as "the Saint of Plymouth." Yet, whenever the " Last Supper" was to be celebrated in this church, its saint arose, and, from the old family pew near the pulpit, walked down the aisle and out of the church. This was not because she did not honour the rite, but because she held its maintenance as a condition of church-membership to be its perversion and dishonour. Mrs. Emerson brought some pecuniary addition to his means, and the house, with its pleasant garden, in which he loved to work, and several acres were purchased. Emerson now regarded himself as a rich man, with his homestead, about twenty thousand dollars in money, and an increasing demand for his lectures. Then, as always, he and his wife knew the art of spending. Simplicity, good taste, comfort, hospitality, sincerity, were the furniture of this Concord home. There were business men in Boston who revered the scholar and philosopher, and perhaps then as later, if they had a good chance for an investment were glad to get Emerson's surplus into it and forward him good dividends. His mother may have been a little distressed at first by the strange opinions which had separated him from the Church, but she soon found that he had chosen the better part. Surrounded thus by all the resources of happiness, Emerson sorrowed most for his friend Carlyle in his lonely home on the bleak moors, and again urged him to come. He offered Carlyle his home, and even his own destiny. He prophesied and pictured for him a career in America singularly resembling the career afterwards fulfilled by himself. "He used to write," said Carlyle to me, "of solid and honest farmers, and said, 'Horace Greeley does their thinking for them at a dollar a head.'" Whereat Carlyle was mirthful; but one can now see a sad contrast in the environments which the Old World and the New had severally assigned to these representatives of the same era. Carlyle praises poverty, while every posthumous page bears witness to its miserable effects upon himself and his life. Emerson never knew real poverty; even while he drove his mother's cow to pasture, there were prospects of plenty around him in every direction, and no room for fear or misgiving about the future. To a healthy intelligent youth America was already a fortune. Carlyle's

"Blessed be poverty" is not so wise as Solomon's "Give me neither poverty nor riches." After all it is a mean thing, this struggle for existence, to a thinker whose mind should be free to detach the poetic dream of its youth from the local mould, and sound a melody for the young world. "Concordia" lost nothing from its notes by not having passed through that furnace-smoke.

Much more will have to be said about Emerson's home as the birthplace of many souls, but I insert here reminiscences written by Louisa Alcott, whose tales have carried far the morning breath of Concord.

"My first remembrance is of the morning when I was sent to inquire for little Waldo, then lying very ill. His father came to me, so worn with watching and changed by sorrow, that I was startled, and could only stammer out my message. 'Child, he is dead!' was his answer. Then the door closed, and I ran home to tell the sad tidings. I was only eight years old, and that was my first glimpse of a great grief, but I never have forgotten the anguish that made a familiar face so tragical, and gave those few words more pathos than the sweet lamentation of the 'Threnody.'

"Later, when we went to school with the little Emersons in their father's barn, I remember many happy times when the illustrious papa was our good playfellow. Often piling us into a bedecked hay-cart, he took us to berry, bathe, or picnic at Walden, making our day charming and memorable by showing us the places he loved, the wood-people Thoreau had introduced to him, or the wildflowers whose hidden homes he had discovered. So that when, years afterwards, we read of 'the sweet rhodora in the woods,' and 'the burly, dozing humble-bee,' or laughed over 'The Mountain and the Squirrel,' we recognised old friends, and thanked him for the delicate truth and beauty which made them immortal for us and others.

"When the book mania fell upon me at fifteen, I used to venture into Mr. Emerson's library and ask what I should read, never conscious of the audacity of my demand, so genial was my welcome. His kind hand opened to me the riches of Shakespeare, Dante, Goethe, and Carlyle; and I gratefully recall the sweet patience with which he led me round the book-lined room, till 'the new and very interesting book' was found, or the indulgent smile he wore when I proposed something far above my comprehension. 'Wait a little for that,' he said. 'Meantime try this, and if you like it, come again.' For many of these wise books I am waiting still, very patiently, because in his own I have found the truest delight, the best inspiration of my life.

"When these same precious volumes were tumbled out of the window while his house was burning some years ago, as I stood guarding the scorched wet pile, Mr. Emerson passed by, and surveying the devastation with philosophic calmness, only said in answer to my lamentations, 'I see my library under a new aspect. Could you tell me where my good neighbours have flung my boots?'

"In the tribulations of later life this faithful house-friend was an earthly Providence, conferring favours so beautifully that they were no burden, and giving such sympathy in joy and sorrow that very tender ties were knit between this beneficent nature and the grateful hearts he made his own. I have often seen him turn from distinguished guests to say a wise or kindly word to some humble worshipper sitting modestly in a corner, content merely to look and listen, and who went away to cherish that moment long and gratefully."

Emerson had taken a deep interest in everything relating to the village in which he had come to reside. In the month of his marriage he gave the address on the two-hundredth anniversary of the incorporation of Concord. It has been quoted in a previous chapter, but another passage may be set here. "In the eternity of Nature how recent our antiquities appear! The imagination is impatient of a cycle so short. Who can tell how many thousand years, every day, the clouds have shaded these fields with their purple awning? The river, by whose banks most of us were born, every winter for ages has spread its crust of ice over the great meadows which in ages it had formed. But the little society of men who now, for a few years, fish in this river, plough the fields it washes, mow the grass, and reap the corn, shortly shall hurry from its banks, as did their forefathers. 'Man's life,' said the Druid to the Saxon king, 'is the sparrow that enters at a window, flutters round the house, and flies out at another, and none knoweth whence he came or whither he goes.' The more reason that we should give to our being what permanence we can, that we should recall the past, and expect the future."

Emerson's mother resided in his home until her death

in 1853. His aunt Mary was a frequent visitor until her death in 1863. And near by, at Waltham, subsequently at the Old Manse in Concord, was Sarah Ripley, who died in 1867.

He suffered some severe bereavements; especially heavy was that of his beautiful boy Waldo. But he was invincible by any sorrow. Writing of his first visit to Europe (1833) he says, "If Goethe had been still living, I might have wandered into Germany also." But he had little need to know Goethe personally, for he had learned that great man's secret of life. There is a letter which Goethe addressed "To the youthful poets of Germany," every line of which became actual in the early years of Emerson's life at Concord. "When at our entrance into the life of action and effort, scant in pleasures, in which, be what we may, we must all feel ourselves dependent on a great whole, we ask back all our early dreams, wishes, hopes — all the delicious joys and facilities of our youthful fairyland — the Muse abandons us, and seeks the company of the man who can bear disappointment cheerfully, and recover from it easily; who knows how to gather something from every season; who can enjoy the glassy ice-track and the garden of roses, each in its appointed time; who understands the art of mitigating his own sufferings, and looks steadfastly and industriously around him, where he may find another's pain to soothe, another's joy to enhance. Then do no years sever him from the benign goddesses, who, if they delight in the bashfulness of innocence, also give their support to far-looking prudence; here foster the germ of hope and promise; there rejoice in the complete accomplished man in his full development.

> "Jüngling, merke dir, in Zeiten,
> Wo sich Geist und Sinn erhöht,
> Das die Muse zu begleiten
> Doch zu leiten nicht versteht."

XV.

NATURE.

HERMAN GRIMM, writing on Emerson's death (National Zeitung), says, "A picture at Assisi, by Giotto, shows St. Francis restoring to life a woman who had died without confession, long enough to confess to him. The woman raises herself on her bier, and the saint kneels before her. So, it appears to me, Emerson awakened Nature, and gave her a voice, that she might confess to him her secrets, and that he knows of these more than he has told."

With this we may remember one of Emerson's early poems — Musketaquid.

> "Because I was content with these poor fields,
> Low, open meads, slender and sluggish streams,
> And found a home in haunts which others scorned,
> The partial wood-gods overpaid my love,
> And granted me the freedom of their state."

The Indian, and the farmer who has succeeded him, are caught into the procession of natural forms passing through without interrupting his solitude.

> "Beneath low hills, in the broad interval
> Through which at will our Indian rivulet
> Winds, mindful still of sannup and of squaw,
> Whose pipe and arrow oft the plough unburies,

Here in pine houses built of new fallen trees,
Supplanters of the tribe, the farmers dwell.
Traveller, to thee, perchance, a tedious road,
Or, it may be, a picture; to these men
The landscape is an armory of powers,
Which, one by one, they know to draw and use.

. . . .

They fight the elements with elements
(That one would say, meadow and forest walked,
Transmuted in these men to rule their like),
And by the order in the field disclose
The order regnant in the yeoman's brain.

" What these strong masters wrote at large in miles,
I followed in small copy in my acre;
For there's no rood has not a star above it;
The cordial quality of pear or plum
Ascends as gladly in a single tree
As in broad orchards resonant with bees;
And every atom poises for itself,
And for the whole. The gentle deities
Showed me the lore of colours and of sounds,
The innumerable tenements of beauty,
The miracle of generative force,
Far-reaching concords of astronomy
Felt in the plants, and in the punctual birds;
Better, the linked purpose of the whole,
And, chiefest prize, found I true liberty
In the glad home plain-dealing nature gave."

In this poem there is the feeling of Wordsworth, but the presence of a new creative force is revealed in the succession of the scenes. The intellect with its prize — liberty, with its rood beneath and star overhead — looks not on shifting landscapes but through vistas unfolding from the morning cloud to man, from man to the poetic idea which gathers up again the past and enfolds the whole.

In 1834 Emerson gave in Boston a lecture on "The Relations of Man to the Globe." It has never been published, but in it occur illustrations prophetic of Darwin's theory. He said, "The brother of the hand existed ages ago in the flipper of the seal."

While young Darwin was voyaging around the world in the "Beagle," Emerson was voyaging around a larger sphere without quitting the limits of Concord. It would be interesting to know the dates of some poems of his, especially those of which Tyndall has said that "in his case Poetry, with the joy of a bacchanal, takes her graver brother Science by the hand, and cheers him with immortal laughter;" and still more of those in which that grave brother is transfigured, as in the mystic-scientific chant of Nature in "Wood-Notes:" —

> "To the open ear it sings
> The early genesis of things,
> Of tendency through endless ages,
> Of star-dust and star-pilgrimages,
> Of rounded worlds, of space and time,
> Of the old flood's subsiding slime,
> Of chemic matter, force, and form,
> Of poles and powers, cold, wet, warm:
> The rushing metamorphosis,
> Dissolving all that fixture is,
> Melts things that be to things that seem,
> And solid nature to a dream."

Fortunately, however, we are not without dates which show how early Emerson's poetic dreams cohered in an ideal conception of the new Genesis which Science has since verified. "The day of days, the great day of the feast of life, is that in which the inward eye opens to the Unity in things." Whatever may be the day, by calendar, which shone with such splendour on Emerson, we know that its radiance so encircled him forty-six years ago as to move profoundly wise and venerable scholars around him. The Hon. Horace Mann, eminent for his educational work in America, wrote to a friend concerning a lecture, probably one of twelve delivered in 1836 at Boston, on the Philosophy of History, in these terms : —

"Mr. Emerson, I am sure, must be perpetually discovering richer worlds than those of Columbus or Herschel. He explores, too, not in the scanty and barren region of our physical firmament, but in a spiritual firmament of illimitable extent and compacted of treasures. I heard his lecture last evening. It was to human life what Newton's 'Principia' was to mathematics. He showed me what I have long thought of so much — how much more can be accomplished by taking a true view than by great intellectual energy. Had Mr. Emerson been set down in a wrong place, it may be doubted whether he would ever have found his way to the right point of view; but that he now certainly has done. As a man stationed in the sun would see all the planets moving around it in one direction and in perfect harmony, while to an eye on the earth their motions are full of crossings and retrogradations, so he, from his central position in the spiritual world, discovers order and harmony where others can discern only confusion and irregularity. His lecture last evening was one of the most splendid manifestations of a truth-seeking and truth-developing mind I ever heard. Dr. Walter Channing, who sat beside me, said it made his head ache. Though his language was transparent, yet it was almost impossible to catch the great beauty and proportions of one truth before another was presented."

In 1836, when Darwin returned from his voyage on the "Beagle" and sat down to his mighty task, the pattern of what he was to do was seen in the mount at Concord, and published that year in the little book entitled "Nature." A writer in the "Saturday Review," after speaking of "the great men whom America and England have jointly lost" — Emerson and Darwin — remarks that "some of those who have been forward in taking up and advancing the impulse given by Darwin, not only on the general ground where it started, but as a source of energy in the wider application of scientific thought, have once and again openly declared that they owe not a little to Emerson." This just remark may be illustrated by Tyndall's words in 1873: "The first time I ever knew Waldo Emerson was when, years ago, I picked up at a stall a copy of his 'Nature.' I read it with such delight, and I have never ceased to read it; and if any one can be said to have given the impulse to my mind, it is Emerson: whatever I have done the world owes to him."

Dr. Tyndall tells me that in the volume so purchased he wrote, "Purchased by inspiration." And he might have said, "Written by inspiration." The work was inspired by the dawn of a great idea in the writer's mind — Evolution. It has a prelude of six lines —

> "A subtle chain of countless rings
> The next unto the farthest brings;
> The eye reads omens where it goes,
> And speaks all languages the rose;
> And striving to be man, the worm
> Mounts through all the spires of form."

In this essay occur such phrases as — "every chemical change, from the rudest crystal up to the laws of life; every change of vegetation, from the first principle of growth in the eye of a leaf to the tropical forest and antediluvian coal-mine; every animal function, from the sponge up to Hercules," — showing the direction in which his eye is turned. And there are these pregnant sentences: — "Nothing in Nature is exhausted in its first use. When a thing has served an end to the uttermost, it is wholly new for an ulterior service." "Herein is especially apprehended the unity of Nature — the unity in variety — which meets us everywhere. All the endless variety of things make an identical impression." "Each creature is only a modification of the other." "Any distrust of the permanence of laws would paralyse the faculties of man." "If the reason be stimulated to more earnest vision, outlines and services become transparent, and are no longer seen: causes and spirits are seen through them." "The world proceeds from the same spirit as the body of man." "In a cabinet of natural history we become sensible of a certain occult recognition and sympathy in regard to the most unwieldy and eccentric forms of beast, fish, and insect." "Nor has science sufficient humanity so long as the naturalist overlooks that wonderful congruity which subsists between man and the world, of which he is lord, not because he is the most subtile inhabitant, but because he is its head and heart, and finds something of himself in every great and small thing, in every mountain stratum, in every new law of colour, fact of astronomy, or atmospheric influence which observation or analysis lay open."

A careful perusal of the sentences just cited will show that Emerson's mind had fully conceived the idea of relationship between all organic forms, and that of the harmony of each and all with elemental environment. It may now be further noted that the notions of a mechanical creation, and of a creation passed and ended, have disappeared from his thought. God is "the universal spirit," whose "essence refuses to be recorded in propositions." The "universal essence, which is not wisdom, or love, or beauty, or power, but all in one, and each entirely, is that for which all things exist, and that by which they are." "Spirit creates." "That which, intellectually considered, we call reason, considered in relation to nature we call spirit." This spirit now creates through man. "He (man) is placed in the centre of beings, and a ray of relation passes from every other being to him. And neither can man be understood without these objects, nor these objects without man." "Spirit, that is, the Supreme Being, does not build up Nature around us, but puts it forth through us, as the life of the tree puts forth new branches and leaves through the pores of the old." "Who can set bounds to the possibilities of man?" "Man has access to the entire mind of the Creator, is himself the creator in the finite." "The reason why the world lacks unity and lies broken and in heaps, is because man is disunited with himself."

"When a faithful thinker, resolute to detach every object from personal relations, and see it in the light of thought, shall, at the same time, kindle science with the fire of the holiest affections; then will God go forth anew into the creation." "Nature is not fixed, but fluid. Spirit alters, moulds, makes it. The immobility or bruteness of Nature is the absence of spirit; to pure spirit it is fluid, it is volatile, it is obedient." "All good is eternally reproductive. The beauty of Nature reforms itself in the mind, and not for barren contemplation but for new creation."

This, Emerson's first work, ends with these great words:—"The kingdom of man over Nature, which cometh not with observation,—a dominion such as now is beyond his dream of God,—he shall enter without more wonder than the blind man feels who is gradually restored to perfect sight." Forty years later the prophecy rose again when Clifford said: "Those who can read the signs of the times read in them that the kingdom of Man is at hand."

XVI.

EVOLUTION.

ACCORDING to an American myth, when Emerson visited Egypt the Sphinx said to him, "You're another!"

The enigmatic element, of which many complained in Emerson's earliest writings, is now explicable enough. He spoke from a generalisation at once poetic and scientific, which as yet had nothing corresponding to it in the popular mind. He could not prove it, but it was perfectly clear to him that the method of nature is evolution, and it organised the basis of his every statement. Thus in August, 1841, addressing the Literary Society of Waterville College, occur such passages as these: "The wholeness we admire in the order of the world is the result of infinite distribution. Its smoothness is the smoothness of the pitch of the cataract. Its permanence is a perpetual inchoation. Every natural fact is an emanation, and that from which it emanates is an emanation also, and from every emanation is a new emanation." "We can point nowhere to anything final; but tendency appears on all hands: planet, system, constellation, total Nature, is growing like a field of maize in July; is becoming somewhat else; is in rapid metamorphosis. The embryo does not more strive to be man than yonder burr of light we call a nebula tends to be a ring, a comet, a globe, and parent of new stars." " How silent, how spacious, what room for all, yet without place to insert an atom, — in graceful succession, in equal fulness, in balanced beauty, the dance of the hours goes forward still. Like an odour of incense, like a strain of music, like a sleep, it is inexact and boundless. It will not be dissected, nor unravelled, nor shewn. Away, profane philosopher! seekest thou in nature the cause? This refers to that, and that to the next, and the next to the third, and everything refers. Thou must ask in another mood, thou must feel it and love it, thou must behold it in a spirit as grand as that by which it exists, ere thou canst know the law. Known it will not be, but gladly beloved and enjoyed." " There is no revolt in all the kingdoms from the commonweal; no detachment of an individual. Hence the catholic character which makes every leaf an exponent of the world." " The termination of the world in a man appears to be the last victory of intelligence." " See the play of thoughts! what nimble gigantic creatures are these! what saurians, what palæotheria, shall be named with these agile movers." How simple these thoughts have become to the post-Darwinian world!

It is notable that simultaneously with " The Vestiges of Creation" in England, namely, in 1844, Emerson's second essay on " Nature" appeared. It is a prophetic hymn to the ascending star whose light was already leading wise men towards the truth, — taking form in exact science, — whereof the " Vestiges" was a half-clad forerunner. " Let us no longer omit our homage to the Efficient Nature, *natura naturans*, the quick cause before which all forms flee as the driven snows, itself secret, its works driven before it in flocks and multitudes (as the ancients represented nature by Proteus, a shepherd), and in undescribable variety. It publishes itself in creatures, reaching from particles and specula, through transformation on transformation, to the highest symmetries, arriving at consummate results without shock or leap. A little heat, that is, a little motion, is all that differences the bald, dazzling white and deadly poles of the earth from the prolific tropical climates. All changes pass without violence, by reason of the two cardinal conditions of boundless space and boundless time. Geology has initiated us into the secularity of nature, and taught us to disuse our dame-school measures and exchange our Mosaic and Ptolemaic schemes for her large style. We knew nothing rightly for want of perspective. Now we learn what patient periods must round themselves before the rock is formed, then before the rock is broken, and the first lichen race has disintegrated the thinnest external plate into soil, and opened the door for the remote flora, fauna, Ceres and Pomona, to come in. How far off yet is the trilobite! how far the quadruped! how inconceivably remote is man! All duly arrive, and then race after race of men. It is a long way from granite to the oyster; farther yet to Plato and the preaching of the immortality of the soul. Yet all must come as surely as the atom has two sides."

In this passage the "Spirit" of Emerson's first work ("Nature," published eight years before) re-appears as the *Natura Naturans;* but this again, paraphrased as "Efficient Nature," "quick (living) cause," is an intellectual Declaration of Independence. "Man," he says, "carries the world in his head, the whole astronomy and chemistry suspended in a thought. Because the history of nature is charactered in his brain, therefore is he the prophet and discoverer of her secrets. Every known fact in natural science was divined by the presentiment of somebody before it was actually verified."

The publication of "The Vestiges of Creation" had the good effect of popularising the idea of evolution, and the bad effect of stating the facts so inaccurately that men of science were prejudiced against the general hypothesis. The panic of the pulpit also led some to commit themselves against a theory so crudely stated. The book did not advance the theory so far as Emerson had already gone, for it still supposed "leaps" in the development of organisation. But Emerson would admit no shock or leap." He was also repelled by the mechanic Theos which the author of the "Vestiges" imported. The old phrases "Supreme Architect," "Almighty," "Providence," had become fossil to him whose deity had become subjective. However, he once told me that he thought the book had done good service in diffusing many valuable discoveries and generalisations of the German and French *savants;* and while it was trampled on by preachers and professors, he affirmed its main principle to be true. One of his steadfast warnings was that in his essay on "Circles" —printed three years before the "Vestiges:" "Fear not the new generalisation. Does the fact look crass and material, threatening to degrade thy theory of spirit? Resist it not; it goes to refine and raise thy theory of matter just as much."

While Auguste Comte and Mill ignored evolution, and Carlyle reviled it, Emerson was building on it as upon a rock. His friend Agassiz had committed himself rather warmly against it, — though relenting in later life, — and I heard several conversations between them on the subject. Emerson quoted various things from Agassiz's own works, especially his researches in embryology, which seemed to support the new theory. Agassiz said that unquestionably there was an ideal relation between organic forms, an unbroken succession of ascending types, but he denied that one species could be developed from another. This seemed to him atheism. But Emerson held no such theism as could be affected by any scientific discovery or opinion. He worshipped Thought. "Our theism is the purification of the human mind," was his brave word many years before, and it was written again on his face whenever any opinion offered itself authoritatively.

Emerson's theory of evolution was a theory of Ascent. "The gases gather to the solid firmament; the chemic lump arrives at the plant, and grows; arrives at the quadruped, and walks; arrives at the man, and thinks." This was his idealism, that matter and mind, as they are called, are varied movements of one symphony.

On this he rested his idea of " Poetry." His essay on this subject in " Letters and Social Aims," published in 1876, was read to a small company in Divinity College twenty-three years before. Some of us at

Harvard University had found our real professor at Concord, and one winter evening we went out, travelling the seventeen miles in sleighs, to hear a lecture that was to have been given by him. The lecture had been postponed, but Emerson, hearing of our arrival, invited us to his house, and we went back enriched by his conversation, without feeling any disappointment. Nevertheless, Emerson wrote me that if I would make the preparations, he would read a lecture in my room. On that occasion, besides the students who had gone to Concord for the lecture, others were present, including Mr. and Mrs. Longfellow, J. R. Lowell, Mrs. Charles Lowell, J. S. Dwight, Charles Norton and his sister, L. G. Ware, H. G. Denny, and Otto Dresel. In that essay Emerson said: "The electric word pronounced by John Hunter a hundred years ago, — *arrested and progressive development*, — indicating the way upward from the invisible protoplasm to the highest organisms, — gave the poetic key to natural science, — of which the theories of Geoffroy St. Hilaire, of Oken, of Goethe, of Agassiz, and Owen and Darwin in zoology and botany, are the fruits, — a hint whose power is not yet exhausted, showing unity and perfect order in physics.

"The hardest chemist, the severest analyser, scornful of all but the driest fact, is forced to keep the poetic curve of Nature, and his result is like a myth of Theocritus. All multiplicity rushes to be resolved into unity. Anatomy, osteology, exhibit arrested or progressive ascent in each kind, the lower pointing to the higher forms, the higher to the highest, from the fluid in an elastic sack, from radiate, mollusk, articulate, vertebrate, up to man; as if the whole animal world were only a Hunterian museum to exhibit the genesis of mankind."

The Darwin here referred to is the elder Erasmus Darwin; it was five years later than the revelation of the method of this progression appeared in the paper of Charles Darwin published in the Linnæan Society's Journal (1858). And now that the noble Boston Museum is built, whose successive storeys repeat the history and ascent of organisation in the earth, there might be written on its door that which Emerson further said to us in that small company — "Each animal or vegetable form remembers the next inferior and predicts the next higher. There is one animal, one plant, one matter, and one force."

From this pedestal, like some white column resting on lions winged and couching, carved in its ascent with the symbols of every faith, rose Emerson's dream of the true poem. "In poetry we require the miracle. The bee flies among flowers, and gets mint and marjoram, and generates a new product, which is not mint and marjoram, but honey; the chemist mixes hydrogen and oxygen to yield a new product, which is not these, but water; and the poet listens to conversation, and beholds all objects in nature, to give back, not them, but a new and transcendent whole."

There were poets present, but when this great essay paused, and only an ideal poet crowned the exalted shaft, it appeared the truest New World poem that we were gathered there around the seer, in whose vision the central identity in nature flowed through man's reason, gently did away with discords by their promise of larger harmonies. That which the Brahmans had found in the East our little company knew there in the West also: "From the poisonous tree of the world two species of fruit are produced, sweet as the waters of life: Love, or the society of beautiful souls, and Poetry, whose taste is like the immortal juice of Vishnu." When Emerson finished there was still a hush of silence: it seemed hardly broken when Otto Dresel performed some "Songs without Words."

XVII.

SURSUM CORDA.

WHEN the rumour reached the Boston ministers that Emerson had made a visitation at Divinity College, there was some small flutter, and even a little inquisition; whereat our good professors — Dr. Francis and Dr. Noyes — smiled, as old sailors might at the shaken nerves which turn squalls to hurricanes. The breeze was useful as a suggestion of the real tornadoes which followed Emerson's earlier visits to Cambridge, concerning which the traditions remained fresh enough up to the time (1867) when the University surrendered, made Emerson Doctor of Laws, and Overseer, and a Special Lecturer to the young men he had all along been really teaching. To that earlier period we now return.

The little book of 1836, entitled "Nature," was a soft footfall in the solitude of Concord, but clerical readjusters of their religious inheritance, with the keen sense of a threatened race, laid their ear to the ground and heard battalions behind that hermit. "It is a suggestive book," the "Christian Examiner" must admit. "But the effort of perusal is often painful, the thoughts excited are frequently bewildering, and the results to which they lead us uncertain and obscure. The reader feels as in a distracted dream, in which shows of surpassing beauty are around him, and he is conversant with disembodied spirits; yet all the time he is harassed with an uneasy sort of consciousness that the whole combination of phenomena is fantastic and unreal." "Nature" was printed anonymously, but its writer was easily known; and when the question was asked, Who is the author of "Nature?" the reply was, " God and Ralph Waldo Emerson."

The misgivings were chiefly excited by the first paragraph of "Nature," so often quoted — the " Let there be light" of this New World creation. "Our age is retrospective. It builds the sepulchres of the fathers. It writes biographies, histories, and criticism. The foregoing generations beheld God and nature face to face; we through their eyes. Why should not we also enjoy an original relation to the universe? Why should not we have a poetry and philosophy of insight, and not of tradition, and a religion by revelation to us, and not the history of theirs? Embosomed for a season in nature, whose floods stream around and through us, and invite us, by the powers they supply, to action proportioned to nature, why should we grope among the dry bones of the past, or put the living generation into masquerade out of its faded wardrobe? The sun shines to-day also. There is more wool and flax in the fields. There are new lands, new men, new thoughts. Let us demand our own works and laws and worship."

The first response to this was an invitation from the most important literary society of the country, the Phi Beta Kappa, that Emerson should be their orator for the year 1837. The oration was given at Harvard University. Lowell has described it as " an event without any former parallel in our literary annals, a scene to be always treasured in the memory for its picturesqueness and its inspiration. What crowded and breathless aisles, what windows clustering with eager heads, what enthusiasm of eager approval, what grim silence of foregone dissent!" The theme was " The American Scholar." The scholar was defined as man thinking. He touched again on the unity of nature. " To this schoolboy under the bending dome of day, is suggested that he and it proceed from one root; one is leaf and one is flower; relation, sympathy, stirring in every vein." " The ancient precept, ' Know thyself,' and the modern precept, ' Study Nature,' become at last one maxim." He dispersed the illusions of antiquity. " Genius looks forward : the eyes of man are set in his forehead, not in his hindhead : man hopes; genius creates." He repudiates the idea that the scholar should be a dreamer. " The scholar loses no hour which the man lives." From the education of the scholar by nature, by books, and by action, the orator passes to the function of the scholar. His duties are such as belong to the world's eye, and the world's heart, which must be raised above private considerations to breathe and live in public and illustrious thoughts. For the ease and pleasure of treading the old road he takes the cross of making his own, and is to find consolation in exercising the highest functions of human nature. " In self-trust all the virtues are comprehended. Free should the scholar be — free and brave. Free even to the definition of freedom, without any hindrance that does not arise out of his own constitution. Brave; for fear is a thing which a scholar by his very function puts behind him."

The art of Emerson in parts of this oration can best be appreciated by those who know how far the institution of slavery had bound fast the conscience of the North with cotton cords, and that pulpits and professions were largely retained to justify the national wrong. Even the brave were apologetic when claiming their right to speak. The example of slaveholding patriarchs had given a fresh lease of infallibility to the Bible. Longfellow's "Slave Singing at Midnight" might represent the darkness corresponding to that which surrounded the negro — that shadow fallen upon the literature of the land, which Emerson was the first to dispel. Preservation of the existing "order" (now recognisable as disorder) being the main factor of moral selection — Compromise alone able to pay high for brains — the literary tendency was toward imitation of foreign models. Intellect required diversion to questions other than those which concerned the United States, and while pulpits fulminated against stiff-necked Israelites, literature was actively engaged with the Greeks and Romans.

Emerson was not one sided. While he said, "Give me insight in to-day, and you may have the antique and future worlds," he reminded the scholars that the near and far explain each other, and that Goethe, "the most modern of moderns, has shewn us as none ever did the genius of the ancients." "The scholar is that man who must take up into himself all the ability of the time, the contributions of the past, all the hopes of the future." His concern was that the American scholar should bring his genius into harmony with the principles and adequacy to the opportunities of his country, and do justice to the trust which human history had placed in his hands. "Young men of the fairest promise, who begin life upon our shores, inflated by the mountain winds, shined upon by all the stars of God, find the earth below not in unison with these, but are hindered from action by the disgust which the principles on which business is managed inspire, and turn drudges or die of disgust — some of them suicides. What is the remedy? They did not yet see, and thousands of young men as hopeful now crowding to the barriers for the career do not yet see, that if the single man plant himself indomitably on his instincts, and there abide, the huge world will come round to him."

This phrase last quoted is now historical. The feathered thunderbolt sped to its mark. It came from a young man who, following his brother, had slowly earned and made his professional panoply only to find there was no post for him, nor corps in which he could serve, and had to form a new army with a new cause. By one of the many whose lives were influenced by it that word was repeated over Emerson's grave: "He planted himself indomitably on his instincts, and did there abide, and the huge world came round to him."

XVIII.

THE SHOT HEARD ROUND THE WORLD.

IN the year 1836, the year of "Nature," Concord monument was completed, and Emerson's hymn sung, beginning —

> "By the rude bridge that arched the flood,
>   Their flag to April's breeze unfurled,
> Here once the embattled farmers stood,
>   And fired the shot heard round the world.

Two years later, from where that shot announced the birth of a nation, came a farmer to announce the birth of its religion. On July 15, 1838, Emerson delivered before the senior class in Divinity College, Harvard University, that address which stands in the moral history of America where the Declaration of Independence stands in its political history. The Phi Beta Kappa oration of the previous year had excited discussions, questionings, enthusiasm; and the assembly which gathered to hear the new prophet's word on religion was not only large, but included the representative scholars and teachers of the country.

Never to be forgotten was the fatal melody that startled the air when that appeal to the young ministers was made. Its opening was as the outburst of some magically gorgeous season. "In this refulgent summer it has been a luxury to draw the breath of life. The grass grows, the buds burst, the meadow is spotted with fire and gold in the tint of flowers. The air is full of birds, and sweet with the breath of the pine, the balm of Gilead, and the new hay. Night brings no gloom to the heart with its welcome shade. Through the transparent darkness the stars pour their almost spiritual rays. Man under them seems a young child, and his huge globe a toy. The cool night bathes the world as with a river, and prepares his eyes again for the crimson dawn. The mystery of Nature was never displayed more happily. The corn and wine have been freely dealt to all creatures, and the never-broken silence with which the old bounty goes forward has not yet yielded one word of explanation. One is constrained to respect the perfection of this world in which our senses converse. How wide; how rich; what invitation from every property it gives to every faculty of man! . . . But when the mind opens, and reveals the laws which traverse the universe, and make things what they are, then shrinks the great world at once into a mere illustration and fable of this mind. . . . A more secret, sweet, and overpowering beauty appears to man when his heart and mind open to the sentiment of virtue."

The audience sat breathless, expectant. What strange planet was to follow these auroral flushes on the horizon? Meanwhile, this new Hephæstus brings his axe, flashing a curve of light, straight on the head of Zeus. "If a man is at heart just, then in so far is he God; the safety of God, the immortality of God, the majesty of God, do enter that man with justice." "Jesus Christ belonged to the true race of prophets." "One man was true to what is in you and me." "Christianity became a mythus, as the poetic teaching of Greece and of Egypt before." "The test of the true faith certainly should be to charm and command the soul, as the laws of nature control the activity of the hands,—so commanding that we find pleasure and honour in obeying." "The faith should blend with the light of rising and of setting suns, with the flying cloud, the singing bird, and the breath of flowers. But now the priest's sabbath has lost the splendour of Nature; it is unlovely; we are glad when it is done; we can make, we do make, even sitting in our pews, a far better, holier, sweeter for ourselves. . . . The prayers and even the dogmas of our Church are, like the zodiac of Denderah and the astronomical monuments of the Hindoos, wholly insulated from anything now extant in the life and business of the people. . . . The stationariness of religion, the assumption that the age of inspiration is past, that the Bible is closed, the fear of degrading the character of Jesus by representing him as a man, indicate with sufficient clearness the falsehood of our theology."

And at last from the cloven cloud emerged a Western Athena with panoply of light and fire. "I look for the hour when that supreme Beauty which ravished the souls of those Eastern men, and chiefly of those Hebrews, and through their lips spoke oracles to all time, shall speak in the West also. The Hebrew and Greek scriptures contain immortal sentences, that have been bread of life to millions; but they have no epical integrity; are fragmentary; are not shewn in their order to the intellect. I look for the new Teacher that shall follow so far those shining laws that he shall see them come in full circle; shall see their rounding complete grace; shall see the world to be the mirror of the soul; shall see the identity of the law of gravitation with purity of heart; and shall shew that the Ought, that Duty, is one thing with Science, with Beauty, and with Joy.

The Rev. Henry Ware, whose colleague Emerson had been in Boston, addressed to him a friendly expostulation against the doctrines of this discourse. In reply Emerson wrote as follows:—"What you say about the discourse at Divinity College is just what I might expect from your truth and charity, combined with your known opinions. I am not a stock or a stone, as one said in the old time, and could not feel but pain in saying some things in that place and presence which I supposed would meet with dissent, and the dissent, I may say, of dear friends and benefactors of mine. Yet, as my conviction is perfect in the substantial truth of the doctrines of this discourse, and is not very new, you will see at once that it must appear very important that it be spoken; and I thought I could not pay the nobleness of my friends so mean a compliment as to suppress my opposition to their supposed views, out of fear of offence. I would rather say to them—These things look thus to me, to you otherwise. Let us say our uttermost word, and be the all-pervading truth,' as it surely will, judge between us. Either of us would, I doubt not, be equally apprised of his error. Meantime I shall be admonished by this expression of your thought to revise with great care the address before it is printed (for the use of the class), and I heartily thank you for this expression of your tried toleration and love."

This was followed by a sermon from the same minister against Emerson's views, a copy of which was sent to him with a letter, to which he replied as follows: —
"I ought sooner to have replied to your kind letter of last week, and the sermon it accompanied. The letter was right manly and noble. The sermon, too, I have read with attention. If it assails any doctrine of mine — perhaps I am not so quick to see it as writers generally — certainly I did not feel any disposition to depart from my habitual contentment that you should say your thought whilst I say mine. I believe I must tell you what I think of my new position. It strikes me very oddly that good and wise men, and Cambridge and Boston, should think of raising me into an object of criticism. I have always been, from my very incapacity of methodical writing, 'a chartered libertine,' free to worship and free to rail, lucky when I could make myself understood, but never esteemed near enough to the institutions and mind of society to deserve the notice of the masters of literature and religion. I have appreciated fully the advantages of my position, for I well know that there is no scholar less willing or less able to be a polemic. I could not give account of myself, if challenged. I could not possibly give you one of the arguments you cruelly hint at, on which any doctrine of mine stands. For I do not know what arguments mean in reference to any expression of a thought. I delight in telling what I think;

but if you ask me why I dare say so, or why it is so, I am the most helpless of mortal men. I do not even see that either of these questions admits of an answer, so that in the present posture of affairs, when I see myself suddenly raised to the importance of a heretic, I am very uneasy when I advert to the supposed duties of such a personage, who is to make good his thesis against all comers. I certainly shall do no such thing. I shall read what you and other good men write, as I have always done, glad when you speak my thoughts, and skipping the page that has nothing for me. I shall go on just as before, seeing whatever I can, and telling what I see; and, I suppose, with the same fortune that has hitherto attended me — the joy of finding that my abler and better brothers, who work with the sympathy of society, loving and beloved, do now and then unexpectedly confirm my perception, and find my nonsense is only their own thought in motley. And so I am your affectionate servant, — R.W.E."

Little wonder that the New England shepherds watching their flocks by night should have been sore afraid when this light shone round about them. But their terror could not quench the star that had risen. "It is of no use," said an eminent divine, when he heard of the censure on the Address; "henceforth the young men will have a fifth Gospel in their Testaments."

But the heroic spirits born in that day, had it been predicted that in 1870 the heretic of 1838 would be an official instructor of Harvard youth, would have been amazed, as might Paul had he been told that a Cæsar would one day hold the stirrup for a Christian pontiff.

XIX.

SANGREAL.

IN the "Morte d'Arthur" we see the knights gathered at the Round Table of Arthur, flower of kings. We find portrayed the splendour of the court, the tournaments, luxuries, gallantries of the knights and dames. But one day, while they sit at the table, there is a voice of thunder, then a sunbeam; as the stricken knights gaze the Sangreal floats in shrouded in white, and, when it has floated out again, each feels that he has tasted that which he most desires in this world. Then rose up all those knights and vowed that they would no more rest until they had found the Sangreal and seen it unveiled. King Arthur pleaded against their resolution, but they must leave him. Then they go about the world, wandering in many a wild place, righting wrongs, delivering imprisoned maidens, sitting at the feet of wise hermits, fighting down fiends, until at length Sir Galahad, just after he has casually helped a cripple, finds the unveiled Sangreal and ascends to heaven with it. The great British myth is repeated at intervals in history. There arrives a period in the progress of the people when their best heads discover the fictitious character of the rites to which they are sacramented, and when the best hearts learn their secret, and then the thunder and the sunbeam lead on the true thing above the sham; the *sang real* shames the *sang unreal*, and the Round Table of conventions is broken up. Amid traditional chalices and fonts, and flameless lamps, unable even to borrow oil from other ages, appears the burning glory appealing to every brave heart to win for itself — to leave the dead symbol and possess the reality. Then are true souls revealed. They make their vow of knighthood; no bribe or persuasion of church or court can detain them; they are compelled by a noble discontent; they are drawn by a pure vision; they have tasted that which turns detaining dainties to poison; they must seek a truth and honour as living and real as was ever known by saint or saviour.

Of such a period we are the children. The sanctities, sacraments, symbols, of an exhausted revelation no longer satisfy any heart or intellect. We have seen in our own time what the life-blood of great hearts, freely shed like the blood of Christ, can accomplish, and the Round Table of Jerusalem breaks up. The great men of our time, by whose fresh graves we stand — Darwin, Emerson, Carlyle, Lincoln, Garibaldi — were men whose lives are traced in transformations; millions of slaves have been liberated, nations set free, science advanced, torpid intelligence awakened; they have been on earth as the Sangreal, or its prototype the cornucopia, from which all have been nourished, and have risen to be a constellation beneath which their words and works shall ripen to the new earth that follows the new heaven.

The quest of the Sangreal is a bosom experience to

all who share the development of their generation. Every youth, whose soul suffers no arrest, is certain to arrive at a period of perception when the old symbols no longer satisfy him, when he turns from the conventional chalice however cunningly mixed, and is seized with a longing to make every drop of his blood real, and held in the cup of a flawless heart.

When our virginal Sir Galahad in America, our Emerson, refused any longer to touch the chalice of his Boston church, the knights around him did not at once catch his vision of the radiant cup floating above it. They thought him mad. The thunder and the sunbeam came to them later, when they had gathered to the Round Table of their old university. There each knightly soul found that he had tasted that which he most loved of all on earth. They could no more rest in that to which they had been sacramented.

Among those who listened to that oration, one preacher, before wont to discourse on such themes as the duties and trials of milkmen, went home to enter in his journal: "My soul is roused, and this week I shall write the long-meditated sermons on the state of the Church and the duties of these times." So under the electric touch of Emerson rose Theodore Parker.

John Weiss — an effective leader of the new religion — has well said of Emerson's oration, "The liberal gesture itself was worth a whole body of divinity." The agitation reached the form of a coherent controversy in the following year, when the chief professor of the Divinity College, Andrews Norton, delivered in the same place an answer to it, afterwards published under the title, "The Latest Form of Infidelity." This was replied to by George Ripley and Theodore Parker. Ripley maintained that Christianity was sufficiently proved by intuition. Parker supported him, and maintained that miracles are true, being signs of all great religious teachers (Buddha, Zoroaster, as well as Jesus), but not proofs of their doctrine! Norton replied to them, and the controversy filled America with excitement. It also set the youth to reading the works of the great German, French, and English philosophers whose views were discussed by the Harvard disputants.

By far the most important figure in this controversy (from which Emerson was conspicuously absent) was that of Andrews Norton, Professor of Sacred Literature in Harvard University. His great learning and his admirable force and clearness as a writer were still of less importance than his intellectual character and his severity towards every kind of sham, whether conscious of itself or not. The young men who undertook to controvert the statements of Andrews Norton concerning the anti-christian nature and tendency of Emerson's views — George Ripley and Theodore Parker — wrote well, and were defeated. They were trying to base the Christian ontology on intuition in order to cast discredit on supernatural evidences and authority. "Consciousness or intuition," said Norton, "can inform us of nothing but what exists in our own minds, including the relations of our own ideas. It is therefore not an intelligible error, but a mere absurdity, to maintain that we are conscious or have an intuitive knowledge of the being of God, of our own immortality, of the revelation of God through Christ, or of any other fact of religion." "Christianity claims to reveal facts, a knowledge of which is essential to the moral regeneration of men, and to offer in attestation of those facts the only satisfactory proof — the authority of God evidenced by miraculous displays of His power." "The latest form of infidelity is distinguished by assuming the Christian name while it strikes at the root of faith in Christianity, and indirectly at all religion, by denying the miracles attesting the divine mission of Christ." These affirmations, buttressed by impregnable logic, were never shaken.

Thirty years ago this aged scholar, surrounded by his beautiful daughters, — to describe whom we used to borrow the title of his book, "The Evidences of Christianity," — was the ideal of an Arthur. In the depths of that grove behind Divinity College, an Avilion to those who remember the home it embowered, the old man sat, his grand face haloed with whitest locks and on it written the perfect peace that follows victory over all that can harm the spirit of man. In early life he had suffered pain, long and keen, by failure in all his attempts to preach, after carefully preparing himself. He had to abandon the pulpit. Then he wrote the beautiful hymn so widely sung in America, "My God, I thank Thee!" The last verse is —

> Thy various messengers employ,
> Thy purposes of love fulfil;
> And 'mid the wreck of human joy
> May kneeling faith adore thy will!"

With such piety had he looked forth over the desolation beyond which he was to find this earthly paradise! He was now calm, and mention of the controversy of fifteen years brought no flash to his eye. I remember that his eye did flash when he spoke of " the practical atheism " which reigned over the nation, disregarding every principle of justice and humanity. "Theological and philosophical controversies," he said, " seem of small importance in the presence of such evils." " *Flos theologorum* " he was, and the last of his race.

Emerson was from the first at one with the principle of his honoured antagonist. His bark had passed to another sea. What he afterwards wrote of Swedenborg and Behmen was equally true of his friends Parker and Ripley,—that they " both failed by attaching themselves to the Christian symbol instead of to the moral sentiment which carries innumerable christianities, humanities, divinities, in its bosom." Therefore Emerson could take no part in the controversy. And though each of the young thinkers had tasted the holier sacrament in this heart whose blood was shed for them, the Sangreal was as yet veiled from their eyes. Dr. Lowell would now probably smile at two lines about Emerson in his " Fable for Critics "—

" All admire, and yet scarcly six converts he's got,
To I don't (nor they either) exactly know what."

When he came to write his poem telling how Sir Launfal journeyed far but found the Sangreal at his own door, Lowell had learned the secret.

But it is doubtful whether Theodore Parker ever comprehended the man whose touch had awakened him to the recognition of that task he so faithfully performed. Two minds could hardly be more differently moulded than those of these distinguished contemporaries. Parker was certainly a product of the new era of thought, but he was puzzled by Emerson's utterances even while they stirred him. There was little of the mystic about Parker; he was the old English deist with American sympathies and forms of speech. So although in those days he used to be found in the " Olympicks," where Emerson and his " cosmic questions " formed the chief themes of the New England gods and goddesses in conclave, he would go home to write in his journal such prosaic sentences as this : " Mr. E. says, ' If a man is at heart just, so far he is God.' Now, it seems that he mistakes likeness for identity. My spirit is like God, but is it necessarily God? There are ten peas in a pod, exactly alike in all things : are there not ten peas, and not one alone? Now if a man's spirit could become exactly like God's, would his be the same as God's?" &c. After reading this we cannot wonder that the interviews between the two should have been sometimes disappointing. Thus Parker records a walk with some friends — C. P. Cranch, poet and artist, among them — to Concord, in the following terms : " We all assembled and took tea with R. W. E. He and Ripley had all the talk. . . . Really it was quite too bad. The only good thing he said was, ' Come and look at this print of " Endymion," which is very beautiful ; so likewise is its rival, the " Coming of Morning," drawn by two dappled steeds and attended by some virgins, daughters of the sun.' Carlyle sent it to Mrs. E. In our walk E. expressed to me his admiration of —— and his foolish article in the 'Dial.' He said it was full of life. But, alas! the life is Emerson's and not ——'s, and so it had been lived before." Nevertheless, Parker rejoiced in Emerson; his character and elevation he held up in reply to claims of the Church folk to a monopoly of piety, and one of his stories was that an eminent orthodox preacher, asked whether he supposed Emerson would go to hell, replied that he might go there, but no doubt the devil would be so embarrassed about his disposal that he would have to send him elsewhere! The only time I remember seeing Parker angry was when some Unitarian preacher, alluding publicly to Emerson's great distress at the loss of his son Waldo, attributed it to his lack of religious faith. When the "Massachusetts Quarterly" was projected in 1847, Parker named Emerson as the only one fit to be its editor, a position which the latter accepted, with Parker and Cabot as co-editors. "He is," wrote Parker, "a downright *man;* we never had such a jewel in America before. I think him worth two or three of Dr. Channing."

On the other hand, Emerson strongly admired the courage and fidelity of the great Boston preacher, and after his death spoke of him in these words:

"'Tis plain to me that he has achieved an historic immortality here; that he has so woven himself in these few years into the history of Boston, that he can never be left out of your annals. It will not be the acts of city councils, nor of obsequious mayors, nor, in the State House, the proclamations of governors, with their failing virtue — failing them at critical moments — that the coming generations will study what really befell;

but in the plain lessons of Theodore Parker in the Music Hall, in Faneuil Hall, or in Legislative Committee-Rooms, the true temper and authentic record of these days will be read. The next generation will care little for the chances of election that govern governors now; it will care little for fine gentlemen who behaved shabbily, but it will read very intelligently in his rough story, fortified with exact anecdotes, precise with names and dates, what part was taken by each actor; who threw himself into the cause of Humanity, who came to the rescue of Civilisation at a hard pinch, and who blocked its course."

Emerson had been desired by Theodore Parker's Society to make the chief address on the funeral occasion, but this he declined to do, though he said there the best words in his honour. I received a note from him, dated June 6, 1860, in which he refers to Parker, then recently dead, and to the answer he had sent to the Society. "I know well what a calamity is the loss of his courage and patriotism to the country; but of his mind and genius few are less accurately informed than I. It is for you and Sanborn, and many excellent young men who stood in age and sensibility hearers and judges of all his discourse and action — for you to weigh and report. My relations to him are quite accidental, and our differences of method and working such as really required and honoured all his catholicism and magnanimity to forgive in me."

Theodore Parker's resolution, entered in his journal after hearing Emerson's oration, as already stated, was followed by a steady progress in anti-supernaturalism, and by a valiant effort to introduce that into the Unitarian Church. He was at once fastened upon as a scapegoat for all the "infidelity" of the time. He was by no means so radical as Emerson, who, however, escaped the lifelong martyrdom which Parker suffered. The arch-heretic was too much of an artist to excite animosity. The soothsayer who prophesied to the Eastern monarch that he would lose all his family and friends, then die himself, and he who said, "Your majesty will survive all your relations," were types of the different ways in which the same fact was sometimes put; and as in the fable one soothsayer was beheaded and the other rewarded, so in this religious controversy in America, some suffered hatred and abuse for a radicalism far less formidable than that of Emerson.

If the infinite heart of Emerson was veiled even for many true knights who followed its attraction, it was shrouded for some others who sought to borrow his thought for sectarian uses. When it was proposed in the Society of Alumni of the Divinity College to send a message of sympathy to Theodore Parker, dying in a foreign land, the proposal was stormily refused by a majority which included some always profuse in their admirations of Emerson. This was the old unfailing sign of a prophet who has won the popular heart. No man durst lay hands on him.

I have before me the scrap of a letter written by Emerson to a friend, in early life — to whom, or by whom given me I cannot remember — in which he says: "We hearken in vain for any profound voice speaking to the American heart, cheering timid good men, animating the youth, consoling the defeated, and intelligently announcing duties which clothe life with joy and endear the land and sea to men." With a deliberation equalled only by his humility, Emerson set himself to break this dreary stillness. With perfect conviction that the hunger of hearts was for the truth he found satisfying; with faith in the spirit of man beneath gainsayings of men's lips or fears; without misgiving, without self-defence, as one who brings glad tidings; so he spake, and the human heart answered.

In truth, Emerson never spoke but with the human race behind him, and the flowers of all devout culture around him; he so took to heart the teachings of all sages, poets, prophets, that they beamed in his face; the great seemed near him, as one re-affirming the truth of their lives. His negations were the rescue of things eternal from their ruins. The eye never lost sight of the star that rose above them. Where shrill polemics and scoffing denials had hidden this or that new-born truth as behind uncouth forms of the stable, here appeared the human infant, haloed, and all the gold, frankincense, and myrrh around it. Reverence, art, poetry, literature, all the fair hopes of the home and of society, shone now on the side of ideal right and the religion of reason, while the unreformed institutions were placed on the side of denial, and appeared as if turned to grey fortresses.

XX.

BUILDING TABERNACLES.

AMID the confusion in the Unitarian circle caused by Emerson's oration, the most pathetic figure was that of old Dr. Channing, who sees another ocean ahead just as he was preparing to land. The shore, then, as in the case of Columbus, has turned out to be a tinted cloud on the horizon!

A significant incident has been lately told by Rev. W. C. Gannet, son of Dr. Channing's successor. In Channing's church it had been the custom for many years to sing "Old Hundred" at the close of the services, but one day, about fifty years ago, the choir conspired among themselves to close with another hymn, whereupon they were visited with such wrath from the astounded congregation, that "Old Hundred" sounded on twoscore years longer.

The incident was a fit prelude to the effort made by Channing to introduce the Transcendental theme into Unitarianism. In the earlier days of the movement, Margaret Fuller used to pass much of her time reading to him from the Germans, whose language he did not understand, and Theodore Parker remembered the simplicity with which the aged preacher expressed the hope that some heretic would translate Strauss's

"Leben Jesu." Channing suspected that the Harvard King Arthur had not gone the right way about holding together his Round Table. Professor Norton's severe pamphlets, which really held the knights to veracity in their use of words, seemed to the eloquent preacher somewhat intolerant. "The Unitarian body," he wrote, "seems to be forsaking its first love — its liberality, its respect for the rights of individual judgment, its separation of the essential from the unessential in Christianity. I have felt for years that it must undergo important developments. It began as a protest against the rejection of reason. It pledged itself to progress as its life and end; but it has gradually grown stationary, and now we have a Unitarian orthodoxy." With this feeling he had joined the young thinkers, then known as the "Friends of Progress," who used to meet in country places. They all "regarded themselves as Christians," and, so long as that old flag floated above the company, the Round Table was in happy condition. These "Friends of Progress" had in September, 1836, the year and month in which Emerson's "Nature" had appeared, formed their "Symposium," which subsequently received the name of "The Transcendental Club," and, after Emerson's oration, it began to contemplate some kind of public organisation and work. But Channing had built his new Christianity upon the pre-existence and mediatorial office of Christ. To this idea Emerson's idea was directly fatal. "We must get rid of Christ," he said once to Nathaniel Hawthorne. "No, Mr. Emerson," replied the other, "we cannot do without Christ." But Emerson, who had justified Jesus even in his claim to be divine, was resolute in his adherence to Paul's prophecy, "Then shall also the son be subject unto him who put all things under him, that God may be all in all."

Elizabeth Peabody, in her "Reminiscences of William Ellery Channing," relates an interesting incident of Emerson. When he was revising the proof of the Divinity College oration she suggested the alteration of a letter in the passage where he speaks of Christianity as dwelling "with noxious exaggeration about the *person* of Jesus." "The soul knows no persons," he says. "It invites every man to expand to the full circle of the universe, and will have no preference but those of spontaneous love. But by this Eastern monarchy of a Christianity, which indolence and fear have built, the friend of man is made the injurer of man." Miss Peabody wished him to "put a large F to designate Jesus as the friend of souls." After a moment's thought Emerson replied, "No: directly I put in that large F they will all go to sleep."

There stands the small "f," beautiful as Giotto's O, announcing the true master that had come. There was to be no more sleep among those whom this new word had reached. Parker, Ripley, and others might manage to call themselves Christians for a time, and Channing might endeavour to form again in Boston the Round Table dispersed at Cambridge. In vain! The Quest must go on. At length Dr. Channing sees that, so far from Unitarianism being able to contain the new movement, Christianity itself was an insufficient tabernacle for it. "I see and feel," he writes in 1840, "the harm done by this crude speculation, whilst I also see much nobleness to bind me to its advocates. In its opinions generally I see nothing to give me hope." A year later he says (to James Martineau) of the Transcendentalists: "They are anxious to defend the soul's immediate connection with God, and are in danger of substituting private inspiration for Christianity." With almost the same words the Puritans had banished the Quakers two hundred years before. So wrote Channing in 1841: the next year he was dead.

Over the grave of Channing the Transcendentalists were the chief mourners. Because of his anti-slavery sermons, even more than his other heresies, Boston paid no public honours to his memory. But one organ expressed regret at this — the "Dial." "Dr. Channing," it said "was a man of so much rectitude, and such power to express his sense of right, that his value to this country, of which he was a kind of public *conscience*, can hardly be over-estimated. Not only his merits, but his limitations also, which made all his virtues and talents intelligible and available for the correction and elevation of society, made our Cato dear, and his loss is not to be repaired."

During all this time the lectures of Emerson were going steadily on — diffused also by the "Dial" and in volumes — with increasingly wonderful results. As Dr. Holmes has said, "Here was an iconoclast without a hammer, who took down our idols from their pedestals so tenderly that it seemed like an act of worship." The Unitarians were bewildered as one after another their brightest young men caught the new enthusiasm. At first it brought out a good deal of the New England pulpit humour. One divine, on his return from a visit to Concord, from which much was expected, opened with the hymn "Thou first great cause, least understood," and preached on the text, " I saw an altar with this inscription, To an unknown God." Dr. Frothingham, whose son is the sympathetic historian of Transcendentalism, preached about Emerson from the text " Some said that it thundered, others that an angel spoke." Dr. Burnap of Baltimore described Transcendentalism as "a new philosophy which has risen, maintaining that nothing is everything in general, and everything is nothing in particular."

Some of these ministers, however, were influenced in a way which I heard a young preacher describe in a Western pulpit. "In the early days of California, a preacher went out to save the souls of gold-diggers, who himself was not averse to picking up nuggets with which the New Jerusalem is paved. On one occasion whilst he was praying at a grave, some one stirred the earth heap, and a little yellow dust appeared. One after another of the mourning bystanders rushed off to buy up the 'claim,' and presently the preacher peeped through his eyelids, and, seeing the situation, pronounced an instant Amen, and also ran off to try and secure the treasure. In the same way Germany crumbled a little gold dust beside the grave of orthodoxy; Emerson, Parker, Ripley, and the rest rushed off first, and at length even Channing stopped in his prayers over the dead, to try and catch up with the rest."

There was a multitude simply dazzled by the transfigured man, and at once bent on building a tabernacle for him. Of course it must be along with tabernacles for Moses and Elias, for the Law and Prophecy of tradition, but these they believed might be reconstructed. How deeply the orthodox were stirred was shewn in many ways. George Bradford (in the "Memorial History of Boston") relates that one of the meetings of the Transcendental Club was made memorable by an eloquent outburst from Father Taylor. The subject related to preaching, and the Methodist, present by invitation, was asked for his views. "He had been sitting silent while the others talked, knitting his brows, with his green spectacles thrown up on his forehead, leaning forward or shifting about on his chair. When he began to speak, he soon rose to his feet, and, warming as he went on, in a sort of indignant and sorrowful eloquence, by and by took his hearers off their feet, and they were carried away as by a flood. He rebuked the shortcomings of the various religious sects, not sparing his own, the Methodists, characterising the faults or peculiarities of each with sarcastic wit and a sort of grim but fervent satire. . . . When he got through, the company were so deeply impressed that they were for the most part disposed to entire silence, and though some desultory attempts were made to renew and continue the discussion, all other speech seemed so cold and hard after the glowing words they had heard, and so out of harmony with their mood, that the company soon broke up."

In 1840 the tabernacle-builders held a grand convention in Boston, called by "The Friends of Universal Progress." Emerson attended, but did not speak. We have, however, his report in the "Dial."

"The composition of the assembly was rich and various. The singularity and latitude of the summons drew together, from all parts of New England, and also from the Middle States, men of every shade of opinion, from the straitest orthodoxy to the wildest heresy, and many persons whose church was a church of one member only. A great variety of dialect and of costume was noticed; a great deal of confusion, eccentricity, and freak appeared, as well as of zeal and enthusiasm. If the assembly was disorderly, it was picturesque. Madmen, madwomen, men with beards, Dunkers, Muggletonians, Come-outers, Groaners, Agrarians, Seventh-day Baptists, Quakers, Abolitionists, Calvinists, Unitarians, and Philosophers, — all came successively to the top and seized their moment, if not their *hour*, wherein to chide, or pray, or preach, or protest. The faces were a study. The most daring innovators and the champions until death of the old cause, sat side by side. The still living merit of the oldest New England families, glowing yet after several generations, encountered the founders of families, fresh merit emerging and expanding the brows to a new breath, and lighting a clownish face with sacred fire. The assembly was characterised by the predominance of a certain plain, sylvan strength and earnestness, whilst many of the most intellectual and cultivated persons attended its councils. Dr. Channing, Edward Taylor, Bronson Alcott, Mr. Garrison, Mr. May, Theodore Parker, H. C. Wright, Dr. Osgood, William Adams, Edward Palmer, Jones Very, Maria W. Chapman, and many other persons of a mystical, or sectarian, or philanthropic renown were present, and some of them participant. And there was no want of female speakers: Mrs. Little and Mrs. Lucy Sessions took a pleasing and memorable part in the debate, and that flea of conventions, Mrs. Abigail Folsom, was but too ready with her interminable scroll. If there was not parliamentary order, there was life, and the assurance of that conditional love for religion and religious liberty which in all periods characterises the inhabitants of this part of America.

"There was a great deal of wearisome speaking in each of those three-days' sessions, but relieved by signal passages of pure eloquence, by much vigour of thought, and especially by the exhibition of character and by the victories of character. These men and women were in search of something better and more satisfying than a vote or a definition, and they found what they sought, or the pledge of it, in the attitude taken by individuals of their number of resistance to the insane routine of parliamentary usage, in the lofty reliance on principles, and the prophetic dignity and transfiguration which accompanies, even amidst opposition and ridicule, a man whose mind is made up to obey the great inward commander, and who does not anticipate his own action, but awaits confidently the new emergency for the new counsel."

Emerson selected for publication the speech of a mechanic named Whiting, — hailing from the town of Webster, — in reading which one reflects how often the lowliest of philosophers in praising others was alone unconscious that he was praising himself. Although Emerson did not ascend the tribune nor open his lips, in a sense he made a majority of the speeches. Through the stirred soul and impassioned lips of the mechanic he concluded with these words a speech about the

Bible: "Above all things, maintain the right of the living soul, of every individual man, to judge, unhesitatingly and unqualifiedly, everything in the past and all of the present; remembering always that the soul is its own authority, is bound by its own laws, does not live in the past, but is now. It is greater than all books — is antecedent to them all. It is the maker of them; and cannot be made subject to them until the Creator can be placed in bondage to his own workmanship. When this great truth shall fill the human heart, and be shadowed forth in human life, then the morning of the Universal Resurrection will dawn, then man shall arise from his grovelling position among the coffins, the bones and ashes of a buried Past, and live, and grow, and expand in the bright sunlight of that Eternity in which he dwells."

This congress, long remembered as the "Chardon Street Convention," was pentecost of the new gospel, its translation into many tongues by the fire that burns through personal prejudices; and this phenomenon, now as of old, implies a nearness of some heaven, and expectancy of a kingdom at hand. And as, in this case, the old heavens were faded, and no returning Messiah looked for, it became necessary for the enthusiasts to try and build a heaven of their own. Hence, Brook Farm. They who have known the same spiritual baptism must have all things in common. The preamble of the constitution of Brook Farm must be placed on record.

"In order more effectually to promote the great purposes of human culture; to establish the external relations of life on a basis of wisdom and purity; to apply the principles of justice and love to our social organisation in accordance with the laws of Divine Providence; to substitute a system of brotherly co-operation for one of selfish competition; to secure to our children, and those who may be intrusted to our care, the benefits of the highest physical, intellectual, and moral education which in the progress of knowledge the resources at our command will permit; to institute an attractive, efficient, and productive system of industry; to prevent the exercise of worldly anxiety by the competent supply of our necessary wants; to diminish the desire of excessive accumulation by making the acquisition of individual property subservient to upright and disinterested uses; to guarantee to each other for ever the means of physical support and of spiritual progress; and thus to impart a greater freedom, simplicity, truthfulness, refinement, and moral dignity to our mode of life; — we, the undersigned, do unite in a voluntary association, and adopt and ordain the following articles of agreement." Among "the undersigned" was *not* the name of Ralph Waldo Emerson.

XXI.

A SIX YEARS' DAY-DREAM.

AND so, said Emerson in the first number of the "Dial," "with diligent hands and good intent we set down our 'Dial' on the earth. We wish it may resemble that instrument in its celebrated happiness, that of measuring no hours but those of sunshine. Let it be one cheerful rational voice amidst the din of mourners and polemics. Or, to abide by our chosen image, let it be such a dial, not as the dead face of a clock — hardly, even, such as the gnomon in a garden — but rather such a dial as the garden itself, in whose leaves and flowers and fruits the suddenly awakened sleeper is instantly apprised, not what part of dead time, but what state of life and growth, is now arrived and arriving."

With this sentence, which Rabelais would have set up in gold in his clockless Abbey of Thelema, appeared that magazine which lasted through the morning hours of the movement it registered. It was set upon the earth, and the days were marked by the closing of errors, the unfolding of truths, gently and sweetly as in the floral dial of Linnæus. Some weeds were, indeed, intermingled, but no poisons; and if one would know the spirit of this American movement, let him compare the records of any controversy in Christian annals with these which report the deliverance of America from them all. Margaret Fuller and Emerson edited it, but in the most catholic spirit. Through this organ men and women since eminent gave their early thoughts to the world, and around these for leading strains there is a chorus of clever writers, all of whom are so charged with the new ideas that their voices seem to come from aërial land raised above the every-day world.

But the "Dial" had not been long published before these scattered feeders on honeydew had come to know each other, and it was inevitable that their insulation from the general world should lead to the formation of some project like that which was already leading restless minds westward from Europe. Emerson has traced the origin of the Brook Farm community to a consultation between Dr. Channing and George Ripley upon the practicability of bringing thoughtful and cultivated people together and forming a society that should be satisfactory. "That good attempt," said Mr. Emerson, "ended in an oyster-supper with excellent wines." Afterward, however, it was revived in Brook Farm, which, Emerson thinks, showed sufficiently that farming and scholarship were not exactly synonymous. "The ladies took cold on washing-days, and it was ordained that the gentlemen-shepherds should hang out the clothes, which they punctually did; but a great anachronism followed in the evening, for when they began to dance, the clothes-pins dropped plentifully from their pockets. . . . One hears the frequent statement of the country members that one man was ploughing all day and another was looking out of the window all day — perhaps drawing his picture — and they both received the same wages." Emerson had not faith enough in the feasibility of such a community, had it been possible for him to surrender his time for the disposal of the wisest counsel, to become a resident; but he was a frequent visitor, and his coming caused more sensation than if he had been an archbishop.

The publication of Hawthorne's "Note-Books," which contain such lively descriptions of his life at Brook Farm, elicited an interesting paper in "Harper's Magazine" from George W. Curtis, of whom Hawthorne speaks in "The Blithedale Romance" as the man who could best write the real history of that very interesting movement.

"When the experiment began at Brook Farm, there was no doubt in conservative circles that for their sins this offshoot of Bedlam was permitted in the neighbourhood. What it was, what it was meant to be, were equally inexplicable. Are they fools, knaves, madmen, or mere sentimentalists? Is this Coleridge and Southey again, with their Pantisocracy and Susquehanna Paradise? Is it a vast nursery of infidelity? and is it true that 'the abbé or religieux' sacrifices white oxen to Jupiter in the back parlour? What may not be true, since it is within Theodore Parker's parish, and his house, crammed with books, and modest under the singing pines, is only a mile away? These extraordinary and vague and hostile impressions were not relieved by the appearance of such votaries of the new shrine as appeared in the staid streets and halls of the city. There is always a certain amount of oddity latent in society which rushes to such an enterprise as a natural vent; and in youth itself there is a similar latent and boundless protest against the friction and apparent unreason of the existing order. At the time of the Brook Farm enterprise this was everywhere observable. The freedom of the anti-slavery reform and its discussions had developed the 'come-outers,' who bore testimony in all times and places against church and state. Mr. Emerson mentions an apostle of the gospel of love and no money, who preached zealously, but never gathered a large church of believers. Then there were the protestants against the sin of flesh-eating, refining into curious metaphysies upon milk, eggs, and oysters. To purloin milk from the udder was to injure the maternal affections of the cow; to eat eggs was Feejee cannibalism, and the destruction of the tender germ of life; to swallow an oyster was to mask murder. A still selecter circle denounced the chains that shackled the tongue, and the false delicacy that clothed the body. Profanity, they said, is not the use of forcible and picturesque words; it is the abuse of such to express base passions and emotions. So indecency cannot be affirmed of the model of all grace, the human body. The fig-leaf is the sign of the Fall. Man returning to Paradise will leave it behind. The priests of this faith, therefore, felt themselves called upon to rebuke true profanity and indecency by sitting at their front-doors upon Sunday mornings with no other clothing than that of the pre-fig-leaf period, tranquilly but loudly conversing in the most stupendous oaths, by way of conversational chiaroscuro, while a deluded world went shuddering by to church. These were harmless freaks and individual phantasies. But the time was like the time of witchcraft. The air magnified and multiplied every appearance, and exceptions and idiosyncrasies and ludicrous follies were regarded as the rule, and as the logical masquerade of this foul fiend Transcendentalism, which was evidently unappeasable, and was about to devour manners, morals, religion, and common-sense. If Father Lawson or Abby Folsom were borne by main force from an anti-slavery meeting, and the non-resistants pleaded that those protestants had as good a right to speak as anybody, and that what was called their senseless tattle was probably inspired wisdom, if people were only heavenly-minded enough to understand it, it was but another sign of the impending anarchy. And what was to be said — for you could not call them old dotards — when the younger protestants of the time came walking through the sober streets of Boston and seated themselves in concert-halls and lecture-rooms, with hair parted in the middle and falling on their shoulders, and clad in garments such as no human being ever wore before — garments which seemed to be a compromise between the blouse of the Paris workmen and the peignoir of a possible sister? For tailoring underwent the same revision to which the whole philosophy of life was subjected, and one ardent youth, asserting that the human form itself suggested the proper shape of its garments, caused trousers to be constructed that closely fitted the leg, and bore his testimony to the truth in coarse crash breeches.

"These were the ludicrous aspects of the intellectual and moral fermentation or agitation that was called

Transcendentalism. And these were foolishly accepted by many as its chief and only signs. It was supposed that the folly was complete at Brook Farm, and it was indescribably ludicrous to observe reverend doctors and other dons coming out to gaze upon the extraordinary spectacle, and going about as dainty ladies hold their skirts and daintily step from stone to stone in a muddy street, lest they be soiled. The dons seemed to doubt whether the mere contact had not smirched them. But, droll in itself, it was a thousand-fold droller when Theodore Parker came through the woods and described it. With his head set low upon his gladiatorial shoulders, and his nasal voice in subtle and exquisite mimicry reproducing what was truly laughable, yet all with infinite *bonhomie* and with a genuine superiority to small malice, he was as humorous as he was learned, and as excellent a man as he was noble and fervent and humane a preacher. On Sundays a party always went from the Farm to Mr. Parker's little country church. He was there exactly what he was afterwards when he preached to thousands of eager people in the Boston Music Hall; the same plain, simple, rustic, racy man. His congregation were his personal friends. They loved him and admired him and were proud of him; and his geniality and tender sympathy, his ample knowledge of things as well as of books, his jovial manliness and sturdy independence, drew to him all ages and sexes and conditions.

"The society at Brook Farm was composed of every kind of person. There were the ripest scholars, men and women of the most æsthetic culture and accomplishment, young farmers, seamstresses, mechanics, preachers — the industrious, the lazy, the conceited, the sentimental. But they were associated in such a spirit and under such conditions that, with some extravagance, the best of everybody appeared, and there was a kind of *esprit de corps*, at least in the earlier or golden age of the colony. There was plenty of steady, essential hard work, for the founding of an earthly Paradise upon a rough New England farm is no pastime. But with the best intention, and much practical knowledge and industry and devotion, there was in the nature of the case an inevitable lack of method, and the economical failure was almost a foregone conclusion. But there were never such witty potato patches and such sparkling cornfields before or since. The weeds were scratched out of the ground to the music of Tennyson or Browning, and the nooning was an hour as gay and bright as any brilliant midnight at Ambrose's."

"It is to the Transcendentalism that seemed to so many good souls both wicked and absurd that some of the best influences of American life to-day are due. The spirit that was concentrated at Brook Farm is diffused, but it is not lost. As an organised effort, after many downward changes, it failed; but those who remember the Hive, the Eyrie, the Cottage — when Margaret Fuller came and talked, radiant with bright humour; when Emerson and Parker and Hedge joined the circle for a night or a day; when those who may not be publicly named brought beauty and wit and social sympathy to the feast; when the practical possibilities of life seemed fairer, and life and character were touched ineffaceably with good influence — cherish a pleasant vision which no fate can harm, and remember with ceaseless gratitude the blithe days at Brook Farm."

To this brilliant sketch but little need be added here. The Pilgrim House, Eyrie, Hive, Cottage; the Nest where Marianne Ripley brought some children from her school in Boston; finally the Phalanstery, which was consumed by fire ere completed, are names that may yet appear in a pretty mythology. George Bradford, in his careful account of the community ("Memorial History of Boston"), says that there were always a number of young people boarding there or attending the school, and that a prominent feature was the opportunity given for the exercise of divers gifts and faculties. "There were amusements suited to the different seasons — tableaux, charades, dances; in the winter, skating and coasting, for which the knolls, wide meadows, and river afforded favourable opportunities; in summer, rural fêtes, masquerades, &c., in the charming localities, rocks, and woods around the place."

Hawthorne used to attend the evening gatherings in the hall of the Hive; though admired, he was shy and apt to be silent. Some of the Brook-Farmers have regretted that in his romance he should have connected with a community, which well deserved the name "Blithedale," the ghastly tragedy of Zenobia's death, which occurred elsewhere. Hawthorne himself regretted that so many closely identified Zenobia with Margaret Fuller, and that the death of his heroine by drowning should be associated with the tragic end of a woman whom he admired. But it remains the fact that "The Blithedale Romance" is the truest monument of Brook Farm, and all the pains and losses it cost them might well seem to the inmates a small price to pay for that immortal product which rose out of the ashes of so many fair hopes.

The most energetic person in founding the community was George Ripley, a scholar and theologian, and his accomplished wife, a niece of the poet Dana. J. S. Dwight, the eminent writer on music, was a member, and with him came a circle that secured for the community enjoyment of the finest classics in that art. William Henry Channing gave inspiring discourses which have hallowed the Brook Farm Sundays in many memories. Charles A. Dana, afterwards Assistant Secretary of War under President Lincoln, now editor of the New York "Sun," added much to the social charm of the place. With refined and cultured families such as the Russells, Hoxies, the brothers Curtis, Elizabeth Peabody, Hawthorne, Alcott, and Brisbane, Brook Farm had no reason to envy Boston its social resources. These educated and refined people, with few exceptions, were drawn to Brook Farm by moral enthusiasm. They were not generally impecunious, but had found that in the conventional world they were spending their labour for that which did not satisfy, and for much that was repulsive to their new ideal. But the general world had such a hold on them that they could not go far from Boston, and the only spot they could get was a barren one. Though a small brook named their farm, they did not have any of those vigorous streams which elsewhere compensate New Englanders for the hardness and thinness of their soil with water-power for manufactures. They had to use steam for their mechanical departments. That so many people were able to live at Brook Farm even for seven years is really a good fact for the associative principle. That it was and is remembered by those who dwelt there as a seven years' festivity, cheaply purchased by the funds each sank in it, is an indication of the spiritual exaltation of the time. This it was that made their valley of Baca a well, as they travelled through its dry places, and their wilderness blossom as a rose. But they were reminded by Emerson and Margaret Fuller that they were still but pilgrims, and their tabernacles but tents that must presently be folded for the journey to a farther land of promise.

In 1840, Nathaniel Hawthorne, aged thirty-six, found himself in Salem Custom-House, " murdering the brightest hours of the day." "Never comes any bird of paradise into that dismal region." He resolves to be free — to be young again. " I will go forth and stand in a summer shower, and all the worldly dust that has collected on me shall be washed away at once, and my heart will be a bank of fresh flowers for the weary to rest upon." The next year he is at Brook Farm. He arrived there in a snowstorm. " Through faith I persist in believing that spring and summer will come in due season ; but the unregenerated man shivers within me, and suggests a doubt whether I may not have wandered within the precincts of the Arctic circle." The story of Hawthorne's day-dream may be outlined by a few passages taken from his charming " Note-Books," between April 13 and September 3, 1841 :

" I have not yet taken my first lesson in agriculture,

except that I went to see our cows foddered yesterday afternoon. We have eight of our own, and the number is now increased by a transcendental heifer belonging to Miss Margaret Fuller."

"This morning I have done wonders. Before breakfast I went out to the barn and began to chop hay for the cattle, and with such 'righteous vehemence,' as Mr. Ripley says, that in the space of ten minutes I broke the machine."

"Miss Fuller's cow hooks the other cows, and has made herself ruler of the herd, and behaves in a very tyrannical manner."

"I shall make an excellent husbandman. I feel the original Adam reviving within me."

"I have milked a cow."

"It is an endless surprise to me how much work there is to be done in the world, but, thank God, I am able to do my share of it, and my ability increases daily."

"A colony of wasps was discovered in my chamber."

"It is my opinion that a man's soul may be buried and perish under a dung-heap or in a furrow of the field, just as well as under a pile of money."

"Joyful thought! in a little more than a fortnight I shall be free of my bondage, . . . free to enjoy Nature — free to think and feel! . . . Even my Custom-House experience was not such a thraldom and weariness; my mind and heart were free. Oh, labour is the curse of the world, and nobody can meddle with it without becoming proportionably brutified. Is it a praiseworthy matter that I have spent five golden months in providing food for cows and horses?"

"Other persons have bought large estates and built splendid mansions with such little books as I mean to write; so that perhaps it is not unreasonable to hope that mine may enable me to build a little cottage, or at least to buy or hire one."

"Really I should judge it to be twenty years since I left Brook Farm; and I take this to be one proof that my life there was an unnatural and unsuitable, and therefore an unreal one. It already looks like a dream behind me. The real Me was never an associate of the community; there has been a spectral Appearance there, sounding the horn at daybreak, and milking the cows, and hoeing potatoes, and raking hay, toiling in the sun, and doing me the honour to assume my name. But this spectre was not myself."

Hawthorne returned to Brook Farm for a short time, but happily long enough to witness and describe a characteristic Brook Farm scene.

"A picnic party in the woods yesterday, in honour of little Frank Dana's birthday, he being six years old. I strolled out with Mr. Bradford, and in a lonesome glen we met the apparition of an Indian chief, dressed in appropriate costume of blanket, feathers, and paint, and armed with a musket. Almost at the same time a young gipsy fortune-teller came from among the trees and proposed to tell my fortune. While she was doing this, the goddess Diana let fly an arrow, and hit me smartly in the hand. The fortune-teller and goddess were in fine contrast: Diana being a blonde, fair, quiet, with a moderate composure; and the gipsy (O. G.), a bright, vivacious dark-haired, rich-complexioned damsel,— both of them very pretty, at least pretty enough to make fifteen years enchanting. Accompanied by these denizens of the wild wood we went onward, and came to a company of fantastic figures arranged in a ring for a dance or a game. There was a Swiss girl, an Indian squaw, a negro of the Jim Crow order, one or two foresters, and several people in christian attire, besides children of all ages. There followed childish games, in which the grown people took part with mirth enough, while I, whose nature it is to be a mere spectator both of sport and serious·business, lay under the trees and looked on. Meanwhile, Mr. Emerson and Miss Fuller, who arrived an hour or two before, came forth into the little glade where we assembled. Here followed much talk. The ceremonies of the day concluded with a cold collation of cakes and fruit. All was pleasant enough,— an excellent piece of work,—' would 'twere done!' It has left a fantastic impression on my memory, this intermingling of wild and fabulous characters with real and homely ones, in the secluded nook of the woods. I remember them, with the sunlight breaking through overshadowing branches, and they appearing and disappearing confusedly, — perhaps starting out of the earth, as if the every-day laws of Nature were suspended for this particular occasion. There were the children, too, laughing and sporting about, as if they were at home among such strange shapes, and anon bursting into loud uproar of lamentation when the rude gambols of the merry archers chanced to overturn them. And apart, with a shrewd, Yankee observation of the scene, stands our friend Orange, a thick-set, sturdy figure, enjoying the fun well enough, yet rather laughing with a perception of its nonsensicalness than at all entering into the spirit of the thing."

And now let us turn to the memories of Margaret Fuller.

"All Saturday I was off in the woods. In the evening we had a general conversation, opened by me, upon education in its largest sense, and on what we can do for ourselves and others. I took my usual ground: — The aim is perfection, patience the road. The present object is to give ourselves and others a tolerable chance. Let us not be too ambitious as to our hopes as to immediate results. Our lives should be considered as a tendency, an approximation only. Parents and teachers expect to do too much."

"*Sunday.* — A glorious day; the woods full of perfume. I was out all the morning. In the afternoon Mrs. R. and I had a talk. I said my position would be too uncertain here, as I could not work. —— said they would all like to work for a person of genius. 'Yes,' I told her, 'but where would be my repose when they were always to be judging whether I was worth it or not?'

"All Monday morning in the woods again. Afternoon out with the drawing party. I felt the evils of the want of conventional refinement in the impudence with which one of the girls treated me. She has since thought of it with regret, I notice.

"Here I have passed a very pleasant week. The tone of society is much sweeter than when I was here a year ago. There is a prevailing spirit of mutual tolerance and gentleness, with great sincerity. There is no longer a passion for grotesque feats of liberty; but a disposition, rather, to study and enjoy the liberty of law. The great development of mind and character observable in several instances persuades me that this state of things affords a fine studio for the soul-sculptor.

"My hopes might lead to association too — an association, if not of efforts, yet of destinies. In such a one I live with several already, feeling that each one, by acting out his own, casts light upon a mutual destiny, and illustrates the thought of a master-mind. It is a constellation, not a phalanx, to which I would belong."

XXII.

LESSONS FOR THE DAY.

I HAVE a letter by Emerson, found among the papers of a friend in Cincinnati, now dead, with an inscription showing that it was written in answer to an inquiry concerning his religious opinions. It is dated at Concord in the October of 1838, and contains the following statement of his outlook while the storm was raging over his Divinity College address, delivered three months before : —

" I hasten to say that I read these expressions of an earnest character — of your faith, of your hope — with extreme interest ; and if I can contribute any aid by sympathy or suggestion to the solution of those great problems that occupy you, I shall be very glad. But I think it must be done by degrees. I am not sufficiently master of the little truth I see to know how to state it in forms so general as shall put every mind in possession of my point of view. We generalise and rectify our expressions by continual efforts from day to day, from month to month, to reconcile our own light with that of our companions. So shall two inquirers have the best mutual action on each other. But I should never attempt a direct answer to such questions as yours. I have no language that could shortly present my state of mind in regard to each of them with any fidelity; for my state of mind in each is in no way final and detached, but tentative, progressive, and strictly connected with the whole circle of my thoughts. It seems to me that to understand any man's thoughts respecting the Supreme Being we need an insight into the general habit and tendency of his speculations, for every man's idea of God is the last or most comprehensive generalisation at which he has arrived. But besides the extreme difficulty of stating our results on such questions in a few propositions, I think, my dear sir, that a certain religious feeling deters us from the attempt. I do not gladly utter any deep conviction of the soul in any company where I think it will be contested — no, nor unless I think it will be welcome. Truth has already ceased to be itself if polemically said; and if the soul would utter oracles, as every soul should, it must live for itself — keep itself right-minded, observe with such awe its own law as to concern itself very little with the engrossing topics of the hour, unless they be its own. I believe that most of the speculations and difficulties that infest us we must thank ourselves for — that each mind, if true to itself, will, by living for the right and not importing into itself the doubts of other men, dissolve all difficulties, as the sun at midsummer burns up the clouds.

"Hence I think the aid we can give each other is only incidental, lateral, and sympathetic. If we are true and benevolent, we reinforce each other by every act and word; your heroism stimulates mine, and your light kindles mine. The end of all this is, that I thank you heartily for the confidence of your letter, and beg you to use your earliest leisure to come and see me. It is very possible that I shall not be able to give you one definition; but I will shew you with joy what I strive after and what I worship, as far as I can. Meantime I shall be very glad to hear from you by letter. — Your friend and servant, R. W. EMERSON."

"Yew," said Confucius, "permit me to tell you what is knowledge. What you are acquainted with, consider that you know it; what you do not understand, consider that you do not know it: this is knowledge." This definition is in startling contrast with the tone of nearly all other founders of religions and philosophies. . The student speedily discovers that the most commonplace attribute of this class is omniscience. Long before charts of land or sea were made, the invisible heavens and hells were mapped and reported in detail. The seven or seventy hells, the nine celestial spheres, twenty-eight heavens, twenty chiliocosms, four dhyanas, four orders of being, three energies, six days of creation, elven avatars, three dispensations, two dispensations, and a thousand other arrangements of the universe into sixes and sevens, meet us at every turn in the cosmogonies and scriptures which still command the faith of the majority of mankind. These exact statements concerning things beyond the scope of human faculties, while they escaped the criticism of the ordinary human understanding by soaring above the objects with which it could deal, indulged a very general weakness of the human mind, and there is little reason to wonder that the every-day rules and moral maxims of Confucius were overshadowed by the clear and positive splendours of Buddhism. The scholar of the present day notes this speculative precision as a sign of the infancy of philosophy, and measures the antiquity of a religion by the boldness of its assumptions of particular knowledge in the realm of the unknowable. Nevertheless, he has only to look around him to perceive how large a part of mankind is still prone to follow the teachers who approximate most nearly the attitude of omniscience. Swedenborg gossiping with the angels; Comte assigning love and thought their grooves; Fourier pigeonholing the universe in his French cabinet; mediums interviewing departed spirits at their tea-tables, and fairly slapping the shades of heroes and prophets on the back with joyous familiarity; the popular divines bringing all mysteries down to a rhetorical zodiac around their pulpits: these are the recognised builders of the only new sects and systems of which our age can boast. With the bones of theories and explanations bleaching all along the track by which the human mind has journeyed, we still find the multitude adoring their calves, and steadily demanding for their leaders those who can most glibly fable of the ineffable.

The recognition and attention paid to some thinkers who have not enclosed the heavens and the earth in a nutshell is a novel and significant phenomenon. There is, indeed, no sign of decrease in the numbers of the system-makers and system-mongers. When some one spoke of the distance of the sky, poor William Blake cried, "It is false; the other day I walked down a lane and touched it with my cane!" It is easy to listen, on any Sunday, to preachers who have repeatedly done the same thing. But when Edinburgh called for Carlyle, and Harvard for Emerson, to speak to them, there was a suggestion that the world is beginning to suspect that the sky touched with such facility may be some theologian's umbrella and not the dome of azure.

With more reverence than the builders or upholders of systems and theories, and all their earnestness, Emerson led his followers to ends only to turn those ends into means; the shining walls are no sooner reached than they change to tinted mist, their towers gleaming now far ahead. At times, indeed, he has seemed to rebuild the old temples and rekindle the flames of altars that have grown cold; but it is only to touch them into ruin again, to shew how and why they have perished, and why those that succeed them must perish; while the disciple gradually learns, if he cannot define it, that there is something that endures through them all; and learns, too, that all the piety and humility of those who knelt at those altars dwell with those who respect the limits of human knowledge and action, adhere to simple truth and reality, and, amid the talkers, can look upon the heavens with a silence like their own.

There is, indeed, an unmistakable tendency of this kind in the mind of Emerson shewn by his successive works. In his earlier volumes we find more that is dreamy and visionary than in the later. Although there was in the earlier essays nothing so formal as the idealism of Berkeley and the schoolmen, and nothing so definite as the Hegelian philosophy or any form of Christianity, there was in them a sufficient relation to the metaphysics of modern Germany and to the mystical statements of religion, to draw upon his views the label of transcendentalism. His criticisms of society, too, were accompanied by prophecies so harmonious, in some respects, with the theories of French socialism, that it is not surprising his more ardent and literal friends should have endeavoured to embody them in communities; while the fact that his visions never acquired the consistency of theories is shewn in his steady refusal to commit himself to any such practical schemes, and his evident lack of faith in them. The New England pulpit in which the philosopher began his teachings was not abandoned *per saltum*, and his first essays were modified from those sermons, to whose rare charms many have testified. It was as if, in the determination to explore all things for himself, he began as the race began, with the adoration of sun and star, though vaguely and without ritual. But with increasing reticence concerning incomprehensible problems, he has with every volume aimed less to realise the ideal than to idealise the real.

Thus far, it may be said, the American thinker has but kept step with the culture of the world, passing from other worldly dreams to European realism, from the certainties of ignorance to the scepticisms of science. But there is in his works somewhat not characteristic of the thought of modern Europe, even if occasionally traceable in it. With the culture of the Old World he has none of its intellectual despair. The hand is that of scepticism, the voice is that of faith. The tottering Jerichos crumble, but the blast before which they have fallen winds into a prelude of the strain that builds the hundred-gated walls in their place.

There is no trace of cynicism in his fine humour, no showing of the teeth in his searching radicalism — though he spare not to touch the best, — but always the undertone of hope, as of one who knows that the sunset of one longitude is the sunrise of another. The old religions and institutions pass away because they are false replies to the question that is deepest, but the power of that questioning spirit to set aside such replies at serious earthly cost, is the ever-renewed pledge of the universe that " whatever curiosity the order of things has awakened, the order of things can satisfy." To this attitude of expectation all things become hopefully significant; snowflakes and blossoms are alike superlative effects of the sunshine, and in vanishings from us, as well as in acquisitions, the advancing ideals trace their steps. Before those for whom alone he writes — those who think — Emerson holds up the great aim of absolute truth; it was so in his earliest, it is so in his latest works; but in the latter there is recognition that the thinker's business is for the present with the corner-stone rather than the coping-stone of his tower of vision. The scholar is to gain his freedom, to get rid of his gilded gyves, rather than to try his wings; he is to demonstrate his liberty rather than crudely press it. Here are rules of life that go to the very generation of the thinker, and estimate the virginal elements of which he is born; his diet, health, habits, physical as well as mental, are anxiously discussed; for with him is the hope of the world. He is to correct ancient methods, and sow the grandest formulas for seed. He will sow the very stars for seed, trusting the perfection of the universe. While others deprecate or invoke, the scholar will discover and polish lenses of a higher power, and transmit more exact notations, assured that when all the conditions have been fulfilled, the star-mist shall faintly appear to the watchers of the future, and in the end gather into the golden worlds.

Emerson was not a man to throw away experience. " He has clapped copyright on the world," he has said of Plato. " This is the ambition of individualism. But the mouthful proves too large. *Boa constrictor* has good will to eat it, but he is foiled. He falls abroad in the attempt, and biting gets strangled: the bitten world holds the biter fast by his own teeth. There he perishes: unconquered Nature lives on and forgets him. So it fares with all; so must it fare with Plato." The New World idealist is too aged to be similarly strangled. He does not, indeed, dislike occasional empiricism if it puts on no doctrinaire airs. He will have absoluteness. The abyss between Emerson and Christianity, not to be spanned by any metaphysical casuistry, is that he turned its every tenet into an empiricism, and its historical claims into a subject for speculation, like the life of Shakespeare and his plays.

This idealistic, devout, aspiring genius was the same that in the centuries had bent its searching gaze upon traditional and speculative heavens. Now, for the first time, it is turned earthward; and, for the first time since Socrates, mankind were reminded that " the pure earth is situated in the pure heavens," and that " there are, indeed, many and wonderful places in the earth, and it is neither of such a kind nor of such a magnitude as is supposed by those who are accustomed to speak of the earth." Such was the earth that the lowly should inherit!

Not in any vision of ancient faith, not in Augustine's dream of the city of God, will be found anything fairer than Emerson's picture of the right and true human home. An architect has said, that if the architecture of the Abbey of Thelema, so minutely written out by Rabelais, could be really built, it would be the ideally perfect edifice. The same may be said of the dwelling planned by Emerson for the human mind and heart, and put within their reach.

Here are characteristic sentences from an early lecture, printed in an English journal, "The Truth-Seeker" (1850), as "Mosaics on Home Life," which it is interesting to compare with the corresponding thoughts in his chapter on "Domestic Life:"

"We are eager to make ourselves acquainted with the ancient fossils, foreign manners and customs, the distant parts of the earth, the depths of the sea, and the stars; but the things which are nearest to us, of which we cannot get out of sight, are the strangest to us of all."

"Domestic events immediately concern us; public events may or may not. That which is done and suffered at home — not what is carried on or left undone in the State-house — must be the history of the times and the spirit of the age to us."

"Never subscribe at another's incitement or buy what you do not want. We must not make-believe with our money."

"It is not desirable that labour should be avoided.

It is the birthright and privilege of all. But another age may divide the manual labour of the world more equally. The true acceptance by each man of his vocation — not that chosen for him by others — is that which alone will reform the age."

"Animals know what they want; the human being without his mission found does not."

"There is as much scope for the exercise of the greatest abilities, as much breadth of aim and enlargement of heart and character requisite to be a master of living well, as the hero or statesman require to become masters of their respective arts; nay, indeed, much more."

"It is the vice of our housekeeping, the vice of our conversation, the vice of our religion, that we take so little account of what really is of the most consequence, and do not hold the highest things sufficiently sacred."

"We account circumstance everything, the man himself nothing."

"Every man is furnished with a model which he instinctively applies to others, and does not find it to fit any one; but we still hold fast our belief in a better life, a happier state of things and circumstances. This affords a certain test that we are not what we are capable of."

"Every individual nature has its own interior beauty. There is no human expression but what has its intense interest, its links down into the very depths of being. In each we may see the foundation of a divine building. Every face and every figure is suggestive. The secret power of form, transcending anything we can account for or explain, is a proof that matter is assuredly a vehicle of a higher power than its own. This is the answer to the sceptic who denies the unseen divinity."

"A new friend entering our house is an era in our true history. Our friends illustrate the course of our conduct. It is the progress of our character that draws them about us. Let us cherish around us whatever has a tendency to bring the character into finer life. Beauty has a power transcending all philosophy, which, if sacredly regarded, would assimilate all natures to itself."

"Every statue and picture was public in ancient Greece. They considered it absurd and profane to pretend to property in a work of art, it being the property of him who could see it. Although their theory is not the true one, we are yet indebted to the Socialists for many useful hints."

"Our towns do not fulfil the only object for which men should congregate in masses, namely, the finding for the individual the means of highest convenience and art, which he could not otherwise do for himself. An object or instrument of value becomes more so the more it is accessible. Every man, every child, wishes to see the satellites of Jupiter or Saturn's rings, but he cannot afford to buy, and he does not want the incumbrance of a good telescope. It is the same with chemical and electrical apparatus; with books, casts, pictures, statues. This is the *rationale* of a museum in every town, because every citizen could contribute something which would be rendered more valuable than by each man possessing it himself. Its influence is to bring us more together, making us more of neighbours, elevating our views, and giving us united interests. The law prevails for ever and ever, and is capable of exact demonstration that a part can never equal the whole."

" Why should not the same spirit prevail always as in our best and happiest moments? The consecration of the Sunday is the desecration of the rest of the week; that of the chapel is the desecration of the house. True religion will be found in the bosom of the family every day in the week, and at any time if at all; and of all places, home will constantly be the most sacred."

"There is nothing more profane than the invasion of trade and the encroachments of our modern mechanical improvements and ultra-utilitarian doctrines upon the privacy, the duties, and harmony of domestic life. Can the labour of many for one bring anything half so good as the labour of every man for himself?"

"In these hints and sketches only the edges of the subject have been touched upon. It is one not for description but for action. If we set about reforming the evils of our social conditon one by one, it is lopping the branches while others spring up from the root, and we get disheartened at the extent and uselessness of our labour. We must go to the source of the matter. The Gorgon of convention and fashion must be slain by some master-mind giving birth to a new era, when we can live truly without shame."

Emerson was, as we have seen, a prophet of Art also. Several years before Ruskin had spoken, the

great essay on Art (first series) had appeared; and it
has been an interesting thing to me to find that the
earliest appreciation of Emerson's new poetic idealism
in England was among the Preraphaelist Brothers.
His new view of art grew out of his new view of
nature; if great, it must be supremest nature. The
statue must rise by creative laws akin to those which
formed the marble in its quarry, the pigments must
pass upon the canvas by methods and in combinations
as perfect as those which have grouped and tinted the
forms they are to represent, or there can be no true
Art. "When science is learned in love, and its powers
are wielded by love, they will appear the supplements
and continuations of the material creation." This
sentence closes Emerson's first series of essays. It is
translatable into his view of Art also, so that he is able
to say, "Beauty must come back to the useful arts, and
the distinction between the fine and the useful arts be
forgotten." Thus he anticipated the new utilitarian
who denies that a structure fulfils the laws of use completely unless it is also beautiful. The body cannot
find true repose on a sofa or chair upon which the eye
cannot rest with an equal satisfaction. Therefore works
originally contrived with an eye to utility alone — as
the crenellated parapet or the dormer-windows on a
spire — survive by reason of their decorative beauty.
We are led to a principle uniting the workman employ-
ing the river to turn his wheel, and the statesman leaning upon the power of justice, and every true work of
Art, which is such in the proportion that it accords
with the method of nature, where beauty is always
organic, inhering in the tissues and combined around

the central purpose of each object. Every tinted feather on the wing of bird or butterfly was called there by the struggle between life and death, and the poem or picture, though it may appear as mere decoration, is rooted in the same hard grey strata of Necessity. Such is the final bearing of all of Emerson's essays on Art and Beauty. Therefore, "eccentricity" is fatal to real beauty, which can come only of the laws of Reason, or nature in its highest interpretation, divested therefore of anything whimsical. He once said, a man must be for a time stony-hearted to paint a stone. "Herein is the explanation of the analogies which exist in all the arts. They are the re-appearance of one mind, working in many materials to many temporary ends. Raphael paints wisdom, Handel sings it, Phidias carves it, Shakespeare writes it, Wren builds it, Columbus sails it, Luther preaches it, Washington arms it, Watt mechanises it. The laws of each art are convertible into the laws of every other."

When Raphael and Watt are selected as the terms of the list of representative artists, we see the line of definition between the workers for Use and the workers for Beauty vanishing; we are prepared for the affirmation that all arts rest upon the most real use, and that from the growth and flowering of the institutions actually around us must come arts comparable to those which our painters and sculptors can now only copy from the past.* The old masters were masters because they were not servile to others who preceded them. Emerson appreciated the earnestness of Preraphaelism but deplored its method. They seemed like the Oxonians who took refuge from the barrenness of Protestantism in Romanism, thereby shifting the burthen only. His burden was against all creators, whether scholars, preachers, politicians, or artists, who would borrow the oil of past ages or adjourn worthy work to the future. It is the artist's business to pierce beneath the trivialities of his age and to compensate men for them. If the age is one of scepticism, with no faith in anything but its economical inventions, all the more necessary is it that the artist shall keep the watchfires of the nobler life bright and burning. "Another age!" There is no other age. Turner found London fog and Thames barges, nay, Covent Garden cabbage-leaves, tender and pathetic. There was spiritual grandeur in that railway train he painted, flashing on through rain and wind. If our artists are satisfied to be retained as painters-in-ordinary to the wealthy, who can see no beauty short of a thousand years in anything save their own portraits or lawns, we cannot perhaps help it; but we protest against the ascription of their incompetency to the age. There are flowerings around us as well as buddings. There is a pass at Harper's Ferry as well as at Thermopylæ. The earth, steadily becoming transparent to the eye of science, discloses forms and realms unpainted, unsung, grand as any that ever shone from legendary spheres for Homer or Titian. Under the discoveries of philology every common word suggests a poem ; our mythological science recovers the dead deities, and reveals their shining circle seated in the human mind ; while historic criticism strikes the hour at which the masquerade of the ages comes to a close, and the shows of things fall away from the forms of heroes and events. And with this new heaven and new earth it seems to be among the least pardonable defalcations of our time that Art should imitate the mere outside of ancient works; for the heart of them was in the conviction that wrought them, and that conviction can exist in no sane mind at the present day. Walt Whitman's first work was welcomed by Emerson, despite its faults, because it showed an absolute faith that American Leaves of Grass have for clear eyes a sacredness like that of the Kusa sward which the Brahmin prepares for the seat of his gods. Emerson shewed us that with the telescope and the microscope for our eyes, and the vault of reason and the vault of heaven fast clearing of their cobwebs, there is no reason why we should consent to be mere preparers of the soil for future arts, or accept the delusion that it is not the eyes of Dante and Milton that we lack, but the whorls of hell and the drama of Paradise.

Emerson taught a new secret of eloquence. Carlyle, in his address to the Edinburgh students four years ago, expressed the fear that "the finest nations of the world — the English and the American — are going all away into wind and tongue." One cannot read fine anecdotes of the effects of eloquence without feeling that the best example falls short of the sufferance of the great, when, as the sheep before its shearers, they are dumb. But the stump-orator found nothing to encourage him in the teachings of Emerson; he was told that his habit of oratory disqualifies him for eloquence. When Confucius was urged to speak after he had said he would rather remain silent, he asked, "Do heaven and earth speak?" Emerson's reply is, that unless heaven and earth do speak there can be no eloquence.

There are times when the right word carries the force of a cannon-ball. It must be the word without which nothing was made. If one will obey the Pythagorean rule to be silent, unless it be to say something better than silence, his speech must bear us back to the silent laws out of which it was born. "There is for every man a statement possible of that truth which he is most unwilling to receive — a statement possible, so broad and so pungent, that he cannot get away from it, but must either bend to it or die of it. Else there would be no such word as eloquence, which means this."

Only for this, if for nothing else, Emerson may be called the most helpful teacher of his generation — that he recognised the habitat of the human mind. Recognising the outlooks toward the unsolved nebulæ of thought, he adheres strictly to the realms of actual knowledge and practical life, and sows its sound seed on real soil, and not on any cloudland of theory. Man is dealt with as a being living in lower and higher worlds; but the higher world is as little speculative as the lower, and is subject to the same scientific statement. The moral sentiment is dealt with as a fact, the intellect as a fact, and the social and physical environment of them are respected as related to and blended with these. It is surely a significant sign to the young generation, that this clear and pure intellect, after exploring every epoch of thought, should finally return home to itself and to the near world of realities, as containing the only keys of knowledge entrusted to man. At the same time, it may be safely affirmed that no volumes produced in this generation contain more that is profoundly poetic than those of our teacher.

With eye ever fixed on the central unity of things — as one beholding the dawn in the tinted shell, or reading the signs which galaxies have dropped in the flowers — this seer seems hardly able to hold his sentences from breaking out into song, like chapters of the Koran. If amid the confident speculations of our time the lower tone of this thinker is surprising, amid their pallor the blood and passion of his book are startling. As it used to be said by the rustics that all the ferns have one root, we may say of these manifold thoughts that every one draws us to that moral sentiment which is with their author the ultimate element. "Can you tell me," said an Englishman to his neighbour at one of Emerson's lectures, "what connection there is between that last sentence and the one that went before, and what connection it all has with Plato?" "None, my friend — save in God!" But when this is said, it remains true that the religious sentiment is here purged from every superstition, even the most conventional, and the poetry is never empirical. An American lecturer complained that in his wanderings from town to town he was pretty sure, at each place that he stopped, to be entertained by a company of ladies who drank green tea and asked him his opinion of the Absolute. If Emerson was similarly waylaid, it is to be feared the ladies found him an unmanageable subject. The young student will not find himself "crammed" for the rehearsal of life by Emerson's teachings, nor any couch prepared for those who wish to find repose on a "system of the universe." With Confucius, he "respects the gods, but keeps them at a distance." There is no line in all his books that can encourage any one to waste his powers in the effort to fence in the illimitable or define the infinite, while every sentence shews that by patient thought and honourable living real progress is made and true knowledge is attained. He who still believes that men were sent into this world to devote their attention to another, or to the benefit and equanimity of the Divine Being, will find no confirmation here, but rather a recognition of Arthur Clough's conclusion —

> "It seems His newer will
> We should not think at all of Him, but turn,
> And of the world that He has given us make
> What best we may."

It is now wonderful to hear the anecdotes that shew how puzzling to divines, long familiar with a supernal universe, were the simple aspects of the world they lived in, to which Emerson introduced them. After his lecture at Middlebury College, Vermont, a minister said, in the closing prayer, "We beseech Thee, O Lord, to deliver us from ever hearing any more such transcendental nonsense as we have just listened to from this sacred desk." Emerson's only remark about this supplicant was that "he seemed a very conscientious plain-spoken man." At Middletown, Connecticut, the Methodist professors and divines were affected by his lecture before their college societies as if he had administered laughing-gas. Bishop Janes alone felt the situation to be serious. Afterwards, when some one quoted lines from Emerson, where, alluding to "Taylor, the Shakespeare of divines," he says —

> "And yet, for all his faith could see,
> I would not the good bishop be," —

"What," said Bishop Janes, "not for Jeremy Taylor's hope of heaven!" So it was for a time. But, when Dean Stanley returned from America, it was to report ("Macmillan," June, 1879) that religion had there passed through an evolution from Edwards to Emerson; and that "the genial atmosphere which Emerson has done so much to promote is shared by all the churches equally."

XXIII.

CONCORDIA.

"Herein! herein!
Gesellen alle, schliesst den Reihen,
Dass wir die Glocke taufend weihen!
CONCORDIA soll ihr Name sein.
Zur Eintracht, zu herzinnigen Vereine
Versammle sie die liebende Gemeine!"

CONCORDIA its name shall be!" was the sound of Schiller's Bell in my ears when I began this book about the Sage of Concord. Its name could not be that, for it would promise too much, but none would be truer for a full story of Emerson and his friends. The prophecy of Weimar was fulfilled when from a race passed through furnaces, heated by heavenly and earthly Star-chambers, refined and tempered by love and culture, fashioned in mould of a New World, this pure genius was raised aloft in its tower over the broken forms that had held it, and there, in tones melodious with all sweetness and the nobleness of human life, summoned all souls to inward and outward harmony.

"The town of Concord is one of the oldest towns in this country, far on now in its third century. The selectmen have once in every five years perambulated the boundaries, and yet, in this very year, a large quantity of land has been discovered and added to the town without a murmur of complaint from any quarter. By drainage we went down to a subsoil we did not know, and have found that there is a Concord under old Concord, which we are now getting the best crops from."

When Emerson said this, in one of the hundred lectures he gave at Concord, some of his neighbours reflected that a much greater addition to their wealth, in a strictly economic sense, had been made by his residence among them. He was the selectman who discovered the supersoil, the Concord above Concord, from which the great crops came.

The effect of Emerson's lectures on the country generally was indescribable. It was found that his voice had been heard in all the byways and hedges, and swarms of a mighty fraternity, popularly classified as "come-outers," swarmed to Concord, each to get his recipe for the millenium countersigned by the new teacher. Hawthorne, who had gone to reside in "The Old Manse," has left us a graphic description of the visitors thus attracted.

"There were circumstances around me which made it difficult to view the world precisely as it exists; for, severe and sober as was the Old Manse, it was necessary to go but a little way beyond its threshold before meeting with stranger moral shapes of men than might have been encountered elsewhere in a circuit of a thousand miles.

"These hobgoblins of flesh and blood were attracted thither by the wide-spreading influence of a great original thinker, who had his earthly abode at the opposite extremity of our village. His mind acted upon other minds of a certain constitution with wonderful magnetism, and drew many men upon long pilgrimages to speak with him face to face. Young visionaries — to whom just so much of insight had been imparted as to make life all a labyrinth around them — came to seek the clue that should guide them out of their self-involved bewilderment. Grey-headed theorists, whose systems, at first air, had finally imprisoned them in an iron frame-work, travelled painfully to his door, not to ask deliverance, but to invite the free spirit into their own thraldom. People that had lighted on a new thought, or a thought that they fancied new, came to Emerson, as the finder of a glittering gem hastens to a lapidary to ascertain its quality and value. Uncertain, troubled, earnest wanderers through the midnight of the moral world beheld his intellectual fire as a beacon burning on a hill-top, and, climbing the difficult ascent, looked forth into the surrounding obscurity more hopefully than hitherto. The light revealed objects unseen before — mountains, gleaming lakes, glimpses of a creation among the chaos — but also, as was unavoidable, it attracted bats and owls, and the whole host of night-birds, which flapped their dusky wings against the gazer's eyes, and sometimes were mistaken for fowls of angelic feather. Such delusions always hover nigh whenever a beacon fire of truth is kindled.

"For myself, there had been epochs of my life when I too might have asked of this prophet the masterword that should solve me the riddle of the universe.

But now, being happy, I felt as if there were no question to be put, and therefore admired Emerson as a poet of deep beauty and austere tenderness, but sought nothing from him as a philosopher. It was good, nevertheless, to meet him in the wood-paths, or sometimes in our avenue, with that pure intellectual gleam diffused about his presence like the garment of a shining one; and he, so quiet, so simple, so without pretension, encountering each man alive as if expecting to receive more than he could impart. But it was impossible to dwell in his vicinity without inhaling, more or less, the mountain atmosphere of his lofty thought."

More of these were emptied at Emerson's door from the Hive of Brook Farm, and from other socialistic tabernacles, which folded their tents like the Arabs, but did not silently pass away. There grew up a transcendental cant which threatened to deluge poor Concord, and the number of insane people that thronged the philosopher's door must have severely tried the nerves of the ladies who dwelt there. To this Mecca came pilgrims with long hair, long beard, and long collars; very many with long ears: those who believed that man was to reach the Golden Year by abstinence from meat, committees of all the " Isms," each seeking to get the new candle for its little altar, came in full chase after the millenium, which Mrs. Emerson had much reason to wish would make haste and come. Of course there was abundance of material for the humourists. Dr. Oliver Wendell Holmes expanded the new transcendental dialect to ennoble an already prominent feature: — " And why is the nose set in the front of the face, stretching outward and upward, but that it may attain, as it were, a foresmell of the Infinite!" But there was no humourist more subtle than Emerson. He did not laugh like Carlyle, but his mirth was deeper, and his constitutional faith was "Sport is the sign of health." At a small festivity in our house at Concord, at which he was present, some of us acted as a charade the word "Transcendentalism." The pedants and fanatics of an earlier period would have been scandalised could they have seen their prophet beaming on our travesty. But since the era of the "hobgoblins" there had been a change, whose true history would be a new Timæus, telling of one who, like a god, led things from disorder to order. The sediment of insanities which the new ideas had stirred up gradually sank to its natural place. There is an allegorical story that once, when Theodore Parker had just parted from Emerson on the road to Boston — the importance of which city in the plan of the universe they had discussed — a crazy "Millerite" encountered Parker and cried, "Sir, do you not know that to-night the world is coming to an end?" Upon which Parker replied, "My good man, that doesn't concern me: I live in Boston." The same fanatic presently announced the end of the world to Emerson, who replied, "I am glad of it; man will get along better without it."

Tender as Emerson was to myths and miracles which, with a sufficient perspective, were visible as figures on the stage of antiquity, he gave no quarter to growing superstitions. He was attracted by Swedenborg, largely, I think, because the spectral rout of the old world gathered in him to one neck which he could neatly cut, preserving the head for craniological study.

One who was with him at a meeting of the society for free religious discussion, when somebody happened to be giving his views in favour of all gross delusions of this kind, expressed disgust to Emerson. "Yes," he said, "there are some persons who will suck up the dirty water from every puddle they can find." On one occasion a "spiritualist" approached him with what he used to call the "rat-hole revelation," and Emerson said, "To me the universe is all a spiritual manifestation." All those delusions ultimately vanished from his presence and found their appropriate caves.

Emerson was also very careful to maintain the high and refined standard in regard to manners, and, against all protests, preserved the word "gentleman," as well as the reality implied. Though never ruffled, he was not defenceless before boorish intruders. A boisterous declaimer against " the conventionalities," who kept on his hat in the drawing-room after repeated invitations to lay it aside, was told, "We will continue this conversation in the garden," and genially taken out of doors to enter them no more. Yet no gentleman could be more free from the pretensions often associated with that title; and had any one sought to defend him from the best that Bottom and Snug had to offer, he would have said with the Duke Theseus —

> "I will hear that play;
> For never anything can be amiss
> Where simpleness and duty offer it."

On one occasion he was travelling in a stage-coach with a friend, and a third entered, a very crude youth, who, after listening to the scholarly talk, was inclined to join in, and asked Emerson, "What do you think of

Romulus?" His friend proposed in French that they should converse in that language, but Emerson said. "No; it would hurt the youth's feelings."

When Emerson fixed his abode at Concord, it was partly because it had been the home of his ancestors, and still more because there was no other place where he could hope to find the solitude he desired so near to the literary advantages of Boston and Harvard University. But he sought no morose solitude; he loved the society of kindred minds; he was by nature given to hospitality. For a long time he was, in a spiritual sense, alone. While honouring his name, most of his neighbours were shy or afraid of him. He had come with a reputation for extreme heresy, and the gossip about his insanity had preceded him. He was as a Prospero in this far island, who had not yet learned the might that lay in his book and wand to summon around him ministers more real than the aërial shapes of his masque. But such loneliness is a condition of the exercise of the highest power. There is a fine passage in Browning's "Colombe's Birthday," where Valence, speaking for the Duchess against the claimant of her throne, speaks also this truth:

> "*Val.* (*advancing*). The lady is alone!
> *Berth.* Alone and thus? So weak and yet so bold!
> *Val.* I said she was alone—
> *Berth.*   — And weak, I said.
> *Val.* When is man strong until he feels alone?
> It was some lonely strength at first, be sure,
> Created organs such as those you seek,
> By which to give its varied purpose shape,
> And, naming the selected ministrants,
> Took sword, and shield, and sceptre, each a man."

Emerson created his own world. This is true in a sense more profound than can be fully told. It is not merely that beneath his spirit light was divided from darkness, morning from evening, dry land from the waters, in that formless chaos already described; not only that the brood of ancient Night were dismissed and the children of Light drawn around him; but that he also breathed into these forms the breath of a new life. Goethe's Prometheus says—

> "Here do I sit, and mould
> Men after mine own image."

But here was a better than promethean art, which made a race not in the image of the artist — a varied race, of which some wrote romances, some advanced sciences, others organised higher education, others again uplifted the standard before which slavery disappeared, and better laws arose for woman and for the home. Emerson never "played providence" to the minds he had evoked. He allowed no imitation. The inevitable worship came. There are notable instances in which his voice, manners, and the very expression of his face, could be recognised moving about Concord in persons unrelated to him by blood; but these curious unconscious results of personal affection, wrought in long years of intimacy, were most marked in those whose individuality was especially distinct from that of Emerson. Of this more must be said hereafter. At present we may observe with interest the Goldmaker (to remember Zschokke's tale) at work in the transmutation of his village. One of the pleasantest glimpses of the earlier society there has been supplied by George William Curtis in his "Homes of American Authors." Somewhere about the year 1845 this now eminent author went to live at Concord. He had graduated at Harvard University, but he and his brother, thinking they had not had enough of the rough side of life, hired themselves as farm labourers near Concord. The young scholars worked well for fair wages, and reserved leisure to enjoy the society of the men who had attracted them there. Here the higher graduation of George Curtis took place, and his "Memorabilia," given to the world from time to time, are always charming. Of Emerson's home he says: "It is always morning within these doors," and gives us a glimpse into the Concord of his time.

"Toward the end of the autumn Emerson suggested that they should meet every Monday evening through the winter at his library. I went the first Monday evening, very much as Ixion may have gone to his banquet. The philosophers sat dignified and erect. There was a constrained but very amiable silence, which had the impertinence of a tacit inquiry, seeming to ask, 'Who will now proceed to say the finest thing that has ever been said?' It was quite involuntary and unavoidable, for the members lacked that fluent social genius without which a club is impossible. It was a congress of oracles on the one hand, and of curious listeners on the other. I vaguely remember that the Orphic Alcott invaded the desert of silence with a solemn saying, to which, after due pause, the Hon. Member for Blackberry Pastures (Thoreau) responded by some keen and graphic observation, while the Olympian host, anxious that so much good material should be spun into something, beamed smiling encouragement upon all parties. . . . Miles Coverdale (Nathaniel Hawthorne), a statue of Night and Silence, sat, a little removed under a portrait of Dante, gazing imperturbably upon the group; and as he sat in the shadow, his dark hair and eyes and suit of sable made him, in that society, the black thread of mystery which he weaves into his stories; while the shifting presence of the Brook farmer (Mr. Pratt) played like heat-lightning round the room. . . . Plato (Emerson) was perpetually putting apples of gold in pictures of silver; for such was the rich ore of his thought and the deep melody of his voice."

The "Note-Books" of Hawthorne contain delightful pictures of the life at Concord. One may be given here.

"Entering Sleepy Hollow, I perceived a lady reclining near the path which bends along its verge. It was Margaret herself. She had been there the whole afternoon, meditating or reading; for she had a book in her hand, with some strange title, which I did not understand, and have forgotten. She said that nobody had broken her solitude, and was just giving utterance to a theory that no inhabitant of Concord ever visited Sleepy Hollow, when we saw a group of people entering the sacred precincts. Most of them followed a path which led them away from us; but an old man passed near us, and smiled to see Margaret reclining on the ground and me sitting by her side. He made some remark about the beauty of the afternoon, and withdrew himself into the shadow of the wood. There we talked about autumn, and about the pleasures of being lost in the woods, and about the crows whose voices Margaret had heard, and about the experiences of early childhood, whose influence remains upon the character when the recollection of them has passed away, and about the sight of mountains from a distance, and the view from their summits, and about other matters of high and low philosophy. In the midst of our talk we heard footsteps above us on the high bank; and while the person was still hidden among the trees he called to Margaret, of whom he had gotten a glimpse. Then he emerged from the green shade, and behold! it was Mr. Emerson. He appeared to have had a pleasant time, for he said that there were Muses in the woods to-day, and whispers to be heard in the breezes. There was the most beautiful moonlight that ever hallowed this earthly world; and when I went to bathe in the river, which was as calm as death, it seemed like plunging down into the sky. But I had rather be on earth than in the seventh heaven just now."

The Concord Lyceum, in which lectures were given in the autumn and winter months, was Emerson's pulpit. His literary friends from a distance were always ready to come and lecture there, the substantial honorarium being made the largest in the country by the opportunity afforded of meeting Emerson, who generally entertained such visitors. Schools of high character arose as the culture and wealth of the place increased, and gradually the beautiful Free Public Library was built. In this library there is a large alcove filled with books written in Concord or by authors who have resided there, — Emerson, Margaret Fuller, Mr. and Mrs. Nathaniel Hawthorne, Thoreau,

G. W. Curtis, Ellery Channing, Bronson Alcott, Louisa Alcott, Elizabeth Peabody, Frank B. Sanborn, Fred. M. Holland, George P. Lathrop, Mrs. Horace Mann, Julian Hawthorne, Rev. G. W. Cooke, Mr. Harris, and perhaps others. It is probable that no other village can show a nobler literary monument of more various labours. It is, in a sense, the monument of one man.

It is the greatest advantage of large cities that each mind can find its circle, though it would be eccentric elsewhere. Emerson was as patient as the earth of all varieties of intellect and character. He was sceptical concerning all rumours of "dangerous opinions." George Bradford gave me a sentence, remembered from a lost note, in which, alluding to some teacher of so-called "wild notions," Emerson says, "A meteor shaking from its horrid hair all sorts of evils and disasters may by and by take its place in the clear upper sky and blend its light with all our day."

Margaret Fuller first came to Concord in 1836. She came to visit Mr. and Mrs. Emerson. It was a year that opened with a bitter trial. She had been looking forward for years to a visit to Europe, but the death of her father brought her under circumstances which rendered it impossible. She was in her twenty-fourth year, but possessed a culture far in advance of her years; a culture that was European, and included a knowledge of the literature and art as well as the languages of Europe. "The New Year opens upon me under circumstances inexpressibly sad. I must make the last great sacrifice, and, apparently, for evil to me and mine. Life, as I look forward, presents a scene of struggle and privation only." So opens her journal on January 1, 1836. But in July she was guest of the man who could be and was far more to her than Europe. She had, indeed, listened to Emerson for some years, but she did not seek his friendship until she had accumulated treasures worthy to be exchanged for his own.

Emerson, who was always wont to scold himself for his love of physical beauty, was repelled by her "extreme plainness." I remember well that the eyes of Margaret's mother, whom I well knew, filled with tears when she remembered that a lack of personal beauty had been ascribed to her daughter in the biography that had just appeared. "I do not understand it," she said, "for Margaret was not without beauty." But the mention of it was necessary, for only so could be shewn the splendour that was unsheathed in the conversation of that woman, and the charm which held her circle of friends spell-bound. And, moreover, only so can be understood the morbid tendencies of her nature, of which she was healed by the steadfast sunshine of Emerson's genius.

Such expressions as these are found in her journals: "Of a disposition that requires the most refined, the most exalted tenderness, without charms to inspire it. Poor Mignon! fear not the transition through death; no penal fires can have in store worse torments than thou art familiar with already." Such secret pain led inevitably in one direction — to an appeal from earth to heaven, from the present to the future. She brought to Concord, along with her riches of knowledge and wit, all manner of notions about talismans, charms, dæmonic influences, presentiments. Emerson separated the bits of stained glass from her gems with the skill of a true lapidary; and then the superstition that had lurked in them assumed a more threatening form. "She passed into certain religious states," says Emerson, "which did not impress me as quite healthy or likely to be permanent; and I said, 'I do not understand your tone; it seems exaggerated. You are one who can afford to hear and speak the truth. Let us hold hard to the common-sense, and let us speak in the positive degree.'" She wrote some bitter complaints to this calm physician, and a plaintive fable, but the worshipper of health was tenderly inflexible. And finally, as Margaret had found that the Europe so bitterly lamented lay only twenty miles out from Boston, she discovered that the heavenly friend she had longed for and the new Jerusalem were equally near. It was after she had listened deep and long to the notes of "Concordia" that she wrote the following:—

"The stars tell all their secrets to the flowers, and if we only knew how to look around us, we should not need to look above. But man is a plant of slow growth, and great heat is required to bring out his leaves. He must be promised a boundless futurity to induce him to use aright the present hour. In youth, fixing his eyes on those distant worlds of light, he promises himself to attain them, and there find the answer to all his wishes. His eye grows keener as he gazes, a voice from the earth calls it downward, and he finds all at his feet."

On my second walk with Emerson he took me to a seat in the woods, which in summer days had been a sort of trysting-place for the literary lotus-eaters, and as he talked of Margaret — so gently, and with a reserve as if she were still living — I heard the voice that had called her to the stars at her feet. From what he told me, I knew that none could ever get from her works or from the reports of her friends the real greatness of Margaret Fuller, and felt a personal grief that I had not known her.

Among Margaret Fuller's friends, in her last years, were Mr. and Mrs. Browning. This was after she had married Count Ossoli. The marriage had been private, and some of her friends in Italy suggested that she should make public explanations of her sufficient reasons for that course; but she refused, saying that " no one for whose opinion she cared would be likely to believe that she had done anything wrong in such a matter." It was with the Brownings that she, with her husband and child, spent the last evening she ever passed on land. As she was starting for the ship, Mrs. Browning pressed upon her finger a ring with a carbuncle in it, quite unaware that Margaret, in her superstitious days, had chosen the carbuncle as her stone, going so far as to put one on when writing to certain friends. Later, as Robert Browning informed me, they received from her a letter written — or scratched, rather — at Gibraltar, telling them of the ravages of the small-pox which had deprived them of a captain, and of the rigours by which they were forbidden to land, and compelled to go on to America with disease lurking in the ship and only the mate for captain. This was her last letter. I need not record the tragic end of this strange and heroic life, nor the sorrow of her friends and relatives, who received her and the husband and child only as the waves dashed them to the shore, within hailing distance of which they perished.

The story has been told with all his eloquence by William Henry Channing. This eminent preacher, so well known in England, was, in a sense, chaplain of the socialistic organisations in America. He possessed — what was rare among Unitarian preachers — a power of eloquent extemporaneous speech. There was a tone of prophetic authenticity in his voice, which, with his scholarly enthusiasm, made him fitter for the new movement than his more famous uncle could have been. After the failure of the socialistic experiments, William Henry Channing was known as an earnest champion of every human cause. His spiritual home was Concord, where he was often seen and was always welcomed by the Emersons. While their children were yet very young, as Emerson told me, his wife wished to have their children christened; he had objected, but said he would consent if she could find a minister "as pure as the children." When Channing came to Concord, he agreed with his wife that the right man had been found, and the children were accordingly christened.

Among those who went to reside at Concord (1841) were also Ellery Channing, a cousin of William Henry, and his wife, a sister of Margaret Fuller. This writer of what is "very near poetry," as Emerson described him, still resides there. "Ellery Channing is excellent company, and we walk in all directions," wrote Emerson to Thoreau in 1843; and, when in England in 1848, Emerson read to a circle in Manchester some pieces from this Concord poet; among them, no doubt, "The Poet's Hope," whose last line has taken its place as a familiar quotation —

"If my bark sinks, 'tis to another sea."

Ellery Channing, who still resides in Concord, was an intimate friend of Thoreau, whose life he has told in prose and celebrated in poetry.

A. Bronson Alcott came with his wife and family to live at Concord in 1840, and there he still resides, a happy and hearty octogenarian, with his daughter Louisa, whose tales are the delight of so many households. In early life Alcott had been a pedlar, — one picturesque enough to have been a model for Wordsworth, — and when the transcendental movement began, he became a peripatetic philosopher, carrying about spiritual "notions" instead of those once supplied from his native Connecticut.

In 1834 Alcott opened a transcendental school in Boston, whose "Records," as preserved by Elizabeth Peabody, deserve to be studied by every parent and teacher. He had taken to heart rather literally Wordsworth's faith that "Heaven lies about us in our infancy," and believed that from the commonest children, if suitably addressed, secrets might be gained "of that immortal sea that brought us hither." His schoolroom was ideal, with busts of Socrates, Shakespeare, Milton, and Scott, the image of Silence with uplifted finger, a bookcase surmounted with the bust of Plato, and the figure of Christ above the head of the blond, dignified teacher. As to the value of the replies given by the pupils to questions on high themes, as they may be now read, there may be some doubt; but there is, in my own mind, no doubt of the importance of some features in Alcott's method. For instance, he opened his school with an instruction in behaviour and manners. These children, of ages ranging from four to fourteen, were many of them rude, and from rude surroundings. It is one of the survivals of the notion of innate depravity that, even in this age of popular education, the misbehaviour of children is ascribed to moral causes, to be met by punishment. A child just learning to read is expected to act up to Herbert Spencer's "Data of Ethics," or be flogged! A child is expected to come from among roughs with an instinctive knowledge of how he must behave in school, or to other children, to the aged, to ladies! It is doubtful whether in all the schools of the world any lesson is taught in politeness, kindness, gentleness. In Alcott's school, this lesson, with which the day began, was so interesting to the children, that they stood waiting at the door for it to open, lest they should miss a word.

Another remarkable thing in this unique school was the mode of punishment. The teacher having found by experience that the rod was ineffectual for discipline, announced one day that thereafter it should fall only on — himself! If any pupil offended, that pupil must inflict on the master the blows merited by the offence. After this announcement, there was more complete silence and obedience than had been known before; but at length one or two cases occurred where boys were compelled to strike the master's hand with a ferule. They were boys to whom punishments had been of little consequence, but they found this, as one of them said, "the most complete punishment a master ever invented;" they pleaded with tears and cries to be spared the disgrace of striking their mild and good teacher, but he was inexorable. The plan was effectual, and the ferule appeared no more. In some respects, this school was an improvement on one which might have suggested it, — that of Jean Paul Richter at Schwarzenbach, described in his "Bonmot Anthology."

When Emerson and Carlyle were returning from a visit to Stonehenge, they were entertained by Sir Arthur Helps at Bishops Waltham, with other gentlemen, and to these "Friends in Council" Emerson told an anecdote about Alcott, which I am sorry I did not ask him to repeat literally, for the version I have heard may contain mythical elements. Alcott seemed unable to produce anything for which the great world was willing to trade, and the family was reduced to want. On one occasion, however, he became the owner of a twenty-dollar gold piece, which caused joy in his household. On the same day a traveller in distress knocked at his door, and, telling a piteous story, besought a loan of five dollars to enable him to reach home. Alcott told him he had not a five piece, but could lend him a twenty. The alternative was accepted with a satisfaction not shared by Mrs. Alcott when she presently returned from a walk. The papers next day contained a description of the rogue and how he had swindled others. Alcott was in some domestic disgrace until a letter arrived containing the money, the swindler declaring that he could not make up his mind to rob a man so simple-hearted as to give him four times the amount he asked for. Alcott alone recovered his money. This, or something like it, was the story Emerson told the company. Carlyle sat silent, and when dinner was announced refused to precede Emerson—"he was altogether too wicked." Alcott for many years went about the country presiding at "Conversations" on philosophical subjects. Of course the humourist and the fabulist have had their stories to tell about him. To his announcement of a "conversation" was added, "Ladies invited, without distinction of sex." On one occasion, it was said, when the philosopher had divided the entity *Man* into the Knower, the Thinker, the Actor, a pious lady asked whether this Knower was the same that was saved in the Ark. A Harvard student was reported to have asked the philosopher's opinion "of the late theory of Verdantius Grün, that the moon is a mass of sweitzeroeaseous matter congealed from the uberous glands of the lacteal nebula." These inventions were suggested by the fact that Alcott remained in a Platonic labyrinth, where he was left by the advance of science. He had no relation to the scientific age. Emerson used to say he needed a reporter, but he also needed an interpreter. Nevertheless some of his oracular paragraphs, printed in the "Dial" as "Orphic Sayings," are fine; and unquestionably a good deal of the intellectual activity of America must be ascribed to this last of the Neo-Platonists. Emerson always regarded Alcott as a kind of transcendental institution, a landmark on his own path, long left but affectionately remembered, and when he was near to death asked if it was well with him. "You have a strong hold on life and will keep it," he said.

One of the most remarkable instances of the effect of the new inspiration was represented by one who never resided at Concord, but was well known there, Jones Very. This man was a fulfilment of Emerson's prophecy that what was sometime ecstasy should become daily bread. He moved in a continual exaltation, and there came from him beautiful sonnets and hymns. Some of these are now sung by liberal congregations throughout the United States, and they are not unknown in England. When Brook Farm had broken up, and the glowing dawn of transcendentalism had faded into the light of common day, Jones Very waked as from a trance and became a prosaic farmer. He never published another line. He was changed even in personal appearance, so that his old friends hardly knew him on the street.

It must not be supposed that either Alcott or Jones Very were representative of the influence of Emerson, however closely related to an early phase of it. Concord held fit homes for such, but it appropriated the spirit of its Sage in all practical ways. Judge Rockwood Hoar was none the less indebted to his great friend for aid in his growth to be a pre-eminent jurist and statesman because his argumentative and logical power was so remote from the genius of Emerson. The father of Judge Hoar, Samuel Hoar, from being a distinguished lawyer and statesman, had become, when I first remember Concord, a saint of the village. "He never comes down on earth among us," said Emerson one day as we passed the calm face of the tall aged man, around whom all the spiritual agitations had gone on for years without interrupting his perpetual prayer. The Rev. George Simmons was there also, with his spiritual face, absorbed in critical studies of the age of St. John's Gospel, while yet able, in certain moods, to recognise the Beloved passing his door.

At the Old Manse lived Sarah Ripley, of whom much has already been said, surrounded by her lovely daughters. The story of her life has been told by that lady of Concord who could best tell it—the late Elizabeth Hoar, whose countenance and conversation were to me always as if she had come from communion with angels. Mrs. Ripley was born in 1793, and made speedy and prodigious advances in the study of languages and of science. In her seventeenth year she is an earnest student of English philosophy, and knows by heart Darwin's "Botanic Garden." She already has the Darwinian instinct, and writes, "Even the humble dandelion exhibits an order and regularity of parts admirable as the harmony of spheres." She already knows how to unmask the passing day, and writes in her journal, "Some sweet ingredient is each day mingled in my cup." When she is twenty-one we find her corresponding with her little friend of eleven, Ralph Waldo Emerson, and in one letter says to him, "I suppose you have Euryalus among your companions; or don't little boys love each other as well as they did in Virgil's time? How beautifully he describes the morning!"

A beautiful life she lived, and when the new age came she took it into her heart, and invested it with all loveliness of womanly character and domestic virtues, which were as potent to win homage as the finest intellectual statements. She was the wife of a Unitarian preacher, a relative of Emerson's, but she knew how unsatisfactory was that phase of faith. Of a preacher who filled her husband's pulpit she wrote to a friend, "How the bucket of the gentleman danced up and down on the surface of that deep well of spiritual life, from which the saints in all ages have drawn living water! But he is a pleasant fellow." And what conversations were those between Sarah Ripley and Emerson! "I was walking the other morning with Waldo Emerson in Concord, and I told him I thought the soul's serenity was at best nothing more than resignation to what could not be helped. He answered, 'Oh, no — not resignation; aspiration is the soul's true estate! What have we knees for? what have we hands for? Peace is victory.'" Emerson having promised her to bring "a lecture which has legs," she writes, "But I fear, after all, wings will be sprouting at the heels."

The Rev. Samuel Ripley died while Emerson was lecturing in England, and he wrote to Mrs. Ripley (from Manchester, 26th December, 1847), "And now that he is gone who bound us by blood, I think we must draw a little nearer together, for at this time of day we cannot afford to spare any friends. I wonder to think — here with the ocean betwixt us — that I have suffered you to live so near me and have not won from the weeks and months more frequent intercourse." Nothing could have been more admirable than the conversations, some of which I heard, between these two in the Old Manse. I had heard at Cambridge a story that Audubon called once to consult this lady on the lichens of her neighbourhood, and found her hearing at once the lesson of a Harvard student in differential calculus, correcting the translation of another from Sophocles, at the same time shelling peas, and rocking her grandchild's cradle with her foot; a story not incredible, and quite characteristic of the New England women who were most alive to the intellectual movements of their time. The Old Manse, while Mrs. Ripley and her daughters lived there, and the Emerson house, were systole and diastole of what my friend Stedman called the *Cor Concordia*. Mrs. Ripley and her friend Elizabeth Hoar appeared to me especially in accord with the intellectual opinions of Emerson. Once I mentioned to Mrs. Ripley a heated discussion we had in Divinity College on miracles. She said, with her soft solemnity, "I cannot believe in the miracles, because I believe in God."

There were nearly always visitors at Concord, but from among them I must single out one, whom I saw one morning emerge from Emerson's door — one whose face bore upon it something of the same spiritual light as that of the man he had been visiting. This was Arthur Hugh Clough, whom I afterwards met in Cambridge, and found that the nobleness of his countenance was a reflection from within. I did not then know that the white hair around his youthful face was a true halo, set there by a long spiritual struggle, and marking a costly victory. Knowing that he was an Oxonian poet who had crossed the ocean to be near Emerson, I used to gaze upon him with love as he passed Divinity College almost daily, on his way to the home of the Nortons, who were as brother and sisters to him. Emerson lent me Clough's "Bothie" and the "Ambarvalia," which he loved to quote on his walks.

With what feelings Clough regarded Emerson appears in these notes in the Memoir of him by his wife: —

"*Sunday.* — Loads of talk with Emerson all morning. Breakfast at eight displays two girls and a boy, the family. Dinner at 2.30. Walk with Emerson to a wood with a prettyish pool. Concord is very bare (so is the country in general); it is a small sort of a village, almost entirely of wood houses, painted white, with Venetian blinds, green outside, with two white wooden churches — one with a stone façade of Doric columns, however. . . . There are some American elms, of a weeping kind, and sycamores, *i.e.* planes; but the wood is mostly pine — white pine and yellow pine — somewhat scrubby, occupying the tops of the low banks, and marshy hay-land between, very brown now. A little brook runs through to the Concord river.

"At 6.30, tea and Mr. Thoreau, and presently Mrs. Ellery Channing, Miss Channing, and others."

"Just back at Cambridge after my visit to Emerson. I was rather *sleepless* there, but it is very good to go to him. He appears to take things very coolly, and not to meddle with religious matters of any kind. Since visiting him, I feel a good deal more reconciled to mere 'subsistence.' If one can only have a little reasonable satisfactory intercourse now and then, subsistence may be to some purpose. But to live in a vain show of society would not do long. The Boston people have been too well off, and don't know the realities. Emerson is really substantive."

"Emerson is the only profound man in this country."

Frank Sanborn, in whom are embodied the traditions of Concord, has told its personal history in his "Thoreau."

Some may imagine that in such a town as this all the children, like Zal in Firdusi's epic, were born greyhaired, but rather like Zoroaster they were born laughing. Concord was always remarkable for the large number of its lovely little people, who might be seen in the winter skating on the marble snow through the pine woods, and in the summer bathing in the river, and at all times boating. And for young men and maidens, Goethe's Weimar with its court had hardly more festivities than Emerson's Concord. Over the graves of the Puritans went on dances, picnics, berrying parties; on the Musketaquid, where Eliot the Apostle terrified the red men with a vision of retributions more savage than their own, gay barges were sometimes seen conveying Cleopatra and her dusky beauties to be attacked by "salvages" in war-paint darting from river-sides fringed with waterlilies; and the grim "embattled farmers" who began the revolution sometimes returned on their anniversary to masquerade with their fair descendants.

Once in that neighbourhood I met with an unquiet soul yearning for higher social conditions, which had taken shape in his mind after the pattern shewn by Fourier. "Have you ever heard," I asked, "of the child that went about lamenting and searching for the beautiful butterfly which she had lost? The butterfly had softly alighted upon her head, and sat there while the search went on. May not this fable apply to one who, living in Concord, searches as far as France for a true society?"

But, when I was last in Concord, it was to Germany some seemed wandering, after a philosophy; and the butterfly had changed to a grasshopper, which, near the "Summer School of Philosophy," chirped me a tale of Tithonus, — or Transcendentalism outliving its time and shrivelling to metaphysics. Not such was the voice that spake with no past at its back ! "Concordia" is not to be muffled in metaphysics, as for one whose "Finis" was written in skull-bones instead of flowers.

> "Now break up the useless mould:
> Its only purpose is fulfilled.
> May our eyes with joy behold
> A work to prove us not unskilled.
> Wield the hammer, wield,
> Till the frame shall yield!
> That the bell aloft may rise
> The form in thousand fragments flies."

XXIV.

NATHANIEL AND SOPHIA HAWTHORNE.

ON a day in Concord I saw the two men whom Michael Angelo might have chosen as emblems of Morning and Twilight, to be carved over the gates of the New World. Emerson emerged from his modern home, and the shade of well-trimmed evergreens in front, with " shining morning face," his eye beaming with its newest vision of the golden year. Hawthorne, at the other extreme of the village, came softly out of his earlier home, the Old Manse — the grey-gabled mansion, where dwelt in the past men and women who have gained new lease of existence through his genius — and stepped along the avenue of ancient ash-trees, which made a fit frame around him. A superb man he was! His erect, full, and shapely figure might have belonged to an athlete, were it not for the grace and reserve which rendered the strength of frame unobtrusive. The massive forehead and brow, with dark locks on either side, the strong nose and mouth, with another soul beneath them, might be the physiognomy of a military man or political leader — some man impelled by powerful public passions; but with this man there came through the large soft eyes a gentle glow which suffused the face and spiritualised the form.

No wonder such fascination held his college fellows to him! Longfellow used to talk in poetry when his early days at Bowdoin with Hawthorne were the theme; and the memory of President Pierce has lost some stains through his lifelong devotion to his early friend.

How the personages who had long before preceded him in that first home of his manhood had become his familiar friends and visitors — preferred to others separated from him by reason of their flesh and blood — no reader of "Mosses from an Old Manse" need be told. As he came down the avenue, unconscious of any curious or admiring eye resting on him, every step seemed a leap, as if his shadowy familiars were whispering happy secrets. What was this *genius loci* thinking of as he walked there? It may have been about that time he mentioned the Old Manse to a friend, and wrote: "The trees of the avenue — how many leaves have fallen since I last saw them!" It was always on the fallen leaf that Hawthorne found the sentence for his romance, but to what a beautiful new life did it germinate there!

It is an almost solemn reflection that in that same Old Manse, and in the same room, were written Emerson's "Nature" and Hawthorne's "Goodman Brown."

On the twenty-eighth birthday of the American Republic was born also this last wizard of Salem; and the spirit of the day, as well as of the place, was potent in him. Much of the romance of early American history gathers about Salem. It is a charming old town, with broad streets overarched by the foliage of aged elms, and with memorable houses preserved amid the mansions of its cultured citizens. Its oldest families are sprung from men who began life as seafarers and became merchants. I know not whether it be because Beauty insists on rising from even such distant waves, but the Salem people and their homes always appeared to me to possess a peculiar charm. Here young Nathaniel could read on Gallows Hill, where the witches were hung, the tragical story of that era, to the time when the people arose and broke open the prison doors of those victims, and entered the door of the judge, whom they forced to kneel and ask pardon of outraged humanity. On the neighbouring sea-beach he was wont to wander in the twilight and see — sombre Astarte shall we say? — rising from the waves, where his fathers had commanded ships of war or merchandise. From these years grew many of those mystical " Twice-Told Tales " in which all the moonlight and starlight of New England history is garnered. When they were first read, some thought even the author's name a myth. " Nathaniel " had been suggested by the Puritan's fondness for scriptural names, and " Hawthorne " had an obvious significance; and, indeed, the letter w, which the author inserted in the old Wiltshire name, may have represented some conscious spiritualisation of his family tree. His ancestor who planted the American branch of Hathornes persecuted Quakers, the next persecuted witches. The best compensation for their lives was when they were turned into gloomily picturesque figures by the art of their descendant, and the blood shed by their thorns tinted the blossoms of Hawthorne.

Carlyle used to say a good word for his pet " survival, " Calvin, even in the Servetus affair. Think of

the amount of sincerity and force of purpose required
to make a man burn his fellowman to ashes! Whereon
one's comment might be: But what Medusa must that
creed be which, three centuries after Calvin's death,
can chain the heart of a giant nursed at that stony
breast! The infernal sincerity and force of those
Puritan soldiers, William Hathorne and his son John,
transmitted their spell also to Hawthorne, but not to
bind his heart. "I know not," he wrote, "whether
these ancestors of mine bethought themselves to repent
and ask pardon of Heaven for their cruelties, or
whether they are now groaning under the heavy conse-
quences of them in another state of being. At all
events, I, the present writer, hereby take shame upon
myself for their sakes, and pray that any curse incurred
by them — as I have heard, and as the dreary and
unprosperous condition of the race for some time back
would argue to exist — may now and henceforth be
removed." The last shadow of Calvinism lay in the
persistence of this notion of a transmitted curse,
which, however refined, held the American Merlin in a
prison of air. The transmutation of subjective into
objective facts was a more terrible tendency in Hawthorne than in Swedenborg; for Hawthorne did not
project his fancies into conventionalised, but into
natural forms. He still uses the fossil word "sin."
The punishers of guilt on his stage are palpable, like
the Furies of Æschylus, which were so fatal to sensitive women in Athens; and neither Æschylus nor any
other writer has described the fatal spiritual phenomena with greater intensity of realisation and more
subtle art.

"The Celestial Railway" was the first piece by Hawthorne that penetrated our Southern region. It was copied in the newspapers of that region, and much enjoyed as a satire upon the rationalistic tendencies of the North. When I became old enough to appreciate the humour of that allegory, and the "serene strength" which Emerson found in it, I was also able to recognise its re-actionary spirit. And years later, recognising Hawthorne as the one American whose genius was comparable with that of Emerson for power, it was my conviction that the piece I have mentioned, and the greater part of the "Mosses from an Old Manse," belong to the earlier and unsunned time of his life. "My son," said Goethe's mother, "whenever he had a grief put it into a poem, and so got rid of it." A dismal day cast its last shadows on those "Mosses," and a careful eye may find them sheathing here and there roses of the fairer morning that had come upon his life

In his earliest tales, written in Salem, there is revealed, along with the ever-appealing intellect, a sensitive and loving nature, thirsting for affection, faint with growing despair of finding a nature responsive to his deep heart. In 1836 Margaret Fuller wrote to a friend, "I took a two or three year old 'Token,' and chanced on a story called 'The Gentle Boy,' which I remembered to have heard was written by somebody in Salem. It is marked by so much grace and delicacy of feeling that I am very desirous to know the author, whom I take to be a lady."

Meantime in that same old town, though unknown as the maiden of his fable that stood near slumbering

David Swan, was dwelling near Hawthorne the heart that held his sunbeam. A kind and intelligent physician dwelt in Salem, with his three lovely daughters, dowered only with riches of mind and heart. Of these sisters Peabody, all lived to do honour to the womanhood of America. Mary, as Mrs. Horace Mann, was able to assist her eminent husband in his educational work East and West, recorded but too modestly in her beautiful memoir of that noble man. Elizabeth, by an unwearied zeal in the pursuit of every high ideal, became a kind of saintly abbess at Concord, of whom I heard Emerson say that her recollections and correspondence would comprise the spiritual history of her time. Sophia, as the wife of Hawthorne, aided in the realisation of ideals as beautiful as any she dreamed while a favourite pupil in the studio of Allston.

It was with a certain despair that Hawthorne made his first pilgrimage to the Brook Farm community,— the wild plunge of a starved heart to find some other world. He found his millennium in a heart. He was a stranger in the land of promise, but found his ideal community, which consisted of two, whose model halls were in the most ancient and solitary mansion of Concord village. There was indeed one other member of the Old Manse community,— Poverty; but never was poor relation treated more good-humouredly.

No other! Yes, Happiness. To read Hawthorne's "Notes" of these years starts to the eyes tears that flash prismatic hues. He is still "the obscurest man of letters in America;" he is poor and without prospect of becoming otherwise; and he feels himself supremely blessed. His honeymoon never waned. He compares himself to Adam with Eve beside him, and cannot think Eden could have been very different from their garden with its Balm-of-Gilead trees and its unforbidden apples All the four rivers of paradise were merged in the Musketaquid, gently streaming past, adorned with lilies holding gold of Havilah, and reflecting the scarlet cardinal-flower, which he would have accepted as a confessor had there been any snake in his garden.

He gave his perfect happiness as a reason why he did not seek from Emerson his solution of the riddle of the universe. But Hawthorne could not escape the cloven tongues of his time; therefore was he at Concord. He himself speaks of the effect of "living for three years under the subtle influence of an intellect like Emerson's." While yet his art was working in its labyrinthine grotto, its crystals correspond with the roses of Emerson's bower.

There is an allegorical flower growing out of a grave, so often met with in Hawthorne's pages that it can never fade from his escutcheon. In his early life it promised a fatal quality, like that in "Septimius" which so closely resembled the flower of perpetual life. M. Emile Montégut has spoken of Hawthorne as a *romancier pessimiste;* and, superficial as the criticism is, there are some startling correspondences between the early fancies of Hawthorne and the great pessimistic systems. It is not probable that Hawthorne could have read Firdusi's history of Zohak when he wrote "The Man with a Snake in his Bosom;" and still less that he knew the now familiar legend of Buddha when he wrote the following in his journal at Salem,

1836: — "Two lovers plan the building of a pleasure-house on a certain spot of ground, but various seeming accidents prevent it. Once they find a group of miserable children there; once it is the scene where crime is plotted; at last the dead body of one of the lovers or of a dear friend is found there; and, instead of a pleasure-house, they build a marble tomb. The moral is that there is no place on earth fit for the site of a pleasure-house, because there is no spot that may not have been saddened by human grief, stained by crime, or hallowed by death."

One day there was a Mayday festival for the children of Concord. Emerson gave the use of his woods and a Maypole. While the ladies were out there making the preparations, Hawthorne came up and said he would like to see the children dancing if he could do so without being perceived. There was found for him the hollow trunk of a tree long dead; he hid himself there as the children were coming and gazed upon them. He left unperceived. Was it a tree grown from a slip of Buddha's Bo-tree, brought over by the Puritans to represent their dogma of a curse on nature? It could not live on Emerson's farm, and its last service was to give Hawthorne his outlook on the dance of happy children in which he could not freely unite. Yet was he a charming playmate to his children and a profoundly sympathetic man; though to the last he could not part with his "horse of the night," as Emerson styled it, a more delightful companion when dismounted could not be found.

Emerson feared the melancholy temperament of his most distinguished neighbour, but recognised his genius and his almost magical art. So long as Margaret Fuller frequented Concord, she was an element which enabled them to mingle; but when that mediator was gone, the two shrank a little from each other by elective necessity, while preserving mutual esteem. Hawthorne may have been afraid of casting a shadow across that path of sunshine visible wherever Emerson moved, and he may also have feared to meet the unfamiliar people who sought the Sage. Here was a man whose nerves were without integument, terribly exposed to all kinds of impressions from without. If any person or thing came into real contact with his mind, it sank deeply into him, drew upon his heart's blood, and remained until it was born into some mental offspring. Every new experience was a fatality to him for good or ill. Not every one who saw how reserved and gentle he was knew the great struggle by which a nature full of fiery forces had been brought into harmony with its ideal elements. Beneath these remained the lava soil, which must needs nurse into life every seed fallen in it.

We have seen that his ancestors became his literary offspring. The genesis of "The Scarlet Letter," the New England epic, has been shadowed forth by himself; and there is nothing more thrilling in it than the scene of Hawthorne himself, in the prosaic Customhouse pressing the faded broidered "A" to his breast till it burns. But whence came the letter and the tale? From the brow of Cain. (Two great pieces of imaginative art in New England came from the Bible when its altar-chain was broken. The other is Dr. Holmes's romance of Eve and the Serpent, entitled "Elsie Venner.") The "House of the Seven Gables" was once the doomed House of Agamemnon. Nearly all the tales of Hawthorne, even the smallest, have bloomed from seed taken, as it were, from the cerements of royal mummies, where they symbolised eternal ideas, albeit the bodies they receive from his genius have such an American look. That, I believe, is why they possess the unique character of seeming new and startling every time one reads them. They do not appear like literary creations, but draw the reader at once to the man in whom these things exist. His writings are overcast with the pain of a heart held under a necessity to expose its inmost recesses to the world.

The Misses Hunt, with whom I boarded during my first summer at Concord, told me the sad story of their near relative who drowned herself in the river. Martha Hunt was young and attractive; she had interested George Bradford, Emerson, and other scholars by her serious studies and high aims. Her parents and relatives were poor but affectionate, and anxious to further her intellectual growth; but she could not "beat her music through." The tidings spread through the village that she had disappeared, and her outer garments were found beside the river, somewhat below the Old Manse, where Hawthorne was then residing. He with a friend shoved off in a boat, and late in the night, under a fitful moonlight, brought to the surface the form of the poor maiden. The tragedy wrote itself inevitably in "The Blithedale Romance," and the artist appears simply in setting it where it belonged. Although the Brook Farmers took it to heart that such a tragedy should be associated with their cheery community, the incident sets fairly in "Blithedale." The suicide of Martha Hunt was an incident of the transcendental movement. That there were not other tragedies of the kind is surprising. Many whose story has found no chronicler must have been brought into sad discord with their environment.

I suspect that the Faun in "Transformation" may be partly traceable to an incident which, though found in a book, was of a kind likely to haunt Hawthorne's imagination. In his "Recollections of Byron and Shelley" Trelawney says: "I asked Fletcher to bring me a glass of water; and on his leaving the room, to confirm or remove my doubts as to the cause of his lameness, I uncovered the Pilgrim's feet and was answered — both his feet were clubbed and the legs withered to the knee; the form and face of an Apollo, with the feet and legs of a sylvan satyr." Trelawney's book appeared just as Hawthorne was starting out from Liverpool on his journey to Italy. The incident just quoted was one which would have shocked his moral sense, but also might easily have taken shape in his artistic sense, and re-appeared in the spiritualised Faun. Hawthorne very rarely gained any hint from any other imagination. The only story he ever wrote which might have been suggested by another is "Feathertop." The theme is nearly that of Tieck's "Scarecrow" (*Die Vogelscheuche*), and turns on the career of a scarecrow which a witch has made into a fine gentleman. In Hawthorne's early journal at Concord he speaks of trying to translate a story of Tieck's, and probably this was the one; probably also he never got through it, for the two stories diverge widely.

There is a little story of Hawthorne's which may have flowered out of the tradition of an old house at Concord — "A Virtuoso's Collection." This Virtuoso, who has collected so many mythical things, and such specimens as a sonnet by Jones Very and an humble-bee, contributed by Emerson, turns out to be the Wandering Jew. It was probably about ten years after this was written that Hawthorne purchased the old house at Concord known as the Wayside. Concerning this new residence he wrote to his friend G. W. Curtis, "I know nothing of the history of the house except Thoreau's telling me that it was inhabited a century or two ago by a man who believed he should never die." When the Wayside was prepared for Hawthorne's residence, Mr. Bronson Alcott undertook to make it and the hillside behind it picturesque, and his visionary theories about the duration of life may have unfolded for Hawthorne another leaf on the stem which was growing from the Virtuoso, Ahasuerus, to Septimius. Mr. Alcott once told me that he came in with this century and intended to go out with it. His old theories about the effect on life and character of vegetables ripened in the sun, and such as are underground, demonic, had an irritating effect upon Carlyle. "There is Piccadilly," he broke out once while they walked and talked there; "there it has been for a hundred years, and there it will be when you and your damned potato-gospel are dead and forgotten." But Hawthorne found in Alcott and his speculations a picturesque subject. It is curious enough to find the young writer about the Eternal Jew afterwards dwelling in this house in Concord said to have been occupied by one of the undying, and the scenery of the old Indian settlement with its wizard Sachem re-appearing as Concord and its vegetarian visionary.

It must have seemed to Nathaniel and Sophia Hawthorne a very long pilgrimage that had brought them from the Old Manse to that pretty villa, little as is the distance. It was with a sigh that Hawthorne responded to the kindness of the Hon. George Bancroft, Secretary of the Navy, in appointing him surveyor of the port of Salem. It ended his poverty, but also his paradise. It seemed also a farewell to his literary aims. It was during the years between 1846, when he received his appointment, and 1849, when he was removed, that he was haunted by the spirits of "The Scarlet Letter." One very intimate with him told me a pleasant story about it. One wintry day he received at his office notification that his services would no longer be required. With heaviness of heart he repairs to his humble home. His young wife recognises the change, and stands waiting for the silence to be broken. At length he falters, "I am removed from office." Then she leaves the room; soon she returns with fuel and kindles a bright fire with her own hand; next brings pen, paper, ink, and sets them beside him. Then she touches the sad man on the shoulder, and, as he turns to the beaming face, says, "Now you can write your book!" The cloud cleared away. The lost office looked like a cage from which he had escaped. The book was written; it was welcomed by the publisher, who knew how to think and write — yes, and how to be a friend — James Fields, and who never penned a sentence with more pleasure than when (1851) he wrote to Miss Mitford:

"A few days ago the author of 'The Scarlet Letter' came to Boston after an absence of many months Every eye glistened as it welcomed an author whose genius seems to have filled his native land quite suddenly with his fame. He blushes like a girl when he is praised."

When his old college-friend Franklin Pierce was nominated for the Presidency, Hawthorne wrote a biography of him; and when, after election, Pierce appointed him Consul at Liverpool, some, who did not know Hawthorne, regarded the proceeding as a bargain. The truth was, Hawthorne was intensely loyal to the few intimate friends of his life, and he could not be persuaded of anything against Franklin Pierce, who, indeed, had many amiable qualities. When Pierce had become exceedingly unpopular in the country, Hawthorne stood by him even to his cost, and insisted on dedicating " Our Old Home" to him, despite the protest of his publishers.

This man, who had inherited from an ancestry of soldiers a port and courage equal to the bravest of them, had gained from the record of their cruelties a horror of bloodshed, something like that of a Confederate soldier of my acquaintance, who, since the American war refuses to kill a mosquito. Probably his "democratic" sympathies were largely due to his dread of the conflict to which the anti-slavery agitation was leading.

The shadow that fell upon Hawthorne's patriotic heart from the blackening sky of his country was for a time forgotten in the shadow of death that seemed to be drawing near and nearer his daughter Una. From that long illness in Rome this lovely girl seemed to recover, but not her father. He came back to England and wrote "Transformation." He went to Leamington and other pretty places, but found that he could not write well amid ornamental and social surroundings, so his dear friend Francis Bennoch found a wild and desolate seaside place, Redcar, where, in a seclusion like that of the Concord snowstorms, which protected his hours of inspiration, those exquisite creations were finished

When he foresaw the civil war in America to be inevitable, Hawthorne said to a friend in Liverpool that he meant to "go home and die with the Republic." The war did indeed wear deeply upon his mind and health. He could not share the high hopes which sustained his nearest friends during those terrible years; he could not see beyond the black cloud a country liberated from the blight of slavery. To him the war was an overwhelming tragedy, and the inevitable end seemed to be the end of the Republic.

These forebodings found much to foster them in the earlier course of the war. Hawthorne visited Washington, and on his return wrote that strange account of his observations and reflections there which appeared in the "Atlantic Monthly" for July, 1862. That paper is a notable instance of the subtlety of Hawthorne's art, which in this case has deceived even so subtle an artist as Henry James, jun. "The article," says Mr. James in his Biography of Hawthorne, "has all the usual merit of such sketches on Hawthorne's part — the merit of delicate, sportive feeling, expressed with consummate grace; but the editor of the periodical appears to have thought that he must give the antidote with the poison, and the paper is accompanied with several little notes disclaiming all sympathy with the writer's political heresies." The foot-notes here mentioned are severe, and sometimes contemptuous in their rebuke of the text; but they were written by Hawthorne himself! So, at any rate, I was assured by Emerson at the time, and as also about that time I passed a night at the house of Mr. Fields with Hawthorne, feel certain that this is the case. No doubt Mr. Fields had remonstrated with Hawthorne on some sentiments in the contribution to his magazine, but the sharp criticisms were by Hawthorne on himself.

Moreover, a close examination of these criticisms convinced me that they represented the real Hawthorne as fairly as the article itself. He was at this time painfully divided between his old prejudices against the Northern agitators for disunion in the interest of emancipation, and his growing horror against a war for disunion begun by their opponents for the sake of slavery. His patriotism, however, was impregnable.

I have before me two letters that have not been published. They were written by Emerson and Hawthorne to English correspondents, from whom I have received them. They were written in the midst of the war from the same historic town of Concord, and by the two chief representatives of the genius of New England, dwelling a few steps from each other. They are not presented for the sake of contrast, but as shewing what the two most far-reaching eyes in America beheld as they looked upon the great movement whose results are now history.

The letter of Emerson was written to the late Mrs. Joseph Biggs, at whose home in Leicester he was a guest, and whose friendship, as well as that of her husband, he much valued. In it he refers to "the probity and honour" of a protest she had written him "against what appears the governing opinion in England," and continues : — "I remember that Mr. Biggs in Leicester questioned me on the point, why good and cultivated men in America avoided politics (for so he had heard), and let them fall into bad hands? He will find in our calamities to-day the justification of his warning. Our sky is very dark, but the feeling is very general in the Union, that bad as the war is, it is far safer and better than the foregoing peace. Our best ground of hope now is the healthy sentiment which appears in reasonable people all over the country, accepting sacrifices, but meaning riddance from slavery and from Southern domination. I fear this sentiment is not yet represented by our Government or its agents in Europe, but it is sporadic in the country. Indeed, the Governments of both England and America are far in the rear of their best constituencies : in England, as shewn in the resolution with which the Government shuts its eyes to the building of ships of war in your ports to attack the Republic — *now* in this spasm to throw off slavery. This unlooked-for attitude of England is our gravest foreign disadvantage. But I have gone quite too far into these painful politics, whose gloom is only to be relieved by the largest considerations. I rejoice in so many assurances of sound heart and clear perception as come to us from excellent persons in England, — among which I rank your letter chiefly ; —and the significant sympathy of the Manchester workmen, which I wish had been better met."

The letter of Hawthorne was to Francis Bennoch: —

"MY DEAR B., — I owe you much in many ways, but there is one way in which I ought not to be your debtor, and that is in friendly correspondence.

"The truth is, that at present I have little heart for anything. We are, as you know, at the beginning of a great war — a war the issue of which no man can predicate, and I for one have no inclination to attempt prophesy. It is not long since the acute ruler of France — the epigrammatic speech-maker — announced to a startled Europe and a delighted country that he had gone to war for an idea, — a very nice, if not an absolutely true idea. But we Yankees have cast him entirely into the shade. We also have gone to war, and we seem to have little, or at least a very misty idea of what we are fighting for. It depends upon the speaker, and that again depends upon the section of the country in which his sympathies are enlisted. The Southern man will say: We fight for State rights, liberty, and independence. The Middle Western man will avow that he fights for the Union; whilst our Northern and Eastern man will swear that from the beginning his only idea was liberty to the Blacks and the annihilation of slavery. All are thoroughly in earnest, and all pray for the blessing of Heaven to rest upon the enterprise. The appeals are so numerous, fervent, and yet so contradictory, that the Great Arbiter to whom they so piously and solemnly appeal must be sorely puzzled how to decide. One thing is indisputable, — the spirit of our young men is thoroughly aroused. Their enthusiasm is boundless, and the smiles of our fragile and delicate women cheer them on. When I hear their drums beating, and see their banners flying, and witness their steady marching, I declare were it not for certain silvery monitors hanging by my temples suggesting prudence, I feel as if I could catch the infection, shoulder a musket, and be off to the war myself!

"Meditating on these matters, I begin to think our custom as to war is a mistake. Why draw from our young men, in the bloom and heyday of their youth, the soldiers who are to fight our battles? Had I my way, no man should go to war under fifty years of age, such men having already had their natural share of worldly pleasures, and life's enjoyments. And I don't see how they could make a more creditable or more honourable exit from the world's stage than by becoming food for powder and gloriously dying in defence of their home and country. Then I would add a premium in favour of recruits of three-score years and upwards, as, virtually with one foot in the grave, they would not be likely to run away. I apprehend that no people ever built up the skeleton of a warlike history so rapidly as we are doing. What a fine theme for the poet! If you were not born a Britisher, from whose country we expect no help and little sympathy, I would ask you for a martial strain — a song to be sung by our camp-fires to soothe the feelings and rouse the energies of our troops, inspiring them to meet like men the great conflict that awaits them, resolved to conquer or to die — if dying, still to conquer. Ten thousand poetasters have tried, and tried in vain, to give us a rousing

'Scots wha hae wi' Wallace bled.'

If we fight no better than we sing, may the Lord have mercy upon us, and upon the nation!

"In the excitement raging everywhere, don't you feel as if you could come and see America in time of war? The room bearing your name is ready; the fire is laid; and here we are prepared to give you welcome. Come and occupy the apartment dedicated to you. Come and let us talk over the many pleasant evenings we spent together in dear Old England. Come, and I promise that all distracting thoughts and disturbing circumstances shall be banished from us. And although our children are no longer children, I am sure they would unite with the older folk, and enjoy the opportunity of shewing that Yankee hearts never forget kindnesses, and long for the chance of repaying them, not as a cancelling of debt, but to prove how deeply kindly deeds are appreciated by them. We have national foibles; what nation has not? We have national peculiarities and whimsical caprices, but we are none the worse for them. We have many sins to answer for and many shortcomings, but ingratitude cannot be reckoned among them. So come, and let us prove that we are, one and all, affectionately your friends.—Always, &c., &c.

NATH. HAWTHORNE."

Shortly after Hawthorne's return from Europe, I met him at a dinner of the Literary Club in Boston. A larger number than usual had come together to welcome him home. He was more social and talkative than I had ever supposed he could be, but was much aged in appearance. He had repaired to his Concord home, and, could he only have escaped the sounds of war, perhaps he might have tasted at the Wayside a drop of that elixir which its old Sachem was fabled to possess. But he could not find repose, and instead of dreaming, like Septimius, of endless life, said that he hoped no trumpet, however angelic, would sound over his grave short of a thousand years.

When I passed a night with him under the roof of James T. Fields, after his return from Washington, he had the expression of one who had been wandering amid ruins — the ruins of his country. Mrs. Fields had invited a little company, but after the first arrivals Hawthorne made his escape to his room. At the request of Mrs. Fields, I went to ask if he could not come down, and found him deep in Defoe's "Short Stories." He did not emerge until the next morning at breakfast-time, and then, with the amusing look of a naughty child, pleaded that he had been carried off by Defoe's wicked ghosts. He must, I think, have been contemplating some phantasmal production at that time; for I remember his asking me questions about the ghost-beliefs of the negroes, among whom my early life was passed. One of these was of a negro who saw an enormous conflagration near by, but on reaching the spot found only one firecoal and heard a dog bark. Hawthorne was interested in this, and spoke in a sympathetic way about the negroes that I did not expect. But he evidently suspected that the war conflagration would end in a small ember for the negroes, and I suspect did not believe that race would be made happier than he had been by freedom and culture.

Hawthorne could see between the Old Manse and the Wayside a transformation as beautiful as that which gave Cinderella beauty for ashes: he saw his lovely and gifted children growing around him like fulfilments of what the riverside flowers had promised his early wedded happiness; and perhaps it seemed to him that it was well enough to pass away in that fulness of life. So it was. Amidst hearts that loved him he was carried to his repose in Sleepy Hollow.

And now that wife, whose literary ability the world was presently to know by her charming "Notes on England and Italy," devoted herself to the work of collecting those "Note-Books" of her husband which have made him an intimate friend of every mind worthy of his friendship. In London she made her home while engaged in this work, and she was surrounded by the books and pictures he had treasured. When they were brought over, an edition of "Waverley" which Hawthorne had prized was seized at the Liverpool Custom-house, but the letter she wrote the inspector made him forget all regulations, and the volumes were forwarded.

Hawthorne once wrote from England to a friend: "Of all things, I should like to find a gravestone in one of these old churchyards with my name upon it; although, for myself, I should wish to be buried in America." It was not very long before his name was read on an English gravestone. On March 4, 1871, when I stood beside the open grave of Mrs. Nathaniel Hawthorne in Kensal Green Cemetery, my vision wandered away to another in that little cemetery at Concord, which, though primitive, is also consecrated by the dust of noble spirits; and the two, so sundered, seemed to represent a happy tale suddenly broken off, and ending with heaviness and pain. She was laid to rest by those who had known and loved her — Francis Bennoch, W. H. Channing, Robert Browning, Russell Sturgis; and not far off the face of Leigh Hunt, from the marble over his grave, seemed to beam with sympathy upon the two lonely daughters of his friends. Before the coffin was lowered, these two — Una and Rose — laid upon it, the one a wreath, the other a cross, of white camelias. When the undertaker took up a handful of clay, Una held out her hand for it, and at the words "dust to dust" let the crumbled pieces fall there where lay the form of her mother.

This was the end. As we turned away the birds sang gaily amid the budding trees. I remembered the old scenes amid which these bereaved children first drew breath, and where, amid the budding joys and heart-melodies of his happiest home, their father wrote, "There is a pervading blessing diffused over all the world. I look out of the window and think: O perfect day! O beautiful world! O good God! And such a day is the promise of a blissful eternity. It opens the gates of heaven and gives glimpses far inward."

XXV.

THOREAU.

WHEN Emerson was giving a course of lectures in my church at Cincinnati, he consented to address the children on Sunday morning. Many times have I regretted that no reporter was present to preserve that address. It was given without notes, and its effect upon the large assembly of children could have been no less striking than that extemporaneous speech delivered by Emerson at the Burns Centenary, which so experienced a critic as Judge Hoar declares to be the grandest piece of eloquence he ever heard. Emerson, in this case as in that, held his hearers between smiles and tears. He began by telling them about his neighbour Henry Thoreau, and his marvellous knowledge of nature, his intimate friendship with flowers, and with the birds which lit on his shoulder, and with the fishes which swam into his hand. It was as if he were charming the children with a fairy-tale, or something omitted from the Gospel stories, which at the same time they felt to be true.

Not very long after (1862) Thoreau died — it was at the age of forty-five — and beside his grave at Concord Emerson delivered an address in which he said, "The country knows not yet, or in the least part, how great a son it has lost." And this is still true, although few men have ever had such full and interesting memoirs. Emerson wrote a sketch of his life; Ellery Channing has written a biography and a fine poem concerning him; James Russell Lowell, Wentworth Higginson, and George W. Curtis have written excellent essays upon him; and this year Frank B. Sanborn has published a Life of Thoreau, full of interesting details and shewing his unique relation to Concord, of which he was a native. In England, a book concerning him by "H. A. Page" appeared four years ago, and there have been some articles about him. I remember an able one in the "Saturday Review," in which, however, he was described, not happily I thought, as "an American Rousseau." Notwithstanding all this, there are comparatively few in America or England who have read the works of this rare genius. It was about four years after his "Week on the Concord and the Merrimack" was published that I spoke to him about that charming book, and he told me that the entire edition of it was still on the publisher's shelf with exception of copies he had given to his friends. Although he had found himself in debt for the printing, I thought he spoke of his book's obscurity with a certain satisfaction. Thoreau's books are so physiognomical that they seem to possess his own aversion to publicity. Like the pious Yogi, so long motionless whilst gazing on the sun that knotty plants encircled his neck and the cast snake-skin his loins, and the birds built their nests on his shoulders, this poet and naturalist, by equal consecration, became a part of the field and forest; and he with his books, — to read which is like walking amid meadows and magnolias, or in woods melodious with nightingales,—might naturally be undiscovered in the landscape by the great world thundering past in its train.

In the annals of Tours several hundred years ago this name recurs in connection with its government, but it was from St. Heliers in Jersey that the first American of that name emigrated. I remember well the stolid, taciturn pencil-maker his father, and his simple mother, and long ago came to the conclusion that the great Thoreau was what the Buddha would call a "twice-born" man. He was born in Concord, and entered Harvard University in 1833, the year of Emerson's first visit to England. Emerson had been residing in Concord two or three years when he discovered this scholar, then twenty years of age. The family was poor, and Thoreau taught school a little and made pencils a little, but read and thought a great deal. At an early period he made up his mind that his road to wealth lay in not wanting things. If he were as satisfied not to have a coach as his neighbour was in having one, was he not quite as well off as that neighbour? "If I had the wealth of Crœsus bestowed on me," he was at length able to say, "my aims must still be the same, and my means the same."

Emerson took me to see Thoreau, and I remember that he asked me what we were studying at Divinity College. I answered, "The Scriptures." "Which?" he asked. I was puzzled until Emerson said, "I fear you will find our Thoreau a sad pagan." Thoreau had long been a reverent student of Oriental bibles, and, like Morgana in the story, had marked all the sacred doors with the same sign, so that Hebrew were not distinguishable from Hindu inspirations. He now shewed me his bibles, translated from various races into French and English, presented him by an English friend. Mr. Cholmondeley.

In this conversation with Thoreau I perceived that he was not in the least like his parents, but closely resembled Emerson. His features, expression, tones of voice, were more like those of Emerson than any likeness I have known between brothers. This phenomenon was, no doubt, the result of the naturalist's genius. Emerson may have thought of Thoreau in his quatrain —

> "He took the colour of his vest
> From rabbit's coat and grouse's breast;
> For as the wild kinds lurk and hide,
> So walks the huntsman unespied."

But meanwhile Thoreau, while he hunted the wild kinds with spyglass and microscope, and became friendly with them, was pursuing more ardently winged thoughts and mystical secrets. He cared most, as he said, to "fish in the sky, whose bottom is pebbly with stars." He once said to me that he had found in Emerson a world where truths existed with the same perfection as the objects he studied in external nature, his ideas real and exact as antennæ and stamina. It was nature spiritualised. I also found that Thoreau had entered deeply Emerson's secret, and was the most complete incarnation of the earlier idealism of the Sage. But because this influence was in the least part personal, the resemblance of Thoreau to Emerson was as superficial as a leaf-like creature to a leaf. Thoreau was quite as original as Emerson. He was not an imitator of any mortal; his thoughts and expressions are suggestions of a Thoreau-principle at work in the universe. A lady who had known Wordsworth in her girlhood told me that he looked as if nature had adopted him, the furrows in his face as if stained by lichens; and I at once thought of Thoreau, in whose eye was the clear Walden Water, and on his brow the peace of pastures and purity of the river lilies, as well as the grace of Emerson.

In 1845 Thoreau built himself a hut with his own hands on the shore of Walden, — that lakelet of a mile and three quarters circumference, which is a pure perennial spring, framed in a wood of oak and pine. It is without visible inlet or outlet, and so transparent, that once when Thoreau's axe fell into it, he saw it at a great depth and recovered it. It was then that socialistic experiments were rife, and Thoreau would shew that educated man could build his house and live happily in nature without impawning his hours or sacrificing life to the means of living. The land was given him, I believe, by Emerson; the house cost him twenty-eight dollars twelve and a half cents; and he lived there, from July 4 to March 1, at a total expense of sixty-two dollars, less one mill. But I cannot help suspecting that a perilous Erl-King's daughter lurked in the beauty of Walden Water, and drew away the life of Thoreau. He was not so strong as his frame suggested his right to be, and died of consumption at forty-five.

But they who read the book that came from that Walden hermitage will know that by a true estimate

Thoreau lived very long. This spiritual Pan naturally had a flute, and he drew wild creatures to him with its music. A mouse became familiar, played bo-peep, and ate from his hand. There was a pet mole in his cellar. Of a sparrow that came to sit on his shoulder he was prouder than any warrior of his epaulette. A phœbe built in his shed, the robin in a pine that waved over his house, and a partridge with her brood fed beneath his window. A fox that had been attracted by the light retreated barking " a vulpine curse," but the owl said, "*How der do?*" He observes them all with the eye and ear of a scientific Pilpay. He has a Darwinian dream of his own, though there is more of transmigration than evolution in it. " If we take the ages into our account, may there not be a civilisation going on among brutes as well as men? They seem to me to be rudimental, burrowing men, still standing on their defence, awaiting their transformation."

Over the door of Thoreau's cabin was written for those who could read it : " Entertainment for man, but not for beast." The beasts were welcome too, if they did not come in human disguise. Hither in the snows came the fools of ideas, the victims of crotchets, the running slave, — whom he sheltered on his road to the North Star, — and also the poets and philosophers. In Walden they are all botanised and zoologised upon as precisely as their poor relations who came on fins, wings, or all-fours ; from the man of one idea to the intellectual centipede ; from the minister who spoke of God as if he " enjoyed a monopoly of the subject," to the philosopher with whom he made a new theory of life over a convivial dish of gruel.

On my first walk with Thoreau we started westward, for he liked to order his morning walk after the movement of the race. The sun is the first western pioneer; he sets his Hesperian fruits on the horizon to lure the human race; therefore we will go by Goosepond to Baker's Farm. Of every acre, he contended, the western side was wildest, therefore fittest to explore. *Ex oriente lux, ex occidente frux.* This new acquaintance filled up my idea of Julius Cæsar, such was the courage and repose in his countenance. His nose was Roman-aquiline, strong and bold, like the prow of a ship, above which watched his wonderful eye, that seemed to reach a far horizon. His powers of conversation were great. At every step I was surprised and delighted by his recognition of laws and significant attributes in common things, as a relation between grasses and geologic characters beneath them; the grouping of various pine-needles, and the effect of their differences on the sounds they yield when struck by the wind; and the "shades" of taste, so to say, represented by different herbs. I cannot remember the name of some little herb he gave me to taste; it was acrid and biting, but tastes very sweet in memory along with his talk about the resolute individuality of some of these lowly organisations.

Thoreau had a calendar of the plants and flowers of the neighbourhood, and would sometimes go a long way around to visit some floral friend whom he had not seen for a year. On one occasion when I was living at Poukawtassett Hill, he mentioned the *hibiscus* beside the river, — a rare flower in New England, — and when I desired to see it, told me it would be open "about Monday, and not stay long." I went on Tuesday afternoon and was a day too late — the petals lay on the ground.

Though shy of general society, Thoreau was a hero among children and the captain of their excursions. He was captain of the Concord huckleberry party, which was an institution. To have Thoreau along with us was to be sure of finding acres of bushes laden with the delicious fruit. On these occasions his talk with the children was as a part of the spirit and circumstance which go to make up what is called in American phrase "a good time." A child stumbles and falls, losing his carefully gathered store of berries; Thoreau kneels beside the weeping unfortunate, and explains to him and the pitying group that nature has made these little provisions for next year's crop. If there were no obstacles, and little boys did not fall occasionally, how would berries be scattered and planted? and what would become of huckleberryings? He will then arrange that he who has thus suffered for the general good shall have the first chance at the next pasture.

Sometimes I have gone with Thoreau and his young comrades for an expedition on the river. Upon such excursions his resources for our entertainment were inexhaustible. He would tell stories of the Indians who once dwelt thereabout, until the children almost looked to see a red man skulking with his arrow on shore; and every plant or flower on the bank or in the water, and every fish, turtle, frog, lizard about us was transformed by the wand of his knowledge from the low form into which the spell of our ignorance had reduced its princely beauty. One of his surprises was to thrust his hand softly into the water, and raise up before our astonished eyes a bright fish which lay in his hand as if they were old acquaintances! If the fish had also dropped a penny from its mouth, it could not have been a more miraculous proceeding to us. The entire crew bared their arms and tried to get hold of a fish, but only our captain succeeded. We could not get his secret from him then, for it was to surprise and delight many another merry boat-full; but later I have read in his account of the bream or ruff (*Pomotis vulgaris*) of that river, that it is a simple and inoffensive fish, whose nests are visible all along the shore, hollowed in the sand, over which it is steadily poised through the summer hours on waving fin. "The breams are so careful of their charge, that you may stand close by in the water and examine them at your leisure. I have thus stood over them half an hour at a time, and stroked them familiarly without frightening them: suffering them to nibble my fingers harmlessly; and seen them erect their dorsal fins in anger when my hand approached their ova; and have even taken them gently out of the water with my hand."

Thoreau had taken deeply to heart the one thing needful for a soul born within sound of "Concordia," — that the time and place were cosmical. Margaret Fuller was inclined to rebuke this before she had learned by sad experience how much truth lay in his humourous motto, *Ne quid quæsiveris extra te Concordiamque*. Emerson relates that he returned "Kane's Arctic Voyage" to a friend with the remark, that "most of the phenomena noted might be observed in Concord!" He seemed a little envious of the Pole for the coincident sunrise and sunset, or five minutes' day after six months, a splendid fact which Annursnuc had never afforded him. He found red snow in one of his walks near Concord, and was hoping one day to find the Victoria Regia. He reported to Emerson somewhat triumphantly that the foreign savants had failed to discriminate a particular botanical variety. "That is to say," replied Emerson, "the blockheads were not born in Concord; but who said they were? It was their unspeakable misfortune to be born in London, or Paris, or Rome; but, poor fellows! they did what they could, considering that they never saw Bateman's Pond, or Nine-Acre Corner, or Becky Stow's Swamp. Besides, what were you sent into the world for but to add this observation?" He would not read the newspapers, which demanded his attention most impertinently for Europe or Washington instead of Walden Pond. One of his beatitudes ran — "Blessed are the young, for they do not read the President's Message." Of friends who read to him of the Crimean war he asks, "Pray, to be serious, where is Sevastopol? Who is Menchikoff?" and goes on to meditate on the white oak in his stove.

Thoreau was so resolute in his anti-slavery principles that he refused to pay taxes which might be used for the enormities of a Pro-slavery Government, and for this went to prison, of which he wrote an account that makes it all look now like a little comedy got up between him and the authorities. I remember on an occasion he addressed an anti-slavery meeting and said, "You have my sympathy; it is all I have to give you, but you will find it important to you." This transcendental remark impressed some who heard it as egotistical, but they discovered ere long that to have with them such impartial and solitary thinkers and scholars as Thoreau meant a force which partisans could not resist. He remembered with satisfaction that he rang the town-bell in 1844, when Emerson delivered his great anti-slavery address; now audible as "Concordia" sounding a first note in the chimes of liberty.

Thoreau was a profoundly religious man, and I fear it must be confessed that it was due to this that, in the absence of resources to win popularity, he could never gain an audience in the country, and readily adapted himself to obscurity. Of course, if he had been superficially religious it would have been another thing; but he was convinced that the only way to understand Christ was to get rid of Christianity, and that theology was the only blasphemy. His articles were repeatedly refused by papers and magazines because he would interpolate sentences of this kind in them. Emerson told me one day that an editor had begged him to persuade Thoreau to write him an article containing no allusion to "God." How can I better shew the religiousness of this noble nature or close this little sketch than by reporting his answer to one who approached him on his death-bed to speak of a future life? Thoreau simply said — "One world at a time."

XXVI.

"THE COMING MAN."

THIS phrase became the cant of tabernacle-builders in the transcendental movement, and passed away with their tabernacles — why they never knew, for their eyes were heavy under the splendour of the transfiguration before them; but, in reality, the man had come, only with heart matched with the need of a world, by no means with the need of any socialist or other sect striving to grow amid ruins imported from the past, or imitations of them.

At Paris, on the opening of the International Exposition of 1867, I found many Americans ashamed of the poor display made by their country. The department seemed a wilderness, broken only by a few unopened boxes that promised little. But I could not share their chagrin. Indeed, I was rather glad to have my countrymen taught, even at cost of some humiliation, that Protectionists cannot change the order of the world nor make America excel in works that can be done better and more cheaply elsewhere. Not for fine cloths and cutlery would I see duplicates of Sheffield, of Manchester, and the Black Country in America. Let the banner of stars float over empty spaces in exhibitions until it can wave over original products instead of facsimiles, which only divert hands that might be developing new resources. Let Europe make our knives and boots, and welcome. Yet America was not unrepresented at Paris. At the end of the section were Bierstadt's picture of the Rocky Mountains, Church's Niagara, and close to these a fine portrait of Emerson, and I felt that this group of physical grandeurs, and the best head to match them, constituted the fair symbol and true exposition of that splendid possibility which America is.

I do not know exactly when Nathaniel Hawthorne wrote his tale "The Great Stone Face," but it was amid much talk about the Coming Man, and probably when he recognised the Man Come, who visited Blithedale when he was there. The suggestion, no doubt, came from the Profile Mountain of New Hampshire. I remember a vacation ramble with fellow-students when this wonderful profile came in view. One cried, "It is the face of Carlyle!" That face was familiar to us all by portraits, and the resemblance was unmistakable. The jutting brow, the strong underface, the delicate mouth, are all there; and, above all, the pathetic look, as of a world pain, was in this great stone face, gazing out above the lower earth to a far horizon, as if waiting for a star not yet risen to relieve its weary watch of ages.

This "Old Man of the Mountains," as the peasants call it, requires a long perspective. They who have travelled towards it have found it vanishing at their approach, and have reached at last a few acres of rugged and blanched desolation. Carlyle, too, as we have seen, cannot be approached too closely; even now we are beholding the blanched and jagged points into which he has been resolved. A farther perspective will again restore the majestic face, but it will always be that of a genius fettered in the Puritan creed, from whose stony side he could only gaze above and beyond the laughing plains of human life to Titans bound on summits like his own. Emerson, beginning a new race of Titans, had recognised this lonely face in the Highlands of Scotland, and had sailed the sea like Herakles when he went to unbind Prometheus. There was good reason why he should first recognise the pain in that face, for it was akin to the intellectual despair in America also.

In Hawthorne's tale the country boy gazes upon the Great Stone Face, seeing in it the unfading light of a prophecy that "The Coming Man," of which so much was said, is to resemble it; he loves and almost worships the Face, and whenever any famous personage comes into his region he hastens to gaze upon him, hoping to discover a likeness to the Face. He has to turn away sorrowful from the applauded general or president, until at last he is astounded to find himself hailed, despite his protest, as antitype of the Great Stone Face — the Coming Man!

Hawthorne's tale told truer than even his subtle power of divination could have imagined when he wrote it. On the great stone face of Puritanism Emerson had gazed till he saw the pain and pathos in it, and the prophecy in its look towards the far horizon; its mountain risen from volcanic depths now cold, its summit clouded with scepticism, commanded yet this one vision of a new faith, real as that which drew scholars and tender women from their English universities and homes to the savage shores of New England; and Emerson, who had sought the new word near and far, from the lecture-room of Everett and church of Channing to the hermitage of Wordsworth and Carlyle, was surprised in his own solitude by the youth of America hailing him as their prophet.

The political and social independence which Puritanism sailed across the sea to maintain, then surrendered to the Presbyter or "Priest writ large;" the intellectual liberty which Unitarianism affirmed, then denied to those who passed by its own transubstantiations of the dogmas; these were made real by Emerson. Under his spirit, as if under a tropical breath, arose strange spiritual fauna and flora; he did not tolerate but rejoiced in them. With the divine impartiality of the earth he nourished every variety of thought and aim from his great heart.

In "The White Lotus" Buddha teaches: "The rays of intelligence make the order of venerable teachers. They are all and equally born to unite science and virtue. The Great Repose results from the comprehension of the equality of all laws; there is only one, not two or three. I explain the law to all creatures, after having recognised their inclinations. It is as a cloud with a garland of lightning spreads joy on the earth; the water falls on all creatures, herbs, bushes, trees, and each pumps up to its own leaf and blossom what it requires for its several end. So falls the rain of the law upon the many-hearted world. The law is for millions; but it is one and alike beautiful to all — it is deliverance and repose."

Let my reader compare with this strain of the Eastern this of the Western seer, from the " Dial : " —

" No one can converse much with different classes of society in New England without remarking the progress of a revolution. Those who share in it have no external organisation, no badge, no creed, no name. They do not vote, or print, or even meet together. They do not know each other's faces or names. . . . This spirit of the time is felt by every individual, with some difference — to each one casting its light upon the objects nearest to his temper and habits of thought — to one coming in the shape of special reforms in the state ; to another, in modification of the various callings of men and the customs of business ; to a third, opening a new scope for literature and art ; to a fourth, in philosophical insight ; to a fifth, in the vast solitudes of prayer. It is in every form a protest against usage and a search for principles. . . . It has a step of Fate, and goes on existing like an oak or a river, because it must."

For this beautiful work Emerson was in every way furnished with ability. On this point, however, I shall here quote Margaret Fuller's account of his lecturing.

" The audience that waited for years upon the lectures was never large, but it was select and it was constant. Among the hearers were some who, though, attracted by the beauty of character and manner, they were willing to hear the speaker through, yet always went away discontented. They were accustomed to an artificial method, whose scaffolding could easily be retraced, and desired an obvious sequence of logical influences. They insisted there was nothing in that which they heard, because they could not give a clear account of its course and purport. They did not see that Pindar's odes might be very well arranged for their own purpose, and yet not bear translating into the methods of Mr. Locke. Others were content to be benefited by a good influence without a strict analysis of its means. 'My wife says it is about the elevation of human nature, and so it seems to me,' was a fit reply to some of the critics. Many were satisfied to find themselves excited to congenial thought and nobler life without an exact catalogue of the thoughts of the speaker. Those who believed no truth could exist unless encased by the burrs of opinion, went away utterly baffled. Sometimes they thought he was on their side; then presently would come something on the other. He really seemed to believe there were two sides to every subject, and even to intimate higher ground, from which each might be seen to have an infinite number of sides or bearings — an impertinence not to be endured! The partisan heard but once and returned no more. But some there were — simple souls — whose life had been, perhaps, without clear light, yet still a search after truth for its own sake, who were able to receive what followed on the suggestion of a subject in a natural manner as a stream of thought. These recognised beneath the veil of words the still small voice of conscience, the vestal fires of lone religious hours, and the mild teachings of the summer woods.

"The charm of the elocution, too, was great. His general manner was that of the reader, occasionally rising into direct address or invocation in passages where tenderness or majesty demanded more energy. At such times both eye and voice called on a remote future to give a worthy reply — a future which shall manifest more largely the universal soul as it was then manifest to this soul. The tone of the voice was a grave body-tone, full and sweet rather than sonorous, yet flexible and haunted by many modulations, as even instruments of wood and brass seem to become after they have been long played on with skill and taste; how much more so the human voice! In the most expressive passages it uttered notes of silvery clearness, winning, yet still more commanding. The words uttered in those tones floated a while above us, then took root in the memory like winged seed.

"In the union of an even rustic plainness with lyric inspiration, religious dignity with philosophic calmness, keen sagacity in details with boldness of view, we saw what brought to mind the early poets and legislators of Greece — men who taught their fellows to plough and avoid moral evil, sing hymns to the gods and watch the metamorphosis of nature. Here in civic Boston was such a man — one who could see man in his original grandeur and his original childishness, rooted in simple nature, raising to the heavens the brow and eye of a poet."

When Emerson's fame among his few first friends, extended only by the noisy resentment of theologians, had drawn "respectable" Boston to hear his early lectures, he had sometimes to speak to audiences that had not yet ears to hear him. The poet Longfellow, who attended a course given in Boston on Human Culture, said to me that it was better than a play to observe the mass of the audience. Things, he said, had so long gone on in their old mill-round in Boston, that the report of something new, and of a preacher who wouldn't administer the sacraments, drew as many as would have come to see a live mermaid combing her hair with a shell. When he began, an awful silence prevailed; every eye was lit up with expectation, every head inclined forward. This was at eight o'clock; at ten minutes past, a kind of despair began to appear on each face, though still inclined forward, and a ray of hope that something would yet be understood still visible in the eye; twenty minutes past, the heads fallen a little back; half-past, bodies returned to comfortable postures, but eyes lowered with a sense of their littleness; forty minutes past, it was as if some one had gone round and turned off the light of every countenance; the last ten minutes was a time of general and profound repose, amid which three or four faces could be seen kindled to ecstasy.

But the three or four kindled ones that Longfellow saw in the heavy-eyed crowd steadily and swiftly multiplied. And they who came to his fontless baptism were never made Emersonians. The new literary age which dates from Emerson has produced works which could not have appeared if he had not lived; and no doubt in some of them thoughts or even phrases of his may be found; but these are exceptional enough to prove the rule to be the reverse. It would be difficult to cite from any generation authors so various in aim and style as those whose minds have been personally and strongly influenced by Emerson.

I recall the vigorous way in which Emerson, warning parents against what he quaintly called disobedience to children, said in a lecture, "Get off that child! You are trying to make that man another you. Once is enough." The patriarch of Concord never made that blunder in the world he created.

This principle lay so deep in Emerson, and so pervaded his influence, that his voice was ultimately heard calming the angry elements even of theology. He was once defining eloquence, and said that it was a power which could soothe and calm a company on a ship foundered in mid-Atlantic. Looking back upon his work, the thinkers and scholars of America would surely consent to this as a true illustration of what the voice of Emerson has done among those who were panic-stricken at the wreck of another kind of ship. Theological polemics are hopelessly vulgarised, and whatever shall follow the foundered faith, it will surely be catholic.

XXVII.

THE PYTHON.

EMERSON was the first American scholar to cast a dart at slavery. On Sunday, May 29, 1831, he admitted an abolitionist to lecture on the subject in his church, and in the following year another was invited to his pulpit. The dates are important. This was six years before even Channing had committed himself to that side. Garrison was at that time regarded as a vulgar street-preacher of notions too wild to excite more than a smile. The despised group of Boston Common was first sheltered by Emerson, and this action was the more significant because he was chaplain of the Massachusetts Legislature, which could hardly have contained one anti-slavery member. Emerson first drew the sympathy of scholars to that side. The voices of the two popular orators, Channing and Phillips, soon followed, and Longfellow began to write the anti-slavery poems collected in 1842.

When, in 1835, Harriet Martineau was nearly mobbed in Boston, and no prominent citizen ventured to her side, Emerson and his brother Charles hastened to her defence. "At the time of the hubbub against me in Boston," she wrote, "Charles Emerson stood alone in a large company in defence of the right of free thought and speech, and declared that he had rather see Boston in ashes than that I or anybody else should be debarred in any way from perfectly free speech. His brother Waldo invited me to be his guest in the midst of my unpopularity."

On November 7, 1837, the Rev. E. P. Lovejoy, an abolitionist, was shot by a mob at Alton, Illinois, while attempting to defend his printing-press from destruction. Some citizens of Boston, headed by Dr. Channing, petitioned the mayor of that city for permission to hold a meeting in Faneuil Hall, "the Cradle of Liberty," and it was refused. The Attorney-General of Massachusetts said that Lovejoy had "died as the fool dieth," and such was the general opinion of "respectability." In a lecture on Heroism, Emerson said, "Whoso is heroic will always find crises to try his edge. Human virtue demands her champions and martyrs, and the trial of persecution always proceeds. It is but the other day that the brave Lovejoy gave his breast to the bullets of a mob for the right of free speech and opinion, and died when it was better not to live." George Bradford says that some of Emerson's friends "felt the sort of cold shudder which ran through the audience at this calm braving of the current opinion." The audience had been "carried on and lifted up" by the speaker's celebrations of heroism in other lands and ancient times, but when he recognised a hero in the lynched abolitionist, they "were wholly unprepared for this unexpected turn and shock;" and Emerson's friends were in terror.

Emerson could not throw himself into any organisation, nor did he encourage the scholars around him to do so; he believed that to elevate character, to raise the ethical standard, to inspire courage in the intellect of the nation, would speedily make its atmosphere too pure for a slave to breathe. He even resented the peremptory demand of the abolitionists that every kind of work should be postponed to their cause. Fearless in vindicating those whose convictions led them to enlist for this particular struggle, Emerson saw in slavery one among many symptoms of the moral disease of the time. "The timidity of our public opinion is our disease, or, shall I say, the absence of private opinion. Good nature is plentiful, but we want justice with heart of steel to fight down the proud. The private mind has the access to the totality of goodness and truth, that it may be a balance to a corrupt society, and to stand for the private verdict against popular clamour is the office of the noble. If a humane measure is propounded in behalf of the slave, or of the Irishman, or of the Catholic, or for the succour of the poor, that sentiment, that project, will have the homage of the hero. That is his nobility, his oath of knighthood, to succour the helpless and oppressed; always to throw himself on the side of weakness, of youth, of hope, on the liberal, on the expansive side, never on the conserving, the timorous, the lock-and-bolt system. More than our good-will we may not be able to give. We have our own affairs, our own genius, which chains us to our proper work. We cannot give our life to the cause of the debtor, of the slave, or the pauper, as another is doing; but to one thing we are bound, not to blaspheme the sentiment and the work of that man, nor to throw stumbling-blocks in the way of the abolitionist, the philanthropist, as the organs of influence and opinion are swift to do."

Emerson had as much practical sagacity as genius; when he spoke the words just quoted (in a lecture in Boston, February 7, 1844) he had reached a commanding position, carrying with it gravest responsibilities; the destinies of best young men and women were determined by his word. But in this early anti-slavery movement he did more than he exacted from others, and recognised it as a far more important reform than others. In 1844, when coloured citizens of Massachusetts had been taken to prison from ships in Southern ports, Emerson delivered an oration in Concord on the anniversary of West Indian emancipation, and spoke sternly on the matter. "If such a damnable outrage can be committed on the person of a citizen with impunity, let the Governor break the broad seal of the State; he bears the sword in vain. The Governor of Massachusetts is a trifler; the State-house in Boston is a playhouse; the General Court is a dishonoured body, if they make laws which they cannot execute. The great-hearted Puritans have left no posterity." He demanded that the representatives of the State should demand of Congress the instant release, by force if necessary, of the imprisoned negro seamen, and their indemnification. "As for dangers to the Union from such demands, the Union is already at an end when the first citizen of Massachusetts is thus outraged."

This address, in which the heroic story of West Indian emancipation was told in simplest words and with thrilling effect, and the lesson plainly applied to America, became of historic importance. Thoreau always remembered with pleasure that he rang the bell which summoned the people to the town-hall that day, where the representatives of thirteen towns assembled. In a contemporary paragraph in the "Herald of Freedom" its effect upon the abolitionists is indicated. "Imagine a face expressive alike of great intellectual power and sweetness of nature; eyes which at times seem to look into another world with far-seeing and prophetic ken; a mouth of chiselled beauty which never speaks but to utter the most melodious, the most exquisite intonations of which the English language is capable. Behold the speaker before you. He appears for the first time on the anti-slavery platform. You expect that he will look at his subject from an intellectual point of view merely; that he will give an impartial judgment on the merits and the faults of abolitionism, and stand on a clear eminence above the dust and turmoil of the movement. But not so. Behold he has descended among us. He grasps our hands with warm and earnest pressure, and says, 'Brothers, I have come to enter with you into this holy war. My arm and my heart are yours, and here do I pledge myself henceforth to do battle in your cause till you have gained the victory.' I wish I could picture to you the audience as it listened in rapt and breathless attention to the speaker as he detailed the progress of British emancipation from its commencement to its close, and then contrasted the noble course of British statesmen with that of their descendants in our own country, and branded the latter with its deserved meed of reproach and contempt. As he pictured the infinite wrongs of the coloured man and his godlike patience, our hearts swayed to and fro at his bidding, and tears found their way down the cheeks of sturdy men as well as of tender-hearted maidens. When the last word was spoken its music still lingered in our ears, and silence alone seemed a fitting expression of our deep and absorbing delight. The faint clapping of hands, which a few attempted, died away immediately as inappropriate to the occasion."

Probably it was this brave note coming from the first battlefield of American independence which led the Governor of Massachusetts to select the Hon. Samuel Hoar, Emerson's friend and neighbour, to repair to South Carolina in order to institute proceedings for the release of the coloured seamen, on which the Legislature had resolved. Mr. Hoar and his daughter, who had been betrothed to Charles Emerson, proceeded to Charleston, South Carolina, from which place they were driven after repeated threats of violence. This incident produced much effect on Emerson's mind, but it could not swerve him from his method. "Let us withhold every reproachful, and, if we can, every indignant remark. In this cause we must renounce our temper and the risings of pride. If there be any man who thinks the ruin of a race of men a small matter compared with the last decorations and completions of his own comfort, who would not so much as part with his ice-cream to save them from rapine and manacles, I think I must not hesitate to satisfy that man that also his cream and vanilla are safer and cheaper by placing the negro nation on a fair footing than by robbing them. If the Virginian piques himself on the picturesque luxury of his vassalage, on the heavy Ethiopian manners of his house-servants, their silent obedience, their hue of bronze, their turbaned heads, and would not exchange them for the more intelligent but precarious hired services of whites, I shall not refuse to shew him that when their free papers are made out it will still be their interest to remain on his estates, and that the oldest planters of Jamaica are convinced that it is cheaper to pay wages than to own slaves."

The nearest thing to hero-worship that had ever been awakened in Emerson's breast probably was his early admiration for Daniel Webster. No one who in his youth has seen and heard that senator can wonder at the enthusiasm and hope with which Emerson once looked up to him as the man of the "Great Stone Face." "He looks like a sort of cathedral," said Carlyle when he saw Webster, forty-four years ago, and Emerson was happy at such admiration of his senator. Besides this, his brother Edward had studied law with Webster and received much kindness from him. It was a heavy blow to Emerson when Webster surrendered to slavery, and gave his aid to pass the Fugitive Slave Bill. The youth of Massachusetts, who worshipped the eloquent senator, were much demoralised by his course and speech; and Emerson, albeit with a heavy heart, for the first time took part in a political campaign. The Hon. J. G. Palfrey, whose opposition to the encroachments of slavery had cost him his seat in Congress, was nominated as Governor of Massachusetts, and Emerson made speeches in favour of his election. One of especial importance was given at Cambridge. The hall was crowded, chiefly by students, and Emerson, in the course of his speech, pictured the car of Slavery and its abominations, with Webster as leading horse straining to drag it. A storm of hisses, perhaps the first Emerson ever heard, broke through the middle of his first severe sentence. Emerson paused, but stood with face unmoved, as if it were an outside wind, then serenely continued with the very next word of the sentence as if there had been no uproar. With the tone of a judge pronouncing sentence he said of Webster, " Every drop of his blood has eyes that look downward. He knows the heroes of 1776, but cannot see those of 1851 when he meets them on the street."

Daniel Webster felt the rebuke of Emerson, at whose house he had been entertained, and in a letter printed in Sanborn's " Thoreau," gave as a reason for not visiting Concord that " many of those whom I so highly esteemed in your beautiful and quiet village have become a good deal estranged, to my great grief, by abolitionism, freesoilism, transcendentalism, and other notions which I cannot but regard as so many vagaries of the imagination.' When Webster died, broken-hearted at having failed in the great object, the Presidency, for which he had sacrificed so much, his best epitaph was the words of Emerson, " He had honour enough to feel degraded."

On the 7th of March, 1854, exactly four years after Webster's speech in defence of slave-hunting, when the country was agitated by a fresh aggression of slavery (the Nebraska Bill), Emerson delivered a remarkable address in New York. It was, he said, the stern edict of progress that liberty shall be no hasty fruit. It is the result of the perfectness of man. Mountains of difficulty must be surmounted, wiles of seduction must be met, dangers encountered. Man must be healed by a quarantine of calamities before he dare say " I am free ! ' The patience required is almost too sublime for mortals when one sees how fast the rot spreads. We demand of superior men that they shall be superior in this, that the mind and virtue of the country shall give their verdict in their day, and help to pull down the wrong. Possession is sure to throw its stupid strength for the existing power; appetite and ambition will go for that. Let the aid of virtue and intelligence be cast where they belong; they are organically ours. The English Earl Grey said on a memorable occasion, that " he should stand by his order." The instructed or illuminated class should know their own flag and not stand for the kingdom of darkness. We should not forgive the clergy of a country for taking on every issue the immoral side; nor should we justify a governor — as the Governor of Pennsylvania did — in sustaining a mob against the laws. The lovers of liberty may tax with coldness the scholars and literary class. They were all lovers of liberty in Greece, but the universities are now seats of conservatism. They grow worldly and political. He remembered an occasion when the university had a distinguished son returning from the political arena to address her. He listened to the speech of this orator, this eminent political man. If sometimes audiences forget themselves, statesmen do not. The low bows to all the crockery gods of the day were duly made — only that in one part of the discourse the orator allowed to transpire, against his will perhaps, a little sober sense. He would not say he said it, but this was what he (Emerson) heard in his ear: "I am, you see, a man virtuously inclined, but only corrupt by my profession of politics. I prefer to be upon the right side. You had the power to make your verdict clear and prevailing in favour of right, and had you done so, you would have found me your willing champion. But you have not done so — you have not armed me. I have to deal with men and things as they are. Abstractions are not for me. I go for such parties as they provide me with. Although I am now to tempt you, you see it is not my will, but my necessities which make me do so." Having made this declaration, he proceeded with his work of denouncing freedom, but with a lingering conscience which qualified each sentence with a recommendation to mercy. "But now, gentlemen," continued Emerson, "I put it to every noble and generous spirit in the land — to every poetic, to every heroic, to every religious heart — that not so are our learning, our education, our poetry, our worship to be declared; not by heads reverted to the dying Demosthenes, nor to Wallace, nor to George Fox, nor to George Washington, but to the dangers and dragons that beset the United States at this hour. Gentlemen, it is not possible to extricate one's self from the questions in which our age is involved. I hate that we should be content with standing on the defensive. Liberty is the crusade of all brave and conscientious men — the epic poetry, the new religion, the chivalry of all gentlemen."

About this time I was often with Emerson, as were other students, and the service we could render in the growing perils of freedom and of the country was often the subject of anxious consultation. Emerson was careful to remind us that slavery, like other wrongs, had invisible roots, and that no reform, however much so in appearance, was really radical, which did not cultivate the spiritual soil so that it would not bear rank and poisonous growths. "There is no man of any importance in our history, and none of our time, who has not spoken or recorded his word against slavery. Generally speaking, a sound man says, 'I have my own affair, and cannot do your affair well, but my opinion shall be given plainly.' But when the ship is in a storm the passengers must lend a hand, and even women tug at the ropes."

In every emergency during the anti-slavery agitation, and at each critical event in the national history, Emerson invariably spoke the right and serviceable word, as well as the profoundest word; he gave leaders their texts and the rank and file their watchwords. These were by no means denunciations of the South, to which he was always magnanimous. During the war he said in a public address that the South had never before appeared to such advantage. But he was a patriot, and was not so lenient to the Northern men who abetted slavery. On one occasion a prominent person, with whom he had travelled pleasantly in Europe, but who had distinguished himself by friendliness with the assailant of his own senator (Sumner), came to Emerson after a lecture and offered his hand. Emerson's voice was never gentler than as he said, "If what I hear be true, I must shake hands with you under protest." When Sumner was assaulted by a Southerner in the Senate, Emerson said, "I think we must get rid of slavery or get rid of freedom. Life has no parity of value in the free State and in the slave State." To a Boston orator who declared the Declaration of Independence a series of "glittering generalities," he replied, "They are blazing ubiquities." When Captain John Brown made his armed attack on slavery in Virginia, and multitudes called him insane, Emerson silenced those "who can only cry 'Madman!' when a hero passes," and said that if Brown should suffer, he would "make his gallows glorious like a cross."

Not long after this Emerson visited us at Cincinnati (whose streets looked over into slave territory), and one evening was in a company where several eminent citizens, who enjoyed his lectures, were still troubled by his reported words about Captain Brown's gallows being glorious like a cross. A wealthy Conservative did not believe that the gentle philosopher had so said, and asked him about it. "Of course," he said, "I do not believe it, but would like to be able to answer the rumour on your own authority." Emerson asked that the reported words should be repeated, and then remarked, "That's about what I said." The questioner, much shocked, said, "Surely you do not approve the bloody raid of John Brown upon the families of Virginia." Emerson slowly replied, "If I should tell you why I disapproved, you might not like it any better."

On the day and hour of John Brown's execution, the people of Concord gathered in their town-hall and were addressed by their eminent men. A striking incident of the meeting was the reading by Emerson of Allingham's poem, "The Touchstone:"

> "A man there came, whence none could tell,
>   Bearing a touchstone in his hand,
>   And tested all things in the land
> By its unerring spell."

With every verse Emerson's tone grew more prophetic, and his eye shone as if the future were close to it as he repeated the last:

> "But, though they slew him with the sword,
>   And in a fire his touchstone burned,
>   Its doings could not be o'erturned,
> Its undoings restored.
>
> "And when, to stop all future harm,
>   They strewed its ashes on the breeze,
>   They little guessed each grain of these
> Conveyed the perfect charm."

This poem was published by the press throughout the Northern States as one written for the occasion by Emerson himself, and much applauded. None was more anxious than he to have due credit awarded his friend Allingham, and "The Touchstone" is among the seven pieces by that poet included in Emerson's "Parnassus." Not long after that solemn assembly gathered at Concord, where the martyr was personally known and loved, the "John Brown Song" became the battle-hymn of the Union armies.

Emerson not only at every critical point spoke the

best and bravest word, but was as prompt to share any personal obloquy or danger as he had been in earlier years, when he took Harriet Martineau to his house in the face of the mob. When the Southern States began to secede, frightened compromisers in the North hoped to soothe them by silencing the abolitionists; roughs were employed to fill the anti-slavery halls, hurl missiles at the speakers, and drown every voice with their yells. When these scenes were occurring in Boston, Emerson repaired thither and took his place on the platform. The Music Hall, on one such occasion, was possessed by a vast throng of screaming roughs, whom the well-known anti-slavery orators vainly tried to address. Even by those near the platform no word could be heard. Garrison was almost in despair, as was Wendell Phillips, who just then caught sight of Emerson looking calmly on the wild scene. He went to him and whispered. Emerson advanced; the roughs did not know this man, and there was a break in the roar, through which was now heard the voice of Emerson, beginning, "Christopher North — you have all heard of Christopher North." There was perfect silence, as if the name had paralysed every man. Not one of them had ever heard of Christopher North, but this assumption of their intelligence by the intellectual stranger disarmed them. Emerson told his story of Christopher North, — that he once defended his moderation in having only kicked some scoundrels out of the door instead of pitching them out of the window, — and went on to shew that under the circumstances the abolitionists had exercised moderation. The power of mind over matter was happily displayed in the attention with which that mad crowd listened to Emerson, who spoke admirably, though without notes or preparation.

During the war, in which many of his friends were slain and his only son wounded, no man did better service than Emerson with voice, pen, and means. It was a terrible trial to him, the war — keeping him, as he said, from sleep; and I do not think he ever quite recovered from the effects of it. Once, when I had just arrived in Boston from Washington, where I had conversed with President Lincoln, and found him waiting for Northern opinion to advance to a demand for the extinction of slavery, I found that Emerson was about to give a lecture there on the condition of the country. I asked him to come to my room at the hotel, and when we were alone I said to him, "The accident of my being born and brought up in the South enables me to give a practical suggestion. You remember how Thoreau used to catch bream with only his hand out of Concord river. He had found that this fish had the peculiarity of hastening to defend its spawn, and by placing his hand under the spawn pulled up the fish. Well, the spawn of the South is its slaves; we have only to put our hands on it, and these armies now resisting us will hasten back to hold on to its slaves. As long as we do not touch slavery, the negroes till the fields, and it is they who point the soldier at us as the soldier points his gun." Emerson proceeded at once to say this in his lecture, unnecessarily mentioning it as my suggestion, and added, "I hope that it is not fatal to this method that it is entirely moral and just." He also, I believe, urged the same plan at Washington, where his lecture was attended by the President and his cabinet. The President was much esteemed by Emerson, and I once heard him say that, in an earlier age, Lincoln's good stories would have earned him the fame of a Pilpay.

Allusion has already been made in this volume to Emerson's "Boston Hymn," read by him on the New Year's Day which brought the President's proclamation of freedom to the slaves. On the eve of that day the negroes of Boston had assembled to keep "watch-night," and, as their preacher said, "to watch and see that the President kept his promise." In that humble assembly there was at midnight a symbolical hissing to indicate the last distress of the dying Python. In the morning the people assembled, and Emerson read his "Boston Hymn." How gently, with all calm enforcement, did his tones march to their climax:

> "Come East and West and North,
> By races, as snowflakes,
> And carry my purpose forth,
> Which neither halts nor shakes.
>
> "My will fulfilled shall be,
> For, in daylight as in dark,
> My thunderbolt has eyes to see
> His way home to the mark."

Thus did the President of the literary, respond to the President of the political Republic, whose Proclamation closed with the words — "Upon this act, sincerely believed to be an act of justice warranted by the constitution upon military necessity, I invoke the considerate judgment of mankind and the gracious favour of Almighty God."

Python appeared to coil and struggle for a time yet, but to the eye of Emerson it lay already dead, and to some other eyes it was his own shining arrow, so softly feathered and sent in the beginning of the generation, which lay nearest its heart.

When the war had ended, he gave one of his grandest orations in Boston, at the close of which he uttered the true American faith. "America means opportunity, freedom, power. The genius of this country has marked out her true policy: opportunity — doors wide open — every port open. If I could, I would have free trade with all the world, without toll or custom-house. Let us invite every nation, every race, every skin; white man, black man, red man, yellow man. Let us offer hospitality, a fair field, and equal laws to all. The land is wide enough, the soil has food enough for all. Let us educate every soul."

It was a sign "gracious as rainbows" that, in the centennial year of American Independence, Emerson delivered the oration before the Literary Societies of the University of Virginia.

XXVIII.

EMERSON IN ENGLAND.

SOME brief account of Emerson's first visit to England, near fifty years ago, has been given in the earlier pages of this book. When Professor Charles Norton, to whom both Carlyle and Emerson intrusted the editing of their correspondence, has completed the task, for which none can be more fit, the world will see both men in a clearer light; and it will also be the best introduction to the history of Emerson's work, friendships, and experiences in England.

Carlyle's preface to Emerson's first series of Essays (London, James Fraser, 1841) is one of his characteristic writings, but it shews that he had not understood the aim of Emerson. He quotes Paul Louis Courrier, "Ce qui me distingue de tous mes contemporains c'est que je n'ai pas la prétention d'être roi;" and regards Emerson as one contemptuously withdrawn from his nation.

Among the first to be stirred by the Essays was John Sterling, who dedicated his "Strafford," to Emerson:

"Teacher of starry wisdom, high, serene,
  Receive the gift our common ground supplies;
  Red flowers, dark leaves, that ne'er on earth had been
  Without the influence of sidereal skies."

In 1845, when Edgar Quinet was lecturing at the College de France, he paid an eloquent tribute to the genius of Emerson. "What we announce in Europe," he said, "from the summit of a ruined past, he also announces in the germinating solitude of a world absolutely new." Although Emerson cared little for French philosophy, the coincidences between his thought and expression and those of Quinet are sometimes striking. On Matthew Arnold the Essays made a deep impression. Matthew Arnold wrote in the volume this sonnet:

> "'O monstrous, dead, unprofitable world!
> That thou canst hear, and hearing, hold thy way.
> A voice oracular hath pealed to-day,
> To-day a hero's banner is unfurled.
> Hast thou no lip for welcome?' So I said.
> Man after man the world smiled and passed by,
> A smile of wistful incredulity,
> As though one spake of noise unto the dead:
> Scornful, and strange, and sorrowful, and full
> Of bitter knowledge. Yet the Will is free.
> Strong is the soul, and wise, and beautiful:
> The seeds of godlike power are in us still:
> Gods are we, bards, saints, heroes, if we will.
> Dumb judges answer, truth or mockery?"

But the world was not so insensate as the sonnet supposes. The tidings spread swiftly around that a "voice oracular" had been heard in America, and it was loudly called for in England. It was slow in responding, but one of its disciples appeared.

In the London "Morning Chronicle" of July 5, 1842, there appeared the following notice: — "PUBLIC INVITATION. — An open meeting of the friends of human progress will be held to-morrow, July 6, at Mr. Wright's, Alcott House School, Ham Common, near Richmond, Surrey, for the purpose of considering and adopting means for the promotion of the great end, when all who are interested in human destiny are earnestly urged to attend. The chair taken at three o'clock, and again at seven, by A. Bronson Alcott, Esq., now on a visit from America." This invitation found about a score sufficiently interested in or curious about " the great end " to turn aside from the great world and seat themselves on the lawn to hear the apostle speak of " the instauration of spirit ; " and they came at length to the following conclusion : —

" In order to obtain the highest excellence of which man is capable, the generation of a new race of persons is demanded, who shall project institutions and initiate conditions altogether original and commensurate with the being and wants of humanity. The germs of this new generation are even now discernible in human beings, but have been hitherto either choked by ungenial circumstances, or having borne fruit prematurely or imperfectly, have attained no abiding growth. It is proposed to select a spot whereon a new Eden may be planted, and man may, untempted by evil, dwell in harmony with his Creator, with himself, his fellows, and with all external natures. Providence seems to have ordained the United States, more especially New England, as the field wherein this idea is to be realised in actual experience."

The " great end " of this fine dream is now represented by the name " Alcott House " on Ham Common, and by a pleasant cottage in Concord, where, with his daughter, who has gained an eminent place among American novelists, a handsome white-haired old man passes his declining years in a peaceful Eden of his own.

The longing to see and hear Emerson was not to be quieted. His friend Alexander Ireland put the matter strongly to him, and he began to yield. "I feel no call to make a visit of literary propagandism in England," he wrote. "All my impulses to work of that kind would rather employ me at home. It would be still more unpleasing to me to put upon a few friends the office of collecting an audience for me, by much advertisement and coaxing. At the same time it would be very agreeable to me to accept any good invitation to read lectures from institutions or from a number of friendly individuals who sympathised with my studies. But though I possess a good many decisive tokens of interest in my pursuits and way of thinking from sundry British men and women, they are widely sundered persons, and my belief is, that in no one city, except perhaps in London, could I find any numerous company to whom my name was favourably known." "You must not suffer your own friendly feelings to give the smallest encouragement to the design."

When it was announced that Emerson would visit England and read lectures, applications from every part of the kingdom came to Mr. Ireland, and in many cases it was found impossible to comply with them. Emerson arrived at Liverpool by the packet ship "Washington Irving," October 22, 1847. Mr. Ireland received a letter from Carlyle, dated at Chelsea ten days after Emerson had sailed. "By a letter I had very lately from Emerson — which had lain, lost and never missed, for above a month in the treacherous post-office of Buxton, where it was called for and denied — I learn that Emerson intended to sail for this country 'about the 1st of October;' and infer, therefore, that probably even now he is near Liverpool or some other of our ports. Treadmill or other as emphatic admonition to that scandalous postmaster of Buxton! He has put me in extreme risk of doing one of the most unfriendly and every way unpardonable-looking things a man could do. Not knowing in the least to what port Emerson is tending, when he is expected, or what his first engagements are, I find no way of making my word audible to him in time, except that of intrusting it, with solemn charges, to you, as here. Pray do me the favour to contrive in some sure way that Emerson may get hold of that note the instant he lands in England. I shall be permanently grieved otherwise; shall have failed in a clear duty (were it nothing more), which will never, probably, in my life offer itself again. Do not neglect, I beg much of you; and, on the whole, if you can, get Emerson put safe into the express train, and shot up hither, as the first road he goes. That is the result we aim at. But the note itself, at all events, I pray you get that delivered duly, and so do me a very great favour, for which I depend on you." These injunctions were faithfully carried out, and Emerson was soon in the hospitable home of his friend in Manchester.

His first course of lectures was delivered at the Manchester Athenæum, its subject, "Representative Men."

He next gave four in the Manchester Mechanics' Institution. It is pleasant to find in a provincial paper of the time such a criticism as the following: — "The first tendril is now wound around your heart and your attention is riveted. He uses no action, save occasionally a slight vibration of the body, as though rocking beneath the hand of some unseen power. Then drop the pearls from his mouth in quick succession, and noiselessly do they sink into the hearts of his hearers, there to abide for ever, and, like the famed carbuncle in Eastern cave, shed a mild radiance on all things therein. Your breath is now hushed, and all eyes are on his lips as on the wand of a magician, stealing away each faculty and leading you captive at his will." During his stay at Manchester, Emerson was entertained at a banquet at the Athenæum, presided over by Sir A. Alison, and attended by Richard Cobden and other eminent men, and made a speech always remembered by those who heard it.

It is not a little curious to trace the first impression made by Emerson upon an English audience. A writer in "Howitt's Journal" begins with expressions of disappointment. He had heard the lecture on Swedenborg, and finds it a misty subject, mistily treated. "Some man near me gravely asked his neighbour if he did not think he could understand it better if they stood on their heads." The tones of the voice are nasal, but at the same time "they now and then come out with musical richness and depth." "His delivery is indifferent and careless. . . . He reads words of passionate admiration, of reprehension, of dissent, and of contempt, and his voice hardly varied; his countenance still less." But now the writer has listened to another lecture, that on Montaigne, and writes as follows: — The stairs were as much and as early crowded; the lecture-room rather less so, but still well filled. He came on the platform in the same simple, quiet, almost careless and indifferent manner. But it grows upon one, does this unconsciousness of anything but the matter in hand No loss of time in bowing, but instant commencement, almost before the clapping (which he seemed not to hear) had subsided. It was a noble lecture. . . . Suddenly he closed his MS., and was off and away while we were yet pondering the full meaning of his last exquisite sentence. It is curious to trace back and perceive how one's admiration and appreciation of him grows. His voice, his delivery, his very carelessness of his audience, his indifference as to whether they understand him or no, seem to become endeared to one as forming part of the individual Emerson, whose thoughtful pathway lies alone through the mental world. For he does not remind me of Carlyle, to whom so many are fond of likening him. In form of sentence, in strange, quaint, and often beautiful similes, in the completely new light in which he views commonplace things, he strikes me as more resembling Jean Paul. But the resemblance of Emerson to any one must spring from internal likeness: he is not one to condescend to catch tricks of manner or style from any other person."

The early appreciation of Emerson in England is so interesting and creditable a fact that I must quote also a discriminating criticism which appeared in the "Gateshead Observer:" — "There is a simplicity about his delivery, in which, to me at least, lies one-half of his intellectual grandeur. He reads with a clear enunciation and a slight American accent, and utters the deepest and sublimest thoughts with an unconsciousness and a modesty, a serene earnestness and a noble catholicity, and all the other highest attributes of genius. There is not the slightest attempt at oratory — no enthusiasm about him; yet his words have a depth, and a warmth, and an emphasis, and a weightiness, and a dignity, and a solemnity, which, I believe, take a deep root in the minds of his hearers, and which many will never forget. He is a thin, tall man, apparently about forty-five, with an oval Yankee countenance, rather sallow and emaciated, and a very prominent Wellington nose."

On the 6th of June, 1848, Emerson began a series of six lectures in London on "The Minds and Manners of the Nineteenth Century." The programme of the course — which was given at the Literary and Scientific Institution, 17 Edwards Street, Portman Square — comprised the following subjects: —

June 6. Powers and Laws of Thought.
" 8. Relation of Intellect to Natural Science.
" 10. Tendencies and Duties of Men of Thought.
" 13. Politics and Socialism.
" 15. Poetry and Eloquence.
" 17. Natural Aristocracy.

These lectures were delivered at four o'clock of each day. During the course the following letter appeared:

"To the Editor of the 'Examiner,' — SIR, — The lectures of Mr. Ralph Waldo Emerson leave only one thing to be regretted — viz., that they cannot be heard by the whole literary and artistic public of the metropolis. The *guinea* for the course renders this impossible. How many there are who love beauty, and know well what it is, and create it afresh every day for their fellow-men, and yet they cannot reap guineas for their own instruction! I would therefore suggest to Mr. Emerson, through your influential trumpet (what I *dare* not suggest as a private friend), that he present the literary men of London with his utterances on a liberal scale. It might be done by fixing a small admission charge commensurate with the means of poets, critics, philosophers, historians, scholars, and the other divine paupers of that class. I feel that it ought to be done, because Emerson is a phenomenon whose like is not in the world, and to miss him is to lose an important informing fact out of the nineteenth century. If, therefore, you will insert this, the favour will at all events have been asked, and one conscience satisfied. It seems also probable that a very large attendance of thoughtful men would be secured, and that Emerson's stirrup-cup would be a cheering and full one, sweet and ruddy with international charity. — Yours always, — AN ATTENDANT ON EMERSON'S PRESENT COURSE. Hampstead, June 14, 1848."

Subsequently Emerson delivered three lectures at Exeter Hall, the surplus proceeds of which were devoted to the objects of the Metropolitan Early Closing Association, by which his services were engaged. The subjects were "Napoleon," "Domestic Life," and "Shakespeare the Poet." In the "Reasoner" (July 5, 1848), "Panthea" (Miss Sophia D. Collet) writes: — "On Friday evening, June 30, Mr. Emerson gave his last lecture in this country (on Shakespeare), at the end of which Monckton Milnes, M.P., who was in the chair, made some remarks on 'the influences which had brought together the diverse elements of Shakespeare, Mr. Emerson, and Exeter Hall,' and called on the audience to manifest their gratitude to the lecturer, which was accordingly done by rising *en masse*, hearty cheering, and waving of hats, &c. Mr. Emerson came forward, and in a very simple and pleasing manner thanked them for their good-will, and spoke gratefully of 'the unbroken kindness he had received from a large number of Englishmen and Englishwomen during his stay here — he had not been aware there was so much kindness in the world.' His visit had enlarged his views on the condition of England. Americans who grow up in the study of English books are apt to think they know all about England,— but they were very glad to come here and know it better. He added that increased knowledge had increased his respect for the English character, sincerely as he had previously esteemed the worth and probity of individuals. He had only one thing more to say to us, 'Let your future be worthy of your past and your present,' he would ask no more."

The lecture referred to by Miss Collet was not, however, to be the last in the country. Emerson had already more applications to visit various towns and cities of the country than he could comply with; but he made a judicious selection. He afterwards went to Sheffield, Worcester, Birmingham, Newcastle-upon-Tyne, and other towns, and was everywhere greeted by large audiences. At Leicester he was so unfortunate as to leave his manuscript at the house of his host and chairman, Mr. Joseph Biggs, two miles distant from the hall, and discovered the fact only on the moment announced for the lecture. As he alone could bring it, the audience enjoyed two lectures,— the chairman having amused them with anecdotes of absent-mindedness in great men, until his friend's return.

The subject for which Emerson had been announced at Newcastle was, "Shakespeare, the Poet;" but when he met his large audience he told them he had resolved to substitute for it one on "New England," not delivered before. Dissatisfaction arose at this announcement, during which the lecturer stood quietly, and then, stating that the change seemed to him necessary because one of the papers had published that morning a full report of the lecture he had meant to give, he gained the consent of the audience to listen to the lecture, by which they were profoundly interested.

A friend related to me a characteristic incident in connection with the visit to Newcastle. He inquired of the gentleman whose guest he was whether a poet named William B. Scott resided there. His host had never heard of such a person. The author of "The Year of the World" had been known in Concord, however, and was speedily sought out and invited to meet the man who knew his worth.

From Newcastle he went to Edinburgh, where he gave three lectures before the Philosophical Institution, the subjects being "Natural Aristocracy," "The Genius of the Present Age," and "The Humanity of Science." He was the guest of the late Dr. Samuel

Brown, and was warmly welcomed by the circle of scholars residing in that city.

The late David Scott, artist and poet, had read Emerson's works before they met in Edinburgh. In the biography of him by his brother the following is quoted from his diary of 1845: — "Read lately the Essays of Emerson — a worthy thinker. The other day mentioned him to Professor Wilson, who proposed to read him, and said he fancied he was both better and worse than Carlyle — higher and lower. . . . In Emerson I find many things that meet conclusions formed and feelings experienced by myself. He is a less sectarian and more unfettered doctrinist than I have yet met. As yet, however, I have not arrived at the basis (if he has indeed defined such) of the superstructure of his mind." It was at a time when the artist was suffering from despondency and failing health that Emerson made his acquaintance, and sat to him for his portrait; and it is perhaps partly due to that circumstance that the following entry is not more hearty: — "Portrait of Emerson nearly done during his stay here. My first impression of him was not what I expected it would have been. His appearance is severe, and dry, and hard. But, although he is guarded and somewhat cold at times, intercourse shews him to be elevated, simple, kind, and truthful." On the other hand, the biographer records, "Emerson was strangely impressed with a sense of the greatness of Scott's character, but noticed the inadequacy of his verbal communications in ordinary circumstances, and said, 'How rich I find him in the studio!'" On one occasion Emerson having said that there was little or no real poetry in Bailey's "Festus," David Scott contested the assertion, and quoted with sadness the line —

"Friendship hath passed me like a ship at sea."

On leaving London Emerson wrote him: "I carry with me a bright image of your house and studio, and all your immortal companions therein, and I wish to keep the ways open between us, natural and supernatural. If the Good Power had allowed me the opportunity of seeing you more at leisure, and of comparing notes of past years a little! And it may yet be allowed in time; but where and when?" But Emerson was destined never again to meet one whom he described as a "man of high character and genius, the short-lived painter, David Scott."

"My portraits," Emerson once remarked to me, "generally oscillate between the donkey and the Lothario." David Scott's portrait he had to admit was the exception; and it is now held by his townsmen as a treasure of their Public Library. It is thought by W. B. Scott to be the best of the few pictures of that kind that his brother painted. This portrait is a very successful rendering of the peculiarities of Emerson's look and manner, which were physiognomically significant of his thought and spirit. The slight depression at the corners of the mouth, with a touch of sternness, the one arm extending from his side as he became more animated by his theme, the two or three fingers of the other hand pressed to the palm as if holding tightly some reservation, all these, and other indefinable characteristics photographed on the mind of one who has attentively listened to Emerson, are in this picture. But some traits but faintly suggested in the picture were developed in after years, of a kind that could not be shewn on canvas.

After leaving Edinburgh Emerson was the guest of Miss Martineau at Ambleside for a few days, and with her once more visited Wordsworth at Rydal Mount.

In the summer of 1848 Emerson went over to Paris, and was there during the exciting scenes of that year, attending many meetings of the clubs. His observations made during that visit were embodied in a brilliant lecture on the French, which I heard him deliver in Concord, but which has not been published. While in Paris a fine crayon sketch of him was made by Oswald Murray, which is now in possession of Mr. Ireland. Mrs. Murray tells me that she was so little aware of the eminence of the man who used to sit to her husband, that when he proposed to hold her baby while she prepared tea, she always allowed him to do so. He was so simple and kindly that she did not feel awe of him. Before leaving England in the autumn he again visited Manchester; and for a few days before sailing he was the guest of Mr. and Mrs. Paulet, of Liverpool, where a number of his friends assembled to take leave of him, among them Arthur Hugh Clough.

A pamphlet written by "January Searle," pseudonym for George Searle Phil, relates an episode in Emerson's Manchester experience:

"Before Emerson left England for America, he invited a number of gentlemen, whose acquaintance he had made during his sojourn amongst us, to a farewell symposium at Manchester. A more motley, dissimilar, heterogeneous mass of persons never before, perhaps, met together at the table of a philosopher.

"It was late in the afternoon of that boisterous winter's day when we, having marched from the far moors of Yorkshire, and crossed the steep and rocky summit of Stanedge, knocked at the gate of Emerson's house in Manchester. It was a small unpretending house, with a little garden in front, and as we entered we found the hall crowded with coats, hats, sticks, and philosophical umbrellas. A large globe lamp stood upon the table, and there was the noise and chatter of many voices, mingled with bursts of laughter, in the room where the guests were assembled.

"We were not expected, although warmly invited, for money was scarce in those days and the journey long. As we entered the room, therefore, the host rose to welcome us all the more cordially, introducing us to many there who were previously unknown to us. And when we had recognised friends and exchanged courtesies with all, we took our seat beside Emerson, who expressed himself happy in seeing so many persons around him who had interested themselves in so many and such various ways in his mission to England. 'There are some men here,' said he, 'to whom I should like more particularly to introduce you as persons of mark and genius;' and whilst he was thus speaking, a tall, thin, ungainly man, about thirty years of age, speaking in squeaks at the top of his voice, making all kinds of grimaces and strange gesticulations, with a small Puritan head, which was more than half *forehead*, approached to our side of the room, book in hand, desirous, as he said, of pointing out a fine passage in

Plato to Emerson, which he had just been reading. Without more ado, he put the volume within half-an-inch of his eyes and read the passage, after which he commenced a long dissertation upon it, twisting his body into all conceivable and inconceivable forms, rolling up the whites of his eyes, and moving his head from shoulder to shoulder with extraordinary activity. Learned and eloquent, he poured forth a stream of talk, not presumptuously, but with a diffident confidence if we may use such an expression, whilst Emerson sat silent and listening, with that calm, pale face of his, the eye thoughtful but not excited, and the mouth occasionally lighted up with a faint moonlight smile. He was evidently pleased, and so were all who listened to that wonderful six feet of brain and nerve. . . .

"Emerson smiled. 'That man,' said he, 'is a fine scholar, has a fine mind, and much real culture. He is well read in literature, in philosophy, in history; and has written rhymes, which, like my friend Ellery Channing's, are very nearly poetry.' We then had a conversation about Channing and Thoreau. 'I will give you,' said Emerson, 'in a few minutes, a copy of Channing's poems, and his "Conversations at Rome." Thoreau,' he added, 'you will hear of by and by. He is now writing a book, most of which I have heard, called "A Week on the Concord and Merrimac Rivers."' We subsequently went with Emerson to his chamber, where he packed his portmanteau and gave us these books of Channing's.

"We had scarcely returned to the room, when a card was put into our hand bearing the name of a friend who had long wished to see Emerson, and who had now come from Nottingham for this purpose. He was well known to Emerson through a book he had written on Divine, and other far sweeter, love; and we went forth to bring in the young philosophical theologian to the host and to the company. He was a thin, timorous young man, not more than twenty years old, with strange mystic eyes, and a head and face like George Herbert's — a very singular young man, loving God and man too much to be a priest, and yet not quite happy out of the pale of the Church — a devout follower of Emerson at this time, and tinged with his thought. He sat at the right hand of Emerson, the introduction being over, and was the St. John of the company. . . .

"At last the dinner was announced, and we sat down to the repast. Emerson sat at the head, and our friend —— at the foot of the table. The Apostle John again sat at the right hand of his master, and that odd compound of stuff from Birmingham sat at his left. Emerson spoke very little, except whilst seeing after the comfort and provisioning of his guests. We remained but a short time at the table after dinner, and returned early to the drawing-room, there being no wine-bibbers present.

"The evening's entertainment was the one redeeming thing in this banquet. It consisted of a reading by Emerson — at urgent request — of his paper on Plato, which has since been published in the 'Representative Men.' After that the evening fell flat and dead.

"The literary men of England made very little impression upon Emerson, although he spoke of some modern works with praise. Of some private and unknown persons he was almost enthusiastic in his laudations. It was life, not literature, that he cared about. And yet he was a great reader of Goethe, and read some chapters of him every morning in the German, and also of Montaigne. . . .

"We all breakfasted together next morning, when the Apostle John and ourselves drove off to the train on our separate journeys homewards, bidding Emerson adieu, perhaps for ever."

Emerson had met a young Oxonian whom his eye held like the wedding guest. This was Arthur Hugh Clough, who used to walk with him to his London lectures, who followed him to the verge of the ocean, and presently across it. He was the last man that parted with him when he passed down the Mersey on that July day, and he straightway wrote to a friend about Emerson's three days' visit to Oxford. "Everybody liked him, and as the orthodox mostly had never heard of him, they did not suspect him. He is the quietest, plainest, unobtrusivest man possible; will talk, but will rarely *discourse* to more than a single person, and wholly declines 'roaring.' He is very Yankee to look at, lank and sallow, and not quite without the twang, but his looks and voice are pleasing, nevertheless, and give you the impression of perfect intellectual cultivation, as completely as would any great scientific man in England — Faraday or Owen, for instance — more in their way, perhaps, than in that of Wordsworth or Carlyle. I have been with him a great deal; for he came over to Paris and was there a month, during which we dined together daily, and since that I have seen him often in London, and finally here. One thing that struck everybody is that he is much less Emersonian than his essays.

There is no dogmatism, or abitrariness, or positiveness about him."

Emerson loved Clough, and loved his poetry. In 1852 he invited him to America, and Clough wrote back, " My best way of thanking you is, I believe, simply to accept your kind proposal."

Arthur Clough did some fine literary work while he was in America, and he became very dear to the best men and women in that country. It was with sorrow that they parted from him; when he was married his American literary friends sent him presents; and when he died, it was nowhere heard of with more pain than at Concord and Cambridge.

When Emerson was last in England he called several times on his old friend W. B. Scott, who lived near Carlyle, with whom Emerson spent some days, and in the course of their conversation Scott asked him why Dante Rossetti received comparatively little attention in America. Emerson said, " We like our own period, and what is vital in these days about us, especially in poetry; but the Rossetti work is not touching us — it is exotic."

It is a notable fact, however, that when Emerson's works appeared in England, among the first to welcome them were the Rossettis, both William and Dante. The Preraphaelist Brothers especially admired his poetry, as one of them tells me, " for its august seer-like qualities, notwithstanding some rustiness on the hinges of verse." Emerson is mentioned with honour in " The Germ." William Rossetti was present at a lecture in Exeter Hall on " Napoleon," and tells me that he well remembers Emerson's " upright figure, clear-cut physiognomy, clear elocution, resolved self-possession." On the other hand, a friend of his was chilled by what he called "the impersonal demeanour of Emerson, his impassivity, total want of sympathetic vital relation towards his audience." The late Goodwyn Barmby had attended Alcott's conversations at Ham in 1842, and was not well pleased with his version of the Emersonian gospel, and he had also had but little satisfaction in his interviews with Margaret Fuller; but he was much impressed by Emerson. Twelve years ago he (Goodwyn Barmby) wrote me : " When Emerson came to tea with me at Bayswater, he was quite enchanted with the trees in Kensington Gardens. I remember well his frequent question, 'Can you shew me any men and women? What life have you here in England?' I knew well that he was aiming at the 'being' before 'knowing and doing,' of James Pierrepont Greaves. He was after biography; I was for history. I had just returned from the French Revolution of '48, and had witnessed the inspiration of a nation, and my harmony was jarred by his not appearing to sympathise with the social movement. He afterwards went to Paris, and took up his abode in the lovely little apartment which I had not long before occupied, in a hotel in the Rue des Beaux Arts, which I think I recommended to him. There he would have seen something of Hugh Doherty. My impression of Emerson was that he was the most beautifully simple and clearest-minded man I ever met with; but I then thought he was too much immersed in biographic ideas, which were after all a certain reflex of egotism, and that he wanted social sympathy and its gospel of self-sacrifice to make him a whole man.

I have no doubt now that your great war has made him greater."

In London Emerson boarded at the house of Dr. Chapman, where he continually wrote on his lectures, and was prone to let his fire go out. At a dinner-party there he met the Hennells, Miss Collet, Mr. Call, the poet, and other liberal thinkers. They were remarkably silent, apparently content to gaze upon Emerson and Carlyle. One or two were in an argumentative state of mind, and Emerson was averse to everything polemical or controversial. "The children of the gods never argue," was one of his puzzling replies. Wherever he was a guest, children were much drawn to him. I have before me a letter written by him to Miss Ashurst Biggs, at the house of whose father he was entertained, when she was about nine years of age. It was written in reply to one from her, and is on a large sheet surmounted by an engraving of Scarborough Castle. "I have been travelling in Yorkshire, and seeing many towns and curiosities, York Minster and Scarborough Castle, and many other things; among other things a great cave at Flamborough Head. I stayed in it listening to the roar of the ocean until the tide rose and the sea came in, and drove me and my friend out at the low passage at the other end, since nobody is admitted when the tide is in except the fishes." He copies two verses written to him by his little daughter, and concludes with the words, "Farewell, my dear child."

Emerson's picture of childhood in one of his London lectures is remembered by some who heard it as unequalled for its charm. His own childlikeness was felt also by those who met him personally; but to others his reputation for that "clean intellect," for which Carlyle said Emerson had not his equal on the planet, carried a certain awe. On one occasion, in London, he was told of a young man who wished to see him, but, added the informant, "he's afraid of you." "So am I afraid of him; let him come!" One lady said he was a man to be approached after fasting and prayer. A lady of Coventry, daughter of an orthodox minister, told me that Carlyle appeared to many in that day as Emerson's John the Baptist at best; for they had been troubled by the ridicule of philanthropy that came from Chelsea. The evangelical were impressed by finding this heretic not a man of the world, like Voltaire and Gibbon, but one whose "righteousness exceeded that of the orthodox."

Emerson had read with much interest a work by Charles Bray, the "Philosophy of Necessity," and this led to a brief but memorable visit to Coventry. I am indebted to Miss Sarah Hennell for a letter written to her by her sister, Mrs. Bray, July 16, 1848, immediately after this visit: "Yes, we have had the great spirit amongst us, and I feel as you do how much greater his thoughts, which we had before, have become from the corroboration they have received from his presence. I have quite a grateful feeling that he has been under this roof, though only for a few hours; but, alas! we shall see his face no more! He is rolling on the waves now towards home. He said his wife insisted on being on the shore to meet him, though they live twenty miles inland. He was taking a rocking-horse for his two little girls, and a crossbow for his son; and his eyes quite sparkled when he spoke of how much they would be grown in these nine months. My head was full of the preparations for our great juvenile fête on Thursday, when Emerson's letter came to say he should be here at midnight, to stay only till Wednesday afternoon. So I ran upstairs to put the best room in order, and directly after in came Mr. and Mrs. Flower and Kate Martineau. Of course they wanted to see Emerson above all things, and had invited him to Stratford. Charles went to meet him at the station. He looked round the drawing-room and said, 'Coventry is a very nice place;' and the next morning was so easy and pleasant that I wondered where all my awe had gone to. He talked about Indian mythology and Stonehenge. After breakfast in walked the Flowers again. They had set off at five, and came to propose taking him back with them to Stratford, as they had found a note from him, on reaching home, expressing a wish to 'see Shakespeare.' We were rather disconcerted, as Mary Ann (Miss Evans) had just come, and we meant to have a nice quiet day all to ourselves. But, however, it was plain Emerson wished to see Stratford, and we all thought it right he should; so we all set off together by train to Leamington, then in cars to Stratford; and had a most delightful ride, we four in an open carriage from Stratford again. This was the pleasantest part of the day to us, and he talked as if we had been old friends. He was much struck with Mary Ann (Miss Evans): expressed his admiration many times to Charles — 'That young lady has a calm serious soul.' He regretted very much he had no more time to stay amongst us. He came home to tea with us. And so he departed, with much warmth pressing Charles to go and see him in America. It is well for us a great benign soul does not often come to disgust us with common life. No, that's a very false sentiment: common life would not be common then. It was a comfort the next day to find that Hannah had been providing the needful for common life while we had been soaring aloft, and that the cakes were made ready for the children at night. The fête was most successful. We had a fiddle and flute to make music, and they danced on the grass."

To this charming account of a visit which Emerson remembered with pleasure, I add a sentence from Mrs. Bray's notebook: " If the law of love and justice have once entered our hearts, why need we seek any other?"—*Emerson* (as he sat in the drawing-room window, July 12, 1848).

Emerson remembered well that visit to the Brays at Rosehill, when he sat with them under the beautiful acacia, and talked with Charles Bray on the "Philosophy of Necessity," which had reached him in Concord and spoke to his mind. George Eliot was then Miss Evans of Birdgrove, where Emerson's essays were among her friends in loneliness. When Emerson had talked a few moments with her he suddenly said, " What one book do you like best?" She instantly answered, " Rousseau's Confessions." He started, then said, " So do I. There is a point of sympathy between us." George Eliot cherished the remembrance of meeting Emerson under these happy auspices, and also in London, where she played the piano at evening, in Dr. Chapman's house, without perhaps knowing that Emerson's ear for such music was what he used to call "marble."

It was wonderful to me, when I was starting for England, to find how Emerson bore in mind the individual traits of the people he had met during his sojourn abroad; and even in 1875, when his memory was already failing, he asked me questions about some of them. He remembered the attention that Sophia Collet had paid to his lectures, and was happy when I was able to tell him that invalidism had not been able to quench the sunshine his works had brought into her study. The extent to which Emerson's thought influenced English freethinkers was largely due to this lady, at that time, under the name "Panthea," the most scholarly writer in the "Reasoner." "In the clear morning light in which he bathes us," she wrote in that paper, "we feel that all the accustomed solutions of the mystery of human existence are but degrading caricatures, which shall never again impose on us; and that the realities, even the (at present) inexplicable ones, which now come forth to view, are more sacred, more dear, and more inspiring than all the christianities of Europe, Asia, Africa, and America, which do but belong to them as one year's blossoms belong to the root from which they spring."

Carlyle's best insight into Emerson's first essays was that which found a fresh and new country in them. "A breath as of the green country — all the welcomer that it is *New England* country, not second-hand but first-hand country — meets us wholesomely everywhere in these Essays: the authentic green earth is there, with her mountains, rivers, with her mills and farms." This was a potent charm of his lectures in England. Wherever he went or spoke, this new world travelled with him and surrounded him while he spoke. His indifference to theology, his aversion to controversy, his affirmative tone, all seemed to come from a land where old dogmas and conventions were unknown. He uttered destructive generalisations of the most startling character as truisms, and swept creeds and institutions out of his path unconsciously, without any tone of radicalism. He might have been the original of the man of the future painted by Weirtz at Brussels, examining with a smile the banners, guns, and crowns of the present time, held in the hollow of his hand. Carlyle once told of a man he found reading Emerson, as he rested from toil and looking out over the sea. It was that westward look which carried so many agitated minds to New England, and no doubt Emerson foresaw the disappointment of many of them when he reserved his sympathy with the social dreams of Goodwyn Barmby. There were enough visionary Americans drawing Englishmen to their country with fanciful pictures, one of whom Herman Melville portrayed in his "Confidence-Man," who, in his blended "shrewdness and mythiness," seemed a kind of "cross between a Yankee pedlar and a Tartar priest." Emerson probably never tried to persuade any one to settle in America, except Carlyle; and his word to English youth would have been that of Goethe, "Your America is here or nowhere." His best influence in England has been, and is, represented by those whom he inspired to build a new and better world around them. And of these it has been my lot to know and hear of many. The world knows what he has been to Tyndall, who still cherishes the little volume he picked up in a bookstall. The Emersonian sermon in Kingsley's "Alton Locke," the sonnet of Matthew Arnold, the letters of Clough, and the writings of Quinet, Max Müller, Herman Grimm, Allingham, Ruskin, and many another, attest how much he has been to the best European teachers. But his influence has been as great in other than literary directions. When he was last in England, a philanthropic man, a Lord Mayor, asked to be introduced to Emerson, because, when he was a poor youth, the essay on Self-Reliance stimulated his energies and gave him his start to success. The late Dr. Lankester, coroner of London, similarly regarded Emerson as the chief influence in his life, and when he died, there was found in his pocket a well-pencilled copy of the Essays, which had been his companion through many years. Other similar instances have been related to me.

After Emerson's return from his visit to England of 1847–8, he gave a lecture upon "The English People," in New York, at the close of which he said that the fabulous St. George was not the true emblem of the national character. He saw it rather in the lawgiver, scholar, poet, mechanic, monarch, Alfred; in later times, in Cromwell; and in one not so well known, William of Wykeham, the builder of Windsor Castle, a bishop of Winchester, a putter-down of abuses in his time in his own diocese. He founded a school at Winchester for seventy scholars for ever; he endowed a college at Oxford for seventy fellows for ever; and he established a house in the neighbourhood of Winchester to provide a measure of beer and a sufficiency of bread to every one who asked it for ever. Emerson was curious to test this good man's credit, and knocked at the door, preferred his request, and received his measure of beer and bread, though its donor had been dead seven hundred years!

When Emerson was last in England there was much desire that he should give lectures at the Royal Institution and at Oxford. This, however, he declined. His only public appearance in England was at the Working-Men's College in London, Thomas Hughes being beside him. That extemporaneous address I heard, and when he spoke of the " pathetically noble " effort of English scholars to educate their humbler brethren, there was before us another " pathetically noble " sight in the figure of the white-haired sage beaming his last farewell, and uttering his last animating word to the class that received him as prophet at the dawn of a closing generation.

When tidings came that Emerson's house was burnt down there was a strong desire in England to help to rebuild it. " Will you please say," he wrote me, " to any such benevolent friend, that whilst I am surprised and gratified at such a good-will, I will have no such thing done, as my friends at home have already taken care to more than indemnify me for my material losses by the fire. Not the less hearty thanks to these English friends."

In the spring of 1873, when Emerson was on his way from the South to England, I had also to convey to him a request to accept a banquet in London, but this he declined. "I desire to thank them heartily for their generous good-will, but say to them that they must forgive me for declining the banquet, much preferring to meet new and old friends on more simple and private terms." This note was written from Paris, March 31, and at the close of the week Emerson was in London.

To observe the various men that gathered around Emerson in England, one might say that concord, as a virtue, was organised in and around the Sage of Concord. Carlyle, Dean Stanley; Professors Tyndall, Newman, Huxley, Carpenter, Sayce, Ruskin; Alexander Ellis, J. A. Froude, Lord Houghton, Allingham, Edward Sterling, the Amberleys, Prince Leopold, Max Müller (with whom he stayed in Oxford), these, and many others, gathered around him with fraternal or filial devotion, and would have had him pass the rest of his life in their homes. He visited the Irelands at Manchester, Dr. William Smith and other friends in Edinburgh, Lord and Lady Amberley at Tintern, and the Crawshays at Cyfarthfa Castle. He also visited again the Flowers at Stratford-on-Avon.

His eldest daughter accompanied him on this journey, and was already beginning to be needed as "his memory." In meeting with new persons his failing memory was noticeable, but his friends of twenty-five year before thought him even nobler and sweeter than in the old times. It was during this last visit, I suppose, that Emerson visited Stratford Church with James Walter on a Sunday morning, and remained beside Shakespeare's grave during the service and sermon.

The Englishman was ashamed of the sermon, and relieved when Emerson asked naïvely, "Did he preach?" To which his English friend answered, "Who? Shakespeare?" "Yes!"

My wife and I had the pleasure of being guests with him and his daughter at Cyfarthfa Castle (Merthyr Tydfil). Mrs. Crawshay told me that she was afraid such a devotee of nature might not enjoy her forced strawberries, and rather evaded his question concerning their season in Wales. The Welsh spring might well break forth into earlier strawberries in honour of his visit. At a dinner-party given at Cyfarthfa Castle the most cultivated people of the neighbourhood were invited, but among them was a gentleman more familiar with the antiquities of Wales than with Emerson. At any rate, after the ladies had retired, when Emerson asked him whether traces of Merlin in his prison of air survived in the neighbourhood, he said, Yes, but that he had passed the place at all times and never heard the legendary sighs, nor did he believe the story. "You must be a bold man," said Emerson in his sweetest voice, but with the old twinkle in his eye.

In Wales I had opportunities of walking alone with Emerson, and conversing with him on those great subjects which had been the theme of his teaching in the sacred years at Concord. I discovered, however, that he had become more inclined than formerly to hesitate about stating religious opinions. These opinions he declared unchanged since we had conversed in former years. He was even more optimistic after twenty years, and advised me to trust more to time than destructive criticism in the combat with error. He held his old sentiment about prayer, and said, " If I saw a man on his knees, I should not like to tell that man to get up." Even the attitude of reverence for something above self he thought to be of some value, and suggested that it was a sort of witness against the notion of mediation.

Max Müller dedicated his work on the " Science of Religion " to " Ralph Waldo Emerson, in memory of his visit to Oxford in May, 1873, and in acknowledgment of constant refreshment of head and heart derived from his writings during the last twenty-five years."

Emerson's friends in England "marked round with vermilion " that festal year when he visited the homes he had made nobler and happier; and many were the children brought to him that they might say to their children and children's children, " This hand has been kept purer because it was once touched by Ralph Waldo Emerson."

XXIX.

THE DIADEM OF DAYS.

SOME years ago Emerson was asked by a friend which of his own poems he most valued. He replied, " Days." This piece of eleven lines, as printed in " May-Day," begins " Damsels of Time ; " but I prefer the original word.

> " Daughters of Time, the hypocritic Days,
> Muffled and dumb like barefoot dervishes,
> And marching single in an endless file,
> Bring diadems and fagots in their hands.
> To each they offer gifts after his will,
> Bread, kingdoms, stars, and sky that holds them all.
> I, in my pleached garden, watched the pomp,
> Forgot my morning wishes, hastily
> Took a few herbs and apples, and the Day
> Turned and departed silent. I, too late,
> Under her solemn fillet saw the scorn."

Rare if not imaginary must have been the " day " that did not bear fruit in Emerson's garden. Let us record here the list of his works : —

> Right Hand of Fellowship at the Ordination of H. B. Goodwin. February 17, 1830.
> Sermon and Letter, to the Second Church, Boston. 1832. (Reprinted in " Frothingham's Transcendentalism," 1876.)

Historical Discourse delivered before the Citizens of Concord, 12th September, 1835, on the Second Centennial Anniversary of the Incorporation of the Town. Concord, 1835 (reprinted 1875).

Nature. Boston, 1836.

Carlyle's "Sartor Resartus," edited in conjunction with Le Baron Russell. Introduction by Emerson. Boston, 1836.

Michael Angelo. "North American Review." 1837.

Milton. "North American Review.' 1838.

Letter to President Van Buren (concerning certain wrongs of the Cherokee Indians). "National Intelligencer." Washington, 1838.

Address before the Senior Class in Divinity College. Cambridge, July 15, 1838.

Carlyle's Critical and Miscellaneous Essays. (Edited.) Boston, 1838.

"The Dial." Boston, 1840–44. Emerson's contributions are:— Vol. I.— No. 1, "The Editors to the Reader," "The Problem" (a poem); No. 2, "Thoughts on Modern Literature," "New Poetry," "Woodnotes" (poem); No. 3, "The Sphinx" (poem), "Thoughts on Art;" No. 4, "Man the Reformer."

Vol. II. — No. 2, "Painting and Sculpture," "Fate" (poem), "Walter Savage Landor;" No. 3, "The Senses and the Soul."

Vol. III. — No. 1, "Lectures on the Times," "Tact." "Holidays" (poems), "Prayers," "Fourierism and the Socialists," "Chardon Street and Bible Convention;" No. 2, "Lectures on the Times" ("The Conservative," "English Reformers"), "Saadi" (poem); No. 3, "Lectures on the Times" ("The Transcendentalist"), "Literary Intelligence;" No. 4, "Europe and European Books."

Vol. IV. — No. 1, "Past and Present," "To Rhea" (poem); No. 2, "The Comic," "Ode to Beauty," "A Letter;" No. 3, "Tantalus," "Eros," "The

Times" (poem); No. 4, "The Tragic," "The Young American," "The Visit" (poem).
Essays. First Series. (12.) Boston, 1841. (With Preface by Carlyle. London, 1841.)
Obituary Notice of Ezra Ripley, D.D. "Concord Republican," October 1, 1841.
Carlyle's "Past and Present" (edited). Boston, 1843.
Essays. Second Series. (9.) Boston, 1844.
Address delivered in Concord, August 1, 1844, on the Anniversary of the Emancipation of Negroes in the British West Indies. Boston, 1844. (Reprinted in "The Dial," Cincinnati, November and December, 1860.)
Editors' Address — To the Public. First number of the Massachusetts "Quarterly Review." 1847.
Poems. Boston, 1847.
War — Miss Peabody's Æsthetic Papers. Boston, 1849.
Nature — Addresses and Lectures. Boston, 1849.
Representative Men. Boston, 1850. (Translated into Danish by Thorson, and published at Copenhagen, 1857).
Memoirs of Margaret Fuller Ossoli. (Chapters on Margaret in Concord and in Boston.) Boston, 1852.
English Traits. Boston, 1856. (Translated by Spielhagen. Hanover, 1857.)
Samuel Hoar. "Putnam's Magazine," December, 1856.
The Chartist's Complaint (poem). "Atlantic Monthly," November, 1857.
The Rommany Girl. "Atlantic Monthly." 1858. In same year and magazine, the poems "Days," "Brahma," "Two Rivers," "Waldensamkeit," and essays on "Illusions," "Solitude and Society," "Books," "Persian Poetry," and "Eloquence."
The Sacred Dance. From the Persian. Printed in "The Dial," Cincinnati, January, 1860.
Quatrains. (12.) Cincinnati "Dial," February and March, 1860.
Domestic Life. Printed in "The Dial," Cincinnati, October, 1860.

Speeches concerning John Brown. (At Boston, November 18, 1859; at Concord, December 2; at Salem, January 6, 1860.) "Echoes of Harper's Ferry," 1860.
Culture. "Atlantic Monthly." 1860. Also the "Song of Nature."
Conduct of Life. Boston, 1860.
The Test (poem). "Atlantic Monthly," January. 1861.
American Civilisation. "Atlantic Monthly," April, 1861.
Old Age. "Atlantic Monthly." 1862. In same year and magazine, "The Titmouse" and "Compensation" (poems).
Thoreau. "Atlantic Monthly," August, 1862. (Preface to Thoreau's "Excursions," edited by Emerson, 1866.)
The President's Proclamation. "Atlantic Monthly," November, 1862.
The Boston Hymn. Read in Boston Music Hall, New Year's Day, 1863. "Atlantic Monthly." 1863.
Voluntaries. "Atlantic Monthly." 1863.
Saadi. "Atlantic Monthly." 1864.
Gulistan, or Rose Garden of Saadi. (Gladwin's translation, edited by Emerson, with preliminary essay on Persian Poetry.) Boston, 1865.
Remarks at the Funeral Services of the President (Lincoln) at Concord. April 19, 1865. Boston: "Living Age," May 13, 1865.
Thoreau's Letters (edited). Boston, 1865.
My Garden. "Atlantic Monthly." 1866.
Character. "North American Review." 1866.
Terminus. "Atlantic Monthly." 1867.
Address at a Meeting to Organise the "Free Religious Association." 1867.
Aspects of Culture. Phi Beta Kapa Address at Harvard University, 1867. "Atlantic Monthly," January, 1868.
May-Day, and other pieces. Boston, 1867.
Address before the "Free Religious Association." Proceedings of Second Annual Meeting, 1869.
Society and Solitude. Boston, 1870. (Haarlem, translated into Dutch by Augusta Pease.)

Introduction to Goodwin's edition of Plutarch's "Morals." Boston, 1870.
Preface to W. E. Channing's poem, "The Wanderer." Boston, 1871.
Speech at Howard University. Washington, 1872.
Address at the Opening of Concord Free Public Library. 1873.
Verses quoted in W. E. Channing's "Thoreau." 1873.
Address at Unveiling of the "Minute Man" Monument on the Hundredth Anniversary of the Concord Fight, April 19, 1875.
Select Poems. Boston, 1876. (Containing several not in previous volumes.)
Letters and Social Aims. Boston, 1876.
Parnassus. A volume of choice poems selected from the whole range of English Literature, by Emerson, with a prefatory Essay. Boston, 1874.
Demonology. "North American Review." 1877.
Perpetual Forces. "North American Review." 1877.
Fortune of the Republic. Lecture given at Old South Church, Boston, March 30, 1878.
The Sovereignty of Ethics. "North American Review." 1878.
The Preacher. (Originally written as a parlour lecture to some divinity students in 1867; afterwards enlarged from earlier writings and read in the chapel of Divinity College, Harvard University, May 5, 1879.) "Unitarian Review.' 1879.
Preface to "One Hundred Greatest Men." London, 1879.
Paper on Carlyle read before the Massachusetts Historical Society. "Scribner's Magazine." 1881.
Superlatives. "The Century." February, 1882.

But these books do not represent all the diadems and fagots that Emerson received from his days. For he distributed them far and wide; they are the treasure and strength of innumerable hearts and homes. One day as we walked in that garden he gave me a plum, saying, "At its best it is the fruit of paradise." Such indeed I found it; the light and warmth of many days were garnered in the lustrous fruit, and the last subtle touch of its perfection was added by the ripening beam in the giver's eye. The divine genius was in all his herbs and apples, and although he might put on the mask of the Days, and veil his gifts in casual humourous phrase, his every word and action were of the organic beauty of his nature. Such gifts as he had could not be given, any more than those of the Days, except to enterprise.

It may seem a light thing that Emerson should give me a plum in his garden and call it the fruit of paradise. It was lightly said and done; nevertheless I began to realise that the secret of wisdom is to be able to recognise the day while it is shining, as it will be recognised in the long perspective of memory, and every day that I was able to bear that in mind, while with Emerson, brought its plum. Some of these are gathered in this chapter of further personal recollections.

"The Day cannot be known to the Day," says Goethe. But Emerson shewed us that it can be. When did he learn this art of living out all his days? I have already told of one who in his youth drove with Emerson on Sunday to his appointment at East Lexington and heard him repeat George Herbert's hymn, "Sweet day! so cool, so calm, so bright." Twenty years later he used to teach us along the same road that every day is a splendour of opportunity, and that immortality is but a verbal counter unless it be an instant experience.

"Deb Socco hopes that her Deb Soccoism will last for ever. She should be encouraged to get rid of her Deb Soccoism." "An actually existent fly is more important than a possibly existent angel." This last was said in reference to some new speculation in eschatology. "When I talked with Coleridge and others about immortality, it soon became slain that they had nothing to say equal to Plato's phædo.' Their talk was only a fine apology for nability to help me where I desired help, and so you would find any opinion of my own if I should give it you to-day. But of what use were even the certainty of an eternity of days until we have learned how to realise the fulness of one? Eternity is not duration. The artist said *pingo in æternitatem*, and this *æternitatem*, if I paint for it, is already mine."

In every way possible, and with every hint, did our loving teacher try to save us from delusions that might defraud us of our lives; if any one nodded and fell into teleology, Emerson's eye was sure to be caught at that moment by a curious wildflower, or unique grass blade, or a spider's web in which our speculative fledgling was softly enmeshed. But the great instruction was that he made our day so beautiful and so luminous that it seemed always festal when he was near, and one's heart spake as Glauco to Socrates, "The whole of life, O Teacher, is the measure of hearing such discourse as thine."

It was afternoon when I first met Emerson, but the morning was in his face as he welcomed me. He was now fifty years of age, but seemed younger; his manner was cordial and simple, and his voice at once relieved me of the trembling with which I stood before him — the first great man I had ever seen. (I had seen, however, the President and Senators whose names were upon the tongue of the nation.) Mrs. Emerson sent in an invitation that I should dine with them. Afterwards he took me on a walk; and while he was preparing I had an opportunity of looking around his library. Over the mantelpiece hung his " Parcæ : " on it was a statuette of Goethe, of whom there was an engraved portrait on the walls, also portraits of Shakespeare, Swedenborg, and Montaigne. Afterwards Emerson shewed me a number of other portraits of Goethe which he had collected, and several of Dante, including a photograph of the Ravenna mask. I also remember a beautiful engraving of Puck, flying through the air under the stars, whose light contrasted with that in the windows of a castle. The furniture of the room was old-fashioned and simple. The shelves at which I looked most hungrily were those occupied by Emerson's own manuscript lectures and essays, of which there seemed to be enough to fill many volumes.

On this first walk Emerson took me to Walden Water. A crystal was the lakelet that day, in setting of emerald, clear and calm, the fit haunt of a poet. In its transparent depths were seen the fishes, and around it sang many birds. In a few moments we were swimming in the sparkling water.

Having bathed, we sat down on the shore, near the site of Thoreau's vanished hermitage; then Walden and its woods began to utter their soft spells through the lips of my poet. Emerson's conversation was different from that of any other I have met. The contrast between his talk and that of Carlyle was remarkable. Carlyle was, in a sense, the more striking figure, but his manner and tone revived dreams of historic characters; one said, "Surely this is Jeremias," or presently it might be Diogenes, Hans Sachs, Luther, or some other personage more or less conventionalised in the imagination. But Emerson suggested none other; he was strictly incomparable, and he never appeared to speak what had been thought or said before that moment. One always felt that there was a line around Carlyle's vehemence and wrathful eloquence; there was something that stood for authority; but every word of Emerson began where authority ended. Emerson was an instinctive artist, and never brought out cannon to slay sparrows. Every one who has witnessed the imperial dignity, or felt the weight of authentic knowledge, which characterised Carlyle's conversation to such an extent that his slight utterances seemed to stand out like pillars of Hercules, must also have felt the earth tremble, as if under "the hammer of Thor" (to remember an expression I once heard Emerson use about Carlyle); but though the same falsehood might be fatally smitten by our American, it was by the invisible, inaudible sunstroke, which left the sky as bright and blue as before. Where general truths and principles were discussed, whilst Carlyle astonished by the range of his sifted knowledge, he did not convey an impression of having originally thought out problems involved in other departments than his own; but the mind of Emerson had no special habitat; there was scarcely a realm of science and art in which he could not instruct the academies. I have heard Agassiz say that he preferred Emerson's conversation on scientific subjects to that of any man he knew. Monologues, like those of Carlyle, were impossible to Emerson; they come of the more viviparous mind; whereas Emerson's talk was in phrases of which each was, indeed, felicitous, but more remarkable for its productiveness under further thought and experience. An English physician, a friend of Emerson, told me that Emerson required a little wine to make his table-talk perfect.

I remember him on that day at Walden as Bunyan's pilgrim might remember the Interpreter. He listened to some rough fishermen in boats, far out from shore, calling to each other about their affairs, remarking how their voices were intoned by the distance and the water to music. He pointed out some of the Walden flora, and observing the suggestiveness of some shapes, as the arrowhead, showed that he had already an original plant-lore. He spoke only as occasion arose, and was very gracious to me. There was no need that he should talk; simply to be with him was to me joy enough, and I put no questions. We were having heated debates in theology at the Divinity College, and to leave them for this presence was like a plunge from sultry air into Walden. "I am not much interested in such discussions," he said; "it does seem deplorable that there should be a tendency in some people to creeds which would take man back to the chimpanzee." "I have very good grounds for being a Unitarian and a Trinitarian too. I need not nibble for ever at one loaf, but eat it and thank God for it, and earn another." He told me about Theodore Parker, who was evidently a most picturesque person to him, and I think he compared him with Socrates. He also had once thought of building himself a study out there beside Walden. But Thoreau was "not in awe of early tea, and could do what others cannot." He found in Thoreau that deeper piety vulgarly regarded as impiety, like George Herbert's sweet intimacy with his deity, "with whom he sometimes cracks jokes." What Emerson once called the "wailing sound" coming from the young world struggling to free itself from dogmas, was but faintly heard in woods melodious with the faith and the flute of Thoreau; but whenever that sound reached him, Emerson felt grateful to Theodore Parker. "It is a comfort to remember that there is one sane voice amid the religious and political confusions of the country." He could not go to church, but supported the village minister, because "it is well to have a conscientious man to sit on town committees, to be active in the moral affairs of the place, to attend the sick and the dead." I had been indignant at a remark made publicly by the said minister (Frost) about his (Emerson's) utter hopelessness when his child died, but if he had heard of it, Emerson felt no resentment, and continued his support to this minister and his successors.

Emerson often advised above all things care of health. "Sound sleep is genius," he said. He quoted Dr. Johnson's declaration, "every man is a rascal when he is sick," and in his playful serious way said he thought it might be true that sickness is the result of some wickedness. "One sometimes suspects that outer have something to do with inner complaints, and when one is ill, something the devil's the matter."

He gave me much counsel about books and reading. It was, he said, a great point to get hold of the right book when it was personally needed, and not too soon or too late. "The time comes when one requires quantity rather than quality;" Goethe awaits that. Not everybody is old enough to read the "Elective Affinities." He maintained that the best in every book is translatable, and that to read foreign books in the original after they were translated, was like swimming a river instead of going over the bridge. It might do for an occasional exercise. He delighted in the poetical translations from the German by some of his friends, — J. S. Dwight, Dr. Frothingham; and, especially, a few by Christopher P. Cranch, whose genius was highly valued by Emerson, as I need hardly say to those who have read that charming book, "The Bird and the Bell." He often spoke of Carlyle with warm personal affection, but it was plain to me that the later works of his friend were regarded by Emerson as unhealthy. When the "Life of Friedrich" was appearing he derived great benefit from it, and wrote warm thanks to Carlyle for each volume; but there was some hesitation when it became a question whether any youth should re-enter the old atmosphere of enthusiasm which had surrounded Carlyle's writings. As much care was needed to get at the best in Carlyle's book as to get at the heart of the man. "When I was in England," he said, "young men desired me to introduce them to Carlyle; but I said, 'Why will you have this vitriol thrown over you?'"

In current literature, he said, the really useful books are those that deal seriously with some prominent point or question. "The interest of 'Jane Eyre,' for instance, is that it puts earnestly such a question. There are writers who write much, and much that is not important, but still shew ability to advance thought at some point. Those are the writers to get hold of." "These novels by Elizabeth Shepherd have an interest in the fact that they shew powerful persons recognising character and superiority under whatever plain exterior or in humble position, as in 'Counterparts.'" Talking of Browning's "Paracelsus" he did not think Paracelsus aspired; "it is the mere canine hunger for knowledge for the power it gives." "When nature wants an artist, she makes Tennyson, and everything good is artistic." The work of Tennyson he liked least was "In Memoriam." He valued highly the romances of George Borrow, George Sand, and Manzoni. But Emerson was rarely enthusiastic except about certain ancient books, and especially "scriptures." "The Bhagavat Gita is of high importance, and also the Bhagavat Purana, — ah! there is a book to be read on one's knees! These Oriental bibles are more intellectual than the Hebrew and Christian, but not so fervent." He personally loved Saadi. "I lately found a charming story about Saadi. He was travelling on foot towards Damascus, alone and weary. Presently he overtook a boy travelling the same way, and asked him to point out the road. The boy offered to guide him some distance, and in the course of conversation, Saadi spoke of having come from Persia and from Schiraz. 'Schiraz!' exclaimed the boy, 'then perhaps you can tell me something of Sheik Saadi who resides there.' The other said, 'I am Saadi.' Instantly the boy knelt and kissed the hem of his skirt with tears, and after that could not be parted from Saadi, but guided and served him during all his stay in Damascus." "Von Hammer's 'Redekunste' is one of the precious books; and Hafiz, 'the tongue of the secret,' as they called him, — who, however, wants translating. The Desatir, or Book of the Seven Prophets, is one of the great collections."

Careful readers of Walt Whitman will not wonder that Emerson should have been the first to greet him. The Oriental largeness and optimism which he admired in ancient books are not to be found in any modern page except that of Walt Whitman. There was an outcry when Emerson's enthusiastic letter to Walt Whitman was published, and some friends wrote to him of misfortunes he had led them into by inducing them to try reading the "Leaves of Grass" aloud in the presence of ladies. Emerson agreed that if he had known his letter to Walt Whitman would be published, he might have made some deductions from his praise. "There are parts of the book where I hold my nose as I read. One must not be too squeamish when a chemist brings him to a mass of filth and says, 'See, the great laws are at work here also;' but it is a fine art if he can deodorise his illustration. However, I do not fear that any man who has eyes in his head will fail to see the genius in these poems. Those are terrible eyes to walk along Broadway. It is all there, as if in an auctioneer's catalogue."

Emerson's letter to Whitman says of the "Leaves of Grass," — "It meets the demand I am always making of what seemed the sterile and stingy nature, as if too much handiwork or too much lymph in the temperament were making our Western wits fat and mean. I give you joy of your free and brave thought." This was written in July, 1855. By Emerson's suggestion, being about to visit New York, I went to see Walt Whitman, and, I think, sent a report to Concord. Soon after Emerson had praised Whitman's democratic poetry, some Bohemians invented a story that Emerson had been converted by Walt from his spirituality and solitude, and had come to the conclusion that motley was the only wear. He must enter into the holes and dens and know life. Consequently finding himself one day in Broadway — so ran the fable — he put on the air of a rough as well as he could, and presenting himself at a public bar, demanded " a glass of grog." It was said the barkeeper folded his arms, looked his customer in the eye for a moment, and remarked, " I guess lemonade will do for you.'

When his own poetry was praised Emerson interrupted with, " You forget ; we are damned for poetry." He included his own poetry under his label for much American work of that kind — " verses." None could come up to his unyielding standard. Rufus Griswald he held an interesting person, as the one man who has discovered the existence of American Poetry. Not that he did not love and value his contemporaries and literary friends ; he rejoiced in them ; but he was remorseless in his demands about poetry. Poe was merely " the man who jingles." Of moderns, Carlyle most nearly approached his poetic standard. Of himself he said once, when forced to speak, " My reputation, such as it is, will be one day cited to prove the poverty of this time."

Emerson's poetry was never so much liked as his prose; for the reason, as I believe, that it presupposed in the reader a much wider knowledge of science, philosophy, and mythology.

In my first summer with Emerson he gave me Arthur Clough's "Bothie" to read. He read to me the beautiful lines in which Philip describes the silent look of Elspie as she passed him. The scholar suddenly terminated his flirtations with the Highland maiden and disappeared, and writes back to his vacation-comrades: —

"I was walking along, some two miles from the cottage,
  Full of my dreamings. A girl went by in a party with others;
  She had a cloak on, was stepping on quickly, for rain was beginning.
  But as she passed, from her hood I saw her eyes look at me;
  So quick a glance, so regardless I, that although I had felt it,
  You couldn't properly say our eyes met. She cast it and left it."

In the vacation I found a room to lodge in at Concord, on Ponkawtassett Hill. Emerson had offered to lend me books, and to give me suggestions as to reading; though, indeed, what I most desired was to study his own works, and to be as much as possible in his presence. His mornings I always held sacred, but it was his custom to take a walk in the afternoon, and he invited me to go with him on these. I was fearful about this also, for I knew he loved solitude, but he promised that if he desired to be alone he would let me know. Two or three times every week I went to walk with him. Once or twice I thought I observed a doubt in his face, and proposed to take his children on a boating or other excursion, for I had already been accepted by them as a comrade.

Emerson's mission was to individual minds. Those who were drawn to him, or those in whom he perceived a tendency of growth, found in him a good shepherd who carried them in his arms. He did not like to deal with people on general principles, but recognised the particular talent and the state of each who sought him, and was maternal in his faithfulness no less than his tenderness to them. He was the friend of souls. For this reason few of his conversations would bear to be reported. I was just twenty-one years of age when I first met him, and often since, reflecting how crude I was, his patience and kindness have been remembered with grateful emotion.

He sometimes talked to young men of love and matrimony. He feared that intellectual men were those most apt to make mistakes in this most vital of interests, perhaps through a certain precocity which might be felt as maturity. They were the natural lovers of beauty, and all the more should study beauty to know the farther beauty. The best security of happiness in marriage is that it should follow a fair degree of culture, especially in the taste for beauty. The age waits for that tardy kind of youth who will not rush upon a career, but can wait. "The engineer asked, 'How long shall we wait for that signal to move?' The guard replied, 'Wait till the wheels rust off their axles.' Any delay is better than a collision with the forces that cannot be resisted." With regard to the various schemes of people for reforming the world, he thought that the danger in all such things is the tendency to pedantry. The Quaker making a great point of his hat and buttons was what movements are likely to come to when they are organised. They are alive to the first man, to the next they are a tradition, to the third a dogma. Against " spiritualism " he was strong in his admonitions. If one cannot trust one's senses there is nothing and nobody he can trust.

But on most matters I found him not inclined to give very positive opinions, especially, I suppose, to one then inclined to worship him; his constant aim being to lead out thought, and to excite one to take his own view of a matter. I think if Emerson ever affected anything it must have been the interest he took in the nascent ideas of some of his young admirers. He never snubbed any of those who gathered around him, but gave to each the right word to be cherished for ever.

There could be no question, however, about the delight with which he sometimes sat at the feet of children. I have known him quote the opinions of his own in grave companies. "My son says of Tom Hughes' characters, 'These are real boys,' and I have great faith in his opinion." A host of the poems collected in " Parnassus " were read to his children in the stages of their growth, and I doubt not some are there through domestic suffrage. His talk with any child that approached him was as gracious and dignified as his conversation with elder persons; he was dear to every child that knew him, and these were many.

He was fond of the festivities and pleasure-parties

which form so important a feature of the Concord summer. "Whom shall we invite to the berrying?" cried his daughter, running in. "All children from six years to sixty," was the reply. Edith looked steadily for a moment, then ran off to act in the spirit rather than the letter of the answer. On these occasions Emerson had a way of presently turning up at some point of our march, and his grave conversation with one or two of the elders was rarely so charming as when thus casual, and alternating with remarks to the children.

Emerson's optimism was qualified, if at all, only by a horror of sickness; in all other matters he was so free from all impatience that it seemed to amuse him in others. He sometimes appeared to require defenders, and was not without them. Once when Emerson, in his study, was talking in his finest strain, his farm-hand broke his sentence in two with report of a broken rake. The Celtic head protruding in at the door said, "The hay's not half in, sir, and the rake we got at Mr. Jones's is broke; here it is, sir." "Bring it here, Stephen," said Emerson, and proceeded to examine the implement profoundly. It seemed to me as he held it beneath his half-inspired, half-mirthful eye, that it was not a rake concrete but the rake absolute and eternal. "Stephen," he said at last, "take it to Mr. Smith to be mended." "But," remonstrated Stephen indignantly, "we only got it yesterday, sir; hadn't I better take it back to Jones." "Mr. Jones probably did not know it was bad; we'll take it to Smith, Stephen." When the Irishman had disappeared, Emerson intimated his fear that Stephen would compel poor Jones to mend it after all, not being able to see that, even on his own theory, Jones was the least competent for his great purpose — getting in the hay. Of course I have not the actual names right in this anecdote, which, for the rest, is interesting apart from the gentle dignity and friendly simplicity with which the great man conversed with his workman. In truth, many a lesson did Emerson learn from such humble and faithful workmen. He himself was farming invisible acres above their heads, but with the same reality and necessary method as any sower going forth to sow. He loved to talk with gardener or farmer, if occasion arose, and was no doubt glad to have a rake broken now and then to supply occasion. Many of their hints have blossomed on his page.

I once visited with him Longworth's Catawba wine vaults at Cincinnati, the workmen in which were chiefly Germans. As we were leaving, I mentioned what the wine-makers had told me, that the bottled wine stirred at the vine-blossoming season, and it was then casks and bottles were most apt to burst. He smiled as we passed on, and said, "The idea is very German." Seven years later I read in "May-Day" —

> " When trellised grapes their flowers unmask,
> And the new-born tendrils twine,
> The old wine darkling in the cask
> Feels the bloom on the living vine,
> And bursts the hoops at hint of spring:
> And so, perchance, in Adam's race,
> Of Eden's bower some dreamlike trace
> Survived the Flight, and swam the Flood,
> And wakes the wish in youngest blood

> To tread the forfeit Paradise,
> And feed once more the exile's eyes;
> And ever when the happy child
> In May beholds the blooming wild,
> And hears in heaven the bluebird sing,
> ' Onward,' he cries, ' your baskets bring —
> In the next field is air more mild,
> And o'er yon hazy crest is Eden's balmier spring.' "

Although Emerson's garb was not rustic, it was plain, never smart, and, with his homely speech and simple manners, he did not find the country-folk shy. The phenomena of the universe were going on in and around Concord, and Emerson kept up a good relation with the humblest purveyors of fact and experience. They were richly rewarded when the day came for Emerson to lecture in the town-hall, when many a farming villager saw his prosaic fact risen to a star and shining in its constellation.

What a day was that when Emerson's lecture came on! Remembering what Longfellow had told me about those sophisticated Bostonians whose faces were as extinguished lamps when listening to Emerson's early lectures, I have remarked the contrast when, with illumined countenances, his villagers were gathered before him at Concord. They knew his voice and followed him. All the sermons in the village churches for a year were not so well remembered as some of his sentences. It has seemed to me that Emerson never spoke so well elsewhere as to his Concord audience. When I first heard him there, he appeared, as he arose, to be the very type of the New England farmer, so plain in dress and so thoroughly standing on his own feet. Ere long he was unsheathed, and we were in the hall of Pericles. It was then that I first heard Emerson, and, while it is the most vivid experience of my life, I find it nearly impossible to transcribe it. I recall no gesture, only an occasional swaying forward of the body by the impulse of earnestness. Though nearly every word had been written, the manuscript did not hold his eye, which kept its magnetic play upon the audience. At one time, indeed, he searched his memory for a quotation from Plato which he wished to introduce, his hand going to his chin and his face turning aside from us as if he would find the words written on the wall. The sentence found was well worth the pause. As he proceeded it was as if genial sunbeams dialled themselves on the mind in unfolding buds of beautiful reasons and the closing of errors. Now and then fell a softly consuming sunstroke upon some reptilian baseness of the time coiled in the garden that grew around his thought. One was not the same man after such an experience. There had been a fall and a redemption, vanishings from us, but no blank misgivings, rather a new courage of hearts thenceforth moving about in a realisable new world. Never, once more must I say, were flowers more symbolical than those pinks, pansies, and roses, shaped into an open book above the Sage, as he lay in Concord church, with " Finis " on the page. His weapons against error and wrong were like those roses, in Goethe's *Faust*, with which the angels drove away the demons, and his sceptre was made known by blossoming in his hand.

Emerson's humour as read has lost some of the flavour it possessed when spoken. Indeed, I have noted here and there the omission from a printed essay of some sally which elicited when it was spoken much mirth, and think he was inclined to suspect any passage which had excited laughter. There was omitted from his lecture on "Superlatives," when recently printed in "The Century," a remark about oaths. The oath, he said, could only be used by a thinking man in some great moral emergency; in such rare case it might be the verdict of the universe; but, he added in a low tone, as if thinking to himself as he turned his page — " but sham damns disgust." I remember, too, how quietly a little drama was mounted on his face when he described a pedant pedagogue questioning a little maid at the school-examination about Odoacer and Alaric. Sylvina can't remember, but suggests that Odoacer was defeated; and the professor tartly replies, " No, he defeated the Romans." But it is of no importance at all about Odoacer, and a great deal of importance about Sylvina; and if she says he was defeated, why, he had better, a great deal, have been defeated than give her a moment's annoy. Odoacer, if there had been a particle of the gentleman in him, would rather have been defeated a thousand times, than that Sylvina's feelings should be hurt.

These humourous passages came from Emerson gently, little wayside surprises, and without any air of intention to excite laughter. One of his wittiest lectures, never published, was that on the French; it is full of racy anecdotes derived from his sojourn in Paris during the revolution of 1848. In it he contrasted French love of display with English love of reality. "A Frenchman invented the dickey; an Englishman added the shirt." He delivered this lecture to a large audience in Philadelphia where an incident followed a story he told. "A Frenchman and an Englishman fought a duel in the dark; they were to be let out of the room after two pistol reports had been heard. The Englishman, to avoid wounding his antagonist, crept round to the fireplace; he fired up the chimney and brought down the Frenchman." After the mirth that ensued was over, Emerson passed on to grave discourse with the words, "The French will have things theatrical; God will have things real." But some individual tardily caught the joke about the duel, and his solitary explosion set the house in a roar that made the lecturer pause.

Emerson's conversation on religious topics was always occasional, and it was strictly adapted to the personal conditions. He taught those who would be teachers that truth could never be upheld by any word that would make it repulsive. We should remember that all liberal people were once orthodox, and that the tenacity of orthodoxy was a good sinew for the farther work. "Every leading man among the Unitarians came from among the orthodox." These born Unitarians he thought lacked momentum. I never knew him dissuade any one from entering the pulpit which he had abandoned; he left us to adjust ourselves to practical exigencies as we could, only always reminding his young friends that there was a goal to be reached, and expecting the most of them." "Well, yes," he wrote to one just ordained, "go bravely onward, and we seniors shall wait, with a hope that may become homage, the experiences of faithful years, and the fulfilment of generous promises."

One evening, in a small company, I had the misfortune to get into a controversial conversation with some ladies who were evidently pained by some of my opinions, or the crude expression of them. Emerson sat in silence, but when we were going home said, "I thought at one time I would put in an oar, but concluded it were better not. You were quite right in your criticisms, but, after all, one need not remind a child enjoying a play that the scene is all pasteboard, all those jewels are paste." "But," I pleaded, "it did not occur to me they were children." "Well, that is a fair reply. People ought not to remain children."

On a berrying party, just before my graduation, Emerson spoke to me about our studies in Divinity College. I enumerated them, and he said, "I cannot feel interested in Christianity. The thoughts and words of a great man becoming at last the inheritance of donkeys, they make them into a system suitable to themselves and into institutions; for these they will lie, and will hate and malign others who have different thoughts; and they do not see that their arguments are refuted by their lack of the mind and character which alone might prove their case."

I can only give the substance of this pregnant thought, with exception of the first sentence, that startled me, and I have not forgotten the words. "It would seem," he said again, "that there should be an end sometime to these controversies and this casuistry. Why should one ask me an opinion about miracles? I am familiar with similar narratives in other books than the Bible, and have no difficulty in dealing with them there. Look into the diamond eyes of that child, and see her hair of sunshine. What is a Jewish or Christian miracle beside it?"

What we used to call the problem of evil was no problem to Emerson. He told me it had been made clear to him when he first came to a perception of the law of development in nature — " from the sponge up to Hercules," to remember his phrase of 1835. The fact lay in that phrase, " arrested development." There is no evil in nature, in the theologic sense of evil; each organisation is fit for its own purpose, but when it is not fit for mine I call it evil. Cat is evil to mouse. If the obstructed is of higher organisation than the obstructor, he erects his standard of good, and whatever is contrary to it he pronounces bad. Development is shewn in the degree of approach to that; all that falls short of the standard is arrest. Immorality means people living out their several shortcomings, or comings-short of the social standard. Prisons are asylums for arrested developments. This phenomenon of arrest in nature was popularly called the Devil. But since this Devil was adopted by theology he has become a name for some good things, as one calls him " the great Second Best." This is the substance of what Emerson said.

I close these anecdotes of days passed with Emerson with recollections of a Sunday morning when he delivered a discourse to five thousand people in Boston Music Hall, from the desk then recently made vacant by Theodore Parker's death. No doubt when this discourse is published it will shew discrepancies with my notes, but I give my impressions as written shortly after listening to it. He began by calling attention to the tendency to simplification. The inventor knows that a machine is new and improvable when it has a great many parts. The chemists find the infinite variety of things contained in a few elements, and physicists promise that this number shall be reduced. Faraday declares his belief that all things will in the end be reduced to one element with two polarities. Religious progress has similarly been in the direction of simplification. Every great religion has in its ultimate development told its whole secret, concentrated its force, in some simple maxims. In our youth we talk of the various virtues, the many dangers and trials of life; as we get older we find ourselves returning to the proverbs of the nursery.

> " A few strong instincts and a few plain rules,
> Among the herdsmen of the Alps, have wrought
> More for mankind at this unhappy day
> Than all the pride of intellect and thought."

In religion one old book serves many lands, ages, and varieties of character; nay, one or two golden rules out of the book are enough. The many teachers and Scriptures are at last but various routes by which we always come to the simple law of obedience to the light in the soul. "Seek nothing outside of thyself," says one; "Believe nothing against thy own spirit," echoes another part of the world. Jesus said, "Be lowly; hunger and thirst after justice; of your own minds judge what is right." Swedenborg teaches that heaven and hell are the loves of the soul. George Fox removes the bushel from the light within. The substance of all morals is that a man should adhere to the path which the inner light has marked before him. The great waste in the world comes of the misapplication of energy. The tragedies of the soul are strung on those threads not spun out of our own hearts. One records of Michael Angelo that he found him working on his statue with a lamp stuck in his cap, and it might almost symbolise the holier light of patient devotion to his art. No matter what your work is, let it be yours; no matter if you are tinker or preacher, blacksmith or President, let what you are doing be organic, let it be in your bones, and you open the door by which the affluence of heaven and earth shall stream into you. You shall have the hidden joy, and shall carry success with you. Look to yourself rather than to materials: nothing is unmanageable to a good hand; no place slippery to a good foot; all things are clear to a good head. The sin of dogmatism, of creeds and catechisms, is that they destroy mental character. Intellect without character is mere fidgetiness. The youth says that he believes, when he is only browbeaten; he says he thinks so and so, when that so and so are the denial of any right to think. Simplicity and self-trust are thus lost, and with them the sentiment of obligation to a principle of life and honour. In the legends of the Round Table it is told that a witch wishing to make her child supremely wise, prepared certain herbs and put them in a pot to boil, intending to bathe the child's eyes with the decoction. She set a shepherd boy to stir the pot whilst she went away. Whilst he stirred it a raven dropped a twig into the pot, which spattered three drops of the liquid into the shepherd's eyes. Immediately all the future became as if passing before his eyes; and seeing that when the witch returned she meant to kill him, he left the pot and fled to the woods. Now if three drops of that all-revealing decoction should suddenly get into the eyes of every human being crowding along Washington street some day, how many of them would still go on with the affair they are pursuing on the street? Probably they would nearly all come to a dead stand! But there would, let us hope, be here and there a happy child of the Most High, who had taken hold of her or his life's thread by sacred appointment. These would move on without even a pause: the unveiled future would shew the futility of many schemes, the idleness of many labours; but every genuine aim would only be exalted, and shewn in eternal and necessary relations. Finally, Humility was, the speaker declared, the one element to which all virtues are reducible. "It was revealed unto me," said the old Quaker, "that what other men trample on must be thy food." It is the spirit that accepts our trust, and is thus the creator of character and the guide to power. Then, lowering his voice, as one might speak on his knees, he recited the sublime paradoxes of Dante's apostrophe to the Virgin:—

> "O Virgin Mother, daughter of thy son,
> Created beings all in lowliness
> Surpassing, as in height thou art
> Above them all."

In conclusion, Emerson related the story from Manzoni's "I Promessi Sposi" of the nobleman who slew another in a brawl, in penitence for which he became a friar. When the slain man's brother demanded this Fra Cristoforo's humiliation before the proud family — not that he cared much for his brother, a worthless fellow, but to make a page in the family history — the friar was eager so to atone for his deed. There was no attempt at effect in Emerson's descriptions — no gestures — yet the subtlest actor could not more have moved the vast audience. On his face was seen that face of the friar in which every eye read perfect sincerity and courage. We saw the friar, frank and fearless, kneeling to confess his wrong, and, pleading in justification, ask pardon of those he had deprived of a brother. We saw his victory through humiliation, the servants kissing the hem of his coarse garment, the proud lord hastening to raise him, to disown anger, to offer him fine food which he would not taste, begging only a little bread and salt as a token of forgiveness; and finally, when Fra Cristoforo had departed through the company, kneeling for the blessing of him who had knelt, we saw the bewildered nobleman saying, "That devil of a monk, if he had knelt there longer, I believe I should have asked his pardon for killing my own brother." A smile beamed on the face of the speaker, and played on the faces before him, at these his last words; but by the time he gathered up his pages and sat down, his listeners were in tears. For some moments the assembly of five thousand sat in a stillness that was sacred.

This man in the beginning of that generation had been compelled to leave his pulpit because he could not administer an Eastern sacrament: now did we receive from him the substance of that shadow, and the kneeling heart whispered — Take, eat: it is his body and his blood he gives thee.

XXX.

LETHE.

"LIFE is unnecessarily long," was a sentence that once startled an audience listening to Emerson. It might be true enough of those he described as floating balloon-like over lands and seas, and settling down the same bubbles of breath that started; but for this man visibly and audibly growing, it was appalling to contemplate decay and death. Long years afterwards I read in a letter of his an expression of apprehension that he might live too long, and a suggestion that even suicide might be better than to mar or undo one's work. This was near the close of the civil war in America, which, as I have said, was a strain upon Emerson's nerves from which, probably, they never completely recovered. At any rate, those nearest him had observed indications of physical decline before the burning of his house in 1872. He said that, on the morning after this fire, he felt something snap in his brain. It is probable Emerson might not have survived the illness that followed this severe shock, had it not been for the love and devotion which everywhere rose around him. It was the least part of this manifestation that it insisted, despite his reluctance, on rebuilding his house for him; the almost passionate love, not only of his Concordians, but of many whose names he had never heard, breathed new life into him. Some day, perhaps, the correspondence which passed on this subject may be made public, and it will reveal a touching incident in the life of this great heart, so loving and beloved.

When he came to England after the fire, with his daughter Ellen, his head was quite clear of hair, like that of an infant. When he returned from a visit to Egypt his head was covered with a snowy downy hair half an inch long. He was in fair physical condition, and cheerful, but already his memory did him but fitful service. Carlyle contended that Emerson's memory was as good as ever, only " he paid less attention to the foolish things said to him; they came in at one ear and went out at the other." But Emerson knew well enough that this was not the fact. Yet he was good-humoured about it, and when a friend asked after his health replied, " Quite well; I have lost my mental faculties, but am perfectly well."

In 1875, when I stayed at his house in Concord for a little time, it was sad enough to find him sitting as a listener before those who used to sit at his feet in silence. But when alone with him he conversed in the old way, and his faults of memory seemed at times to disappear. There was something striking in the kind of forgetfulness by which he suffered. He remembered the realities and uses of things when he could not recall their names. He would describe what he wanted or thought of; when he could not recall "chair" he could speak of that which supports the human frame, and " the implement that cultivates the soil" must do for plough. Could it be that idealism had such deep root in this mind that even disease, veiling the "nominal" world, was held at bay when assailing mental concepts?

Among the matters we discussed at that time was the report of an interview with him, published in an American paper, in which he had criticised Swinburne severely. He said he could not remember what he had said at the interview, but "its publication was one of the damnable things."

He evinced some emotion when I said the house and rooms were not distinguishable from what they had been before the fire. The loving art with which his friends and neighbours had made this exact restoration, and the welcome they had given him on his last return from England — the music, the hundreds of children singing "Sweet Home," the floral decorations, — had overwhelmed him at the time, but they were now a happy memory that could not be dimmed.

In 1880, when I was last at Concord, the trouble had made heavy strides. The intensity of his silent attention to every word that was said was painful, suggesting a concentration of his powers to break through the invisible walls closing around him. Yet his face was serene; he was even cheerful, and joined in our laughter at some letters his eldest daughter had preserved, from young girls, trying to coax autograph letters, and in one case asking for what price he would write a valedictory address she had to deliver at college! He was still able to joke about his "naughty memory;" and no complaint came from him when he once rallied himself on living too long. Emerson, appeared to me strangely beautiful at this time, and the sweetness of his voice, when he spoke of the love and providence at his side, is quite indescribable.

The answer of the Methodist, Father Taylor, when told Emerson had not the faith that was saving — that if he went to hell, he would change the climate and emigration would set that way — found one day a curious commentary. A number of Methodist ministers began this emigration by going to Concord together to pay their respects to Emerson. One of them described the call to a friend of mine as delightful. "Emerson," he said, " looked a little doubtful at first — as though he thought, perhaps, we had come to put him through the catechism — but became re-assured, affable, and charming, as it dawned on him that it was in compliment to his fame as a wise man and a great scholar." On his death, the Methodist paper, "Zion's Herald," said: "Certainly a beautiful life, that for late years has been like an ancient psalm, full of solemn melody, has ceased to be read among men."

It is to be feared he was not always so happy in his pious visitors. One, at any rate, visited him with the hope of getting some kind of sanction for his own little theology. But Emerson rose to this occasion; and when asked his religious views, walked to the shelf of his works and said, "There are my opinions; I have nothing to take from them."

It is in one sense melancholy to know that Emerson's son was under the necessity of contradicting insinuations that his father had receded from his religious views; while at the same time one cannot wonder that superstition should feel uneasy under its conscious inability to produce or to satisfy the finest head and grandest heart in America. It may be that yet such claims will be made; but, if true, as they certainly are not, they would only be of pathological interest, and shew that the real Emerson had departed this life sooner than had been supposed.

Apart from such liabilities and annoyances as this, it was not without compensation that Emerson's memory failed. His sensitive heart was thereby saved many a pang. This occurred to me when I was walking with him and his wife and son to the house of her brother, Dr. Charles Jackson, then recently deceased. The sorrow had swiftly passed by him.

He was never more sweet and gracious, and never forgot his way of saying the kindliest word. Not long before he was seized with the fatal illness, he returned from a walk and found two young ladies of the village in his study. "It is too bad of us, Mr. Emerson," said one, "to take possession of your study." "It will be all the brighter that you have thought it worth coming to," was the prompt reply.

At the funeral of Longfellow, Emerson twice walked up to the coffin, and gazed intently upon the face of his dead friend. Then he turned to a friend and said, "That gentleman was a sweet, beautiful soul, but I have entirely forgotten his name."

Thus did he pass deeper into his Lethe, and forgot griefs that would have wrung his heart, unto the day when the pain came upon his body. But here, too, as we have seen, a brother's art had provided the anæsthetic draught, of which the mythical Lethe seems a dream. The prophet of love and science by their hands passed painlessly into the elements which henceforth will be gentler because he has lived.

Here, then, ends the long pilgrimage from Plymouth to Concord, from the Rock to the Soul in which all its strength was humanised. The physician brought his draught of Lethe to the bed of pain against all the protests of dogmas which translated blind elements and cherished the curse of nature. Dr. Holmes found it necessary to demand of the medical students at Harvard University that they should not permit the scriptures of ancient Jahve-worshippers to restrain them from soothing human agonies and mitigating maternal pangs! When the wife, her tender care of forty-seven years now ending, saw her great husband soothed in his last hours by her brother's anæsthetic, administered by her son, her solace was from that maternal spirit which everywhere presses gently back inorganic power with charms yielded by itself to love and wisdom. Never was the soothing agent more fitly used than on him who had done more than any other to soften for his age the pangs of its new birth.

THE END.

www.ingramcontent.com/pod-product-compliance
Lightning Source LLC
Chambersburg PA
CBHW032031220426
43664CB00006B/437